NEW PERSPECTIVES
ON PRISONS AND
IMPRISONMENT

Also by James B. Jacobs

Stateville: The Penitentiary in Mass Society

NEW PERSPECTIVES ON PRISONS AND IMPRISONMENT

James B. Jacobs

Cornell University Press

ITHACA AND LONDON

First published 1983 by Cornell University Press.
Published in the United Kingdom by Cornell University Press Ltd.,
Ely House, 37 Dover Street, London W1X 4HQ.

International Standard Book Number (cloth) 0-8014-1586-1
International Standard Book Number (paper) 0-8014-9248-3
Library of Congress Catalog Card Number 82-22222
Printed in the United States of America
*Librarians: Library of Congress cataloging information appears
on the last page of the book.*

The paper in this book is acid-free and meets the guidelines for permanence and durability of the Committee on Production Guidelines for Book Longevity of the Council on Library Resources.

TO JAN, THOMAS, AND SOPHI

Contents

Preface

The twelve essays in this volume represent my efforts over the past half-dozen years to produce a sociolegal history of the American prison since approximately 1960. This book is offered as a serious step toward an integrative social analysis of contemporary American prisons and as a brief in behalf of interdisciplinary research.

My broad goal has been to describe and explain contemporary American prisons, more specifically to illuminate the dynamics that have been transforming them for the past several decades. I have been eclectic in my methodology and choice of data. I have relied on case study, survey research, content analysis, multivariate analysis, and reflective social analysis. In addition, because I am a lawyer, my attention has been continually drawn to prisoners' rights litigation, the controversial role of the federal courts in institutional litigation, and the impact on prisons of antidiscrimination and collective bargaining laws.

My theoretical orientation is presented in the first chapter, "Macrosociology and Imprisonment." I have tried to piece together a tradition of macro-level analysis beginning with the brilliant work of Gustave de Beaumont and Alexis de Tocqueville. This chapter applies a comparative perspective by examining the status of prisons and prisoners in various countries. Merely to ask how prisons differ from one country to another focuses attention on the types of elites who control the institutions of punishment in various societies, the extent of their authority, and their accountability to others for their actions.

Chapter 2, "The Prisoners' Rights Movement and Its Impacts," describes and accounts for the phenomenal transformation of American prisoners' legal status since 1960. This transformation, I believe, has to be analyzed as more than the sum of individual court decisions; it must be understood as a legal and political movement whose participants are prisoners, public interest lawyers, federal judges, and some leaders of the national corrections establishment. Likewise, the impacts of this movement are indirect and subtle as well as direct and palpable. They should be discerned in the emergence of new types of administrators and of many kinds of institutional changes, as well as in the changing expectations of prisoners and staff members.

Chapter 3, "Race Relations and the Prisoner Subculture," began as an effort to critique the massive sociological literature on prisoner subcultures. My previous research had implicitly, sometimes explicitly, criticized this corpus of scholarship for presenting an exaggerated picture of the prison as a closed system or total institution, governed by its own institutional logic and norms, and inhabited by its own bizarre social types. As I immersed myself in this literature, I was astonished at the failure of earlier scholars to take account of racial segregation, discrimination, polarization, and conflict. I decided to trace the history of prison race relations, and to show how recognition of racial divisions and conflict makes the traditional descriptions and explanations of the prisoner subculture untenable. The goal is to develop a new and more realistic model of prisoner subculture.

The following chapter, "The Limits of Racial Integration" deals with the policy consequences of prison race relations. For the most part courts have not asked whether racial integration in the prison context presents legal and moral issues different from those presented by school integration. However, even a casual acquaintance with prisons suggests many possible significant differences. The meaning of "integration" is more complex in prisons than in schools. Must individual prisons, cell houses, and tiers reflect the racial composition of the system's entire inmate population? Is the threat of interpersonal or intergroup racial conflict a justification for keeping members of different races apart? Are any constitutional values affronted by permitting prisoners to choose members of their own race as cell partners?

Chapter 5 presents three empirical studies on prison politics. Curiously, despite being so obvious, prison politics has been virtually ignored by prison scholars. There does not exist a scholarly base from which to construct an integrative edifice. Ideally, we should have studies of prison interest groups, legislative politics, bureaucratic conflict, public relations, and the shaping of mass opinion. I hope the reader will settle for three soundings in these waters. The first study, "Town-Prison Relations as a Determinant of Reform," focuses on the complex relationship between the correctional system and the local community. Why do some communities accept and even welcome prisons and halfway houses while others mobilize enormous resources and energies to prevent their construction? My participant observation study, carried out at a minimum security prison in southern Illinois in 1974, demonstrates how the interdependency of this institution with the small, economically depressed town in which it is located made it possible for the prison to become a national model of progressive penology. By implication, the chapter underscores the difficulties of "selling" new prisons, halfway houses, and other penal facilities to communities that have no economic, political, or social stake in them.

The second sounding in correctional politics, "Mass Media and Prison News," is a content analysis of the prison news carried by two newspapers, all mass circulation magazines, and one television network in 1976. The data reveal that the public is exposed to a large amount and wide range of information about prison conditions and policy issues; of course, the extent to which this information is digested and fed into individual opinion formation is an entirely different question, one that begs for thorough empirical and conceptual analysis.

The third sounding is a case study and electoral analysis of the 1981 New York State bond referendum that proposed to raise five hundred million dollars for construction of three new prisons and renovations of several older ones. The referendum provided a rare opportunity to study a statewide election on a single relatively clear issue of penal policy. It enabled us to examine such questions as: What types of interest groups contest penal issues? What kinds of arguments do they perceive to be effective for influencing public opinion and attracting widespread support? What accounts for the way political jurisdictions, and by implication individuals, vote on prison issues when given the opportunity?

Just as macrosociological study of prisons requires analysis of demographic, social, political, and legal trends affecting the prisoners and their subculture, it also requires an analysis of how such trends affect those who run the prisons, their backgrounds, self-conceptions, ideologies, competencies, and, most important, authority. My research focuses primarily on the uniformed guard force, the most numerous prison employees; parallel research on administrative elites, treatment staff, teachers, and clerical personnel is badly needed.

Few readers will know much about what prison guards do and the conditions under which they work. The short excerpt "The Guard's World," presented as Chapter 6, is meant to provide background for the three following chapters. It describes what being a prison guard entails, the various types of responsibilities, and the divisions within the uniformed ranks. It also identifies the stresses on the guard's role that have been generated by larger societal trends.

Probably the most important development for the guards over the past two decades is unionization and collective bargaining. It has redistributed power so that penal institutions have become tri-polar worlds; the rank-and-file guards now exert considerable influence on almost all aspects of prison administration and issues of penal policy. Chapter 7 is an in-depth case study of the 1979 New York State prison guard strike, the largest and most dramatic guard strike in American history. The causes of the strike can be traced to strains within the guard's role and to an increasing division of interest between the rank and file

[11]

and top departmental administrators. Once the strike was called, the prisons were thrown into a state of emergency that required deployment of the National Guard. The events leading up to the settlement reveal a great deal about state power and its limits.

Chapters 8 and 9 examine two portentous demographic changes in the composition of the uniformed guard force: racial and sexual integration. Up until the 1970s, most prison guard forces were racially and sexually homogeneous. Because of changing societal attitudes and, more important, the pressures generated by Title VII of the 1964 Civil Rights Act, large numbers of blacks and other ethnic minorities, and an increasing number of women, entered uniformed guard forces around the country. It is not surprising that this legal and social change has produced a great deal of organizational strain. At issue is the capacity of the guard force to adapt to an irreversible breakdown in homogeneity and in the guards' subculture. Divisions and conflict among the guards multiply the problems of administration and complicate the pattern of relationships between guards and prisoners.

The final chapter, "The Implications of National Service for Corrections," speculates on the impact that either a compulsory or voluntary national service program might have on prisons. Rotating tens of thousands of young people through the prisons, as staff members, on one-year tours of duty would create an extraordinarily powerful link between the prison and mainstream society. Such a program in the current period might be the only way to provide adequate manpower and at the same time contribute to a more humane correctional system.

Chapter 10 demonstrates how macro-level analysis can inform policy making, or as Morris Janowitz prefers to say, "institution building." The comparative advantage of the academic penologist is surely not second-guessing the day-to-day administration of the prisons. Our task is the continual and intense examination of society's institutions of punishment for what they reveal about the structure and culture of the larger society. In so doing we can contribute to the societal conscience. Pressures toward represssion and brutality are never far below the surface; by keeping the prisons in the limelight, by examining current trends and future possibilities, and by constantly pointing out how closely we are all tied to our institutions of criminal justice, we may make it just that much more unlikely for an eruption of inhumanity to occur.

Many colleagues, friends, students, and professionals in the criminal justice system played a role in the creation of these essays. No one knows better than I the extent to which research and the maturation of one's ideas is a collective endeavor. I hesitate to single out a few individuals for special acknowledgment in fear of appearing to slight the enormous assistance that so many have provided. However, my debts to Morris Janowitz, Norval Morris, and Franklin Zimring are especially great. They have encouraged me, stimulated me, and frequently criticized me for more than a decade. Their collective influence on my work is enormous, although I urge the reader not to hold them responsible for my pitfalls. My friend and colleague at Cornell, Rose Goldsen, although not a criminologist, has given generously of her time and considerable sociological vision in her incisive critiques of my manuscripts. Jess Maghan, a professional corrections administrator, has assisted me with data sources, contacts, insights, and encouragement since I first met him almost ten years ago; our country is fortunate to have people like him, and there are many of them, working hard to achieve rationality and decency in our institutions of punishment. Among the many criminologists who have assisted me, I especially thank Daniel Glaser, Frank Merritt, Sheldon Messinger, William Nagel, and Michael Tonry. Among law colleagues, thanks are due Kevin Clermont, Michael Gold, Ronald Goldstock, Ian Macneil, Henry Monaghan, Charles Morris, Robert Nagel, Robert Sedler, Gary Simson, and Robert Summers. I also acknowledge the assistance of Cornell colleagues Joe Kahl, Donald Cullen, Ron Donovan, and Ronald Ehrenberg. My students have sustained me throughout my tenure at Cornell. I am proud to acknowledge the assistance of five of them by recognizing their coauthorship in five of the chapters. Many others have also helped; three of them, Kate Fitzgerald, Susan Forney, and Ronald Kuby, deserve special mention. Last but not least, I acknowledge and thank my secretary, Jylanda Diles, who has put up with me with patience and good humor and who has assisted me with the greatest efficiency, intelligence, and skill.

All of these essays, except one, were written after the publication of *Stateville*. Nine of them have been previously published, although I have felt free to edit, update, and amend. I have also eliminated all but essential footnotes so that the reader will not be distracted from the main themes. The following publishers have kindly granted me permission to use these essays in this volume: Sage Publications, Inc.; University of Chicago Press; *Criminal Law Bulletin*; *Social Service Review*; New York State School of Industrial & Labor Relations Press; *Industrial & Labor Relations Review*; *Social Problems*; University of Toledo *Law Review*.

JAMES B. JACOBS

Ithaca, New York

NEW PERSPECTIVES
ON PRISONS AND
IMPRISONMENT

[1]

Macrosociology and Imprisonment

Prisons do not exist in a vacuum: they are part of a political, social, economic, and moral order. Besides the intervention of the military to maintain internal order, imprisonment is society's most important instrument of coercive control. Who is sent to prison, the deprivations that are imposed, and the authority vested in the custodians reveal much about a society's values, its distribution of power, and its system of legal rights and obligations. Thus, many of the most important characteristics of a society can be inferred from an examination of its prisons. In part, this insight is captured in the famous observation that the level of a society's civilization can be judged by the state of its prisons.

Prisoners are not drawn randomly from a population. On the contrary, the character of the prisoner population reflects the stratification system of the larger society. The social and occupational origins of the prison staff, especially when compared with those of employees of other state bureaucracies, mark the status of the penal institution. A comparison of the residuum of legal rights left to the prisoner with those rights held by society's members-in-good-standing illuminates the meaning of both citizenship and criminality. The extent to which prevailing humanitarian norms and values apply to prisoners, the most peripheral members of society, indicates a great deal about the overall moral order.

Therefore, the prison is an important institution for those who seek to understand the way in which society is organized. Moreover, a macro-level analysis is essential for explaining the organizational life of the prison and its segments. Living and working conditions, the legitimacy or illegitimacy of various disciplinary mechanisms, and the structure of punishments and re-

Reprinted in slightly different form from David Greenberg, ed., *Corrections and Punishment* (Beverly Hills, Cal.: Sage Pubns., 1977).

wards all depend upon how the prison articulates with the political, economic, and legal systems of the whole society. In this chapter I attempt to direct attention beyond the prison's walls to the society in which the institution is lodged. The theoretical lens that I find most valuable is found in political sociology, more specifically in macrosociology (*see* Janowitz 1970).

A Legacy of Political Sociology

Despite a few useful exceptions (Clemmer 1958:xi; Sykes 1958:8), most sociological studies of prison reflect an organizational perspective that stresses the day-to-day details of prison life for inmates and staff. Therefore, to discover a macrosociological analysis of the prison, one must cast a wider net. For example, in 1833 Gustave de Beaumont and Alexis de Tocqueville (1964), perhaps the first students of the American penitentiary, linked this penal innovation to the culture, social structure, and political system of the young nation. The French travelers compared the institutions of social control in the American and French societies of the period. They emphasized such differences as (1) the philanthropic and religious traditions giving rise to the American penitentiary movement, (2) the egalitarianism of American society responsible for the absence of class privileges inside the penitentiary, and (3) the effect of public opinion in America in setting limits on prison policies and conditions. They hypothesized that it was easier to maintain order in the American penitentiary because of the more pervasive commitment to law and order in American society generally, lamenting that

> this spirit of submission to the established order does not exist in the same degree with us. On the contrary, there is in France, in the spirit of the masses, an unhappy tendency to violate the law, and this inclination to insubordination seems to us to be of a nature to embarrass the regular operation of the [prison] discipline. [De Beaumont and de Tocqueville 1964:121]

A second classic comparative macrosociological study of imprisonment is Georg Rusche and Otto Kirchheimer's (1939) analysis of the evolution of punishment in Europe from the twelfth to the twentieth century. The two German emigré sociologists showed the integral relationship between the institutions of punishment and a society's economic system. They argued that the emergence of the modern prison was linked to the transformation of the European economic system (from feudalism to mercantilism to industrial capitalism) and to demographic changes, which by the nineteenth century had established a situation of chronic surplus labor. By the mid-nineteenth century, the economic function of the precursors of the modern prison (workhouses) was undetermined, and the prison's role of keeping the working poor in the labor market became more explicit.

By the late nineteenth and early twentieth century, the masses were participating more fully in the material advantages of modern society. In addition, according to Rusche and Kirchheimer, there was a wider acceptance of a "sociological" understanding of criminality, which emphasized society's responsibility for crime as well as the need for "scientific treatment" of the criminal. These trends supported the ideology of "rehabilitation." It is impossible to understand what is at stake in most debates about penal policy inside and outside the prison without appreciating the history of rehabilitation as an ideology since the founding of the American penitentiary.

Rusche and Kirchheimer stressed that the way in which prison articulates with the economic system has crucial implications for penal practices and conditions. They pointed to the near universal acceptance of the principle of "less eligibility" as setting limits to the potential for penal reform. This principle holds that if prison conditions were made preferable to the circumstances of the next-best-off segment of the population, the working poor would cease to be deterred from dropping out of the work force and joining the ranks of the criminal lumpen proletariat.

No recent scholars have approached the topic of imprisonment from as broad a comparative macrosociological perspective as de Beaumont and de Tocqueville or Rusche and Kirchheimer. Selected research on the German concentration camps and on prisoner-of-war camps, however, constitutes an important contribution to a prison tradition in political sociology. The ways in which the concentration camps served the race ideology of National Socialism and the economic requirements of the German war economy demonstrate the bases for both slave labor and genocide. One student of the camps, H. G. Adler (1958:514), explicitly embraced political sociology:

One may look at the concentration camp within the system of contemporary society, especially within the authoritarian and terroristic states. In a world made vulnerable, or at least strongly influenced, by the ideas of enlightenment, the purely secular state, the new democracy, and secular socialism, the fate of the man who dissents from the guiding principles and idea of the ruling group has become important: how he is to be rendered innocuous as soon as the ruling group feels threatened by him and how, under whatever pretense, that group discards all protections granted by the constitutional state and the democratic guarantees for personal inviolability. The dissenter is excluded from the community of those who conform, sent to the concentration camp, or killed. This approach to the study of the concentration camp would begin with the position of the ruling group, paying particular attention to political and economic conditions.

The concentration camp research illustrates the most complete exclusion of the imprisoned from the rights of citizenship. It demonstrates the convergence of political, economic, and social circumstances that make it possible for a society to destroy its prisoners without contradicting law, public opinion, or political leadership.

Studies of prisoner-of-war camps also show how institutions of confinement and control articulate with the political and military objectives of the state. In his analysis of Chinese prisons of the early 1950s, Edgar Schien (1960) pointed out that the techniques of coercive persuasion used on Western prisoners were an expression of a cultural emphasis on unanimity and that the treatment of Western prisoners was merely an extension of the policy used to "convert" Chinese peasants to the communist cause.

Albert Biderman (1968) has argued that the administration of prisoner-of-war camps is an extension of broader military and political conflict. The treatment afforded the enemy's prisoners of war will depend upon the captor power's sensitivity to international opinion and its concern for the treatment of its own prisoners. Of more general significance for all prison studies is Biderman's observation that the degree of control exerted over prisoners of war has fateful implications for the type of social system which will develop among the prisoners. The more unlimited (by law, public opinion, and so forth) the captor's recourse to coercive sanctions and the more repressive the organizational regime, the more likely it is that predatory relations will develop among the prisoners. Where administrators are constrained by national or international law, it is more likely that the captives will be able to maintain the structure of military or criminal organization imported from the outside (*see* Jacobs 1976).

This tradition of prison studies in political sociology emphasizes comparative study at the level of the nation-state. While the research constituting this tradition has been important, it suffers from several limitations. The Rusche and Kirchheimer book stressed materialism at the expense of almost all other variables. No room was left in their analysis, for example, for the role of religious thought in the evolution of institutions of social control. De Beaumont and de Tocqueville stressed cultural variables, but their study was cursory and limited to a comparison of America and France. While instructive, neither the concentration-camp nor the prison-of-war research has been integrated with sociological studies of society's more typical penal institutions. In the rest of this chapter I suggest ways to extend the tradition that now exists.

Punishment and Social Structure

From the perspective of political sociology it is important to trace how each prison segment (inmates, guards, administrators, treatment personnel, and so forth) reflects society's systems of stratification. The social origins of the staff, prisoners, and interest groups serve as indicators of the prison's status in a particular society. It makes a difference whether the management of the prison is entrusted to people who share elite status with those who administer other state bureaucracies or whether it is entrusted to members of nonelite groups who cannot get better jobs. It is a worthy hypothesis that where prison administrators are drawn from the same groups as other bureaucrats, the prison will tend to be run more like other state agencies. On the other hand, we should not overlook the possibility that the powerful constraints impinging on prison management might limit the impact of a change in the social class background of the administrators.

Not only the social status of the prison's leadership, but its occupational status as well, is of utmost importance (*see* European Committee on Crime Problems 1963). Whether a country has turned over the administration of its institutions of punishment to the clergy (as in some Latin American countries), or to the top levels of the civil service (as in Austria), or to the national police (as in the Soviet Union), or to the mental health professions (as in some cases in the United States and Western Europe) will have important implications for the formulation of penal policy, the maintenance of discipline, and the promotion of humanitarian objectives.

Just as significant for explaining the day-to-day operation of the prison is the origin of the front line staff. In his classic essay "Good People and Dirty Work," Everett Hughes (1964:33) stated that "it is likely that the individuals recruited to run the Nazi concentration camps were *gescheiterte Existenzen*, men or women with a history of failure, of poor adaptation to the demands of work and the classes of society in which they had been bred." But what is problematic, according to Hughes and to my analysis as well, is not the existence of such elements, but the process by which certain segments of the population are recruited to staff the institutions of punishment and control. Whether the guards are drawn from the ranks of the unemployed, military service veterans, displaced farm workers, or aspiring law enforcement officers and bureaucrats should help to explain day-to-day behavior.

Where the organization's rank and file and the prisoners are drawn from dissimilar and antagonistic segments of a society one would expect the same culture conflicts that occur on the streets to be imported into the prisons. Hostility between rural white guards and urban black prisoners, while frequently exaggerated, has been so often pointed to as a key source of conflict in American prisons that to ignore it would surely be a significant oversight. On the other hand, almost no attention has been paid to conflicts that occur between guards and inmates presumably drawn from the same classes, a common situation in large metropolitan jails in the United States.

Class conflict may also occur between the penal organization's rank and file and its administrative elite. J. E. Thomas's thorough study (1972) of the English prison officer reported how members of the educated middle class gradually dominated the top positions in the prison service, leading to the alienation and demoralization of the guard force. The prison officers perceived (with much justification) that an "alliance" existed between liberal administrators and prisoners, both groups blaming the guards for the "failures" of the prison system.

My own case study of Stateville Penitentiary (Jacobs 1977), Illinois's largest maximum security prison, is consistent with Thomas's research. In 1970 the Stateville warden who had risen through the ranks and who shared a background and ideology identical to the rank and file was replaced by a young college-educated professional oriented toward treatment. The new warden's first expressions of empathy with the plight of the prisoners convinced the guards that he was "for the cons." The subsequent estrangement of the rank and file from the growing number of professional administrators resulted in a deterioration of the prison's ability to provide food, showers, clothing, mail, and other basic services. Ultimately the breakdown of administration led to more and more violence and a "crisis in control."

The trend toward bureaucratizing and professionalizing the prisons in Great Britain and the United States has been strong, at least since the mid-1960s. (Indeed, John Conrad [1965] has suggested the existence of a professional cadre of prison administrators throughout Western and Eastern Europe.) Whether this trend will continue and whether the same trend is evident in societies with different political, economic, and social systems and at different "stages of development" are questions worthy of extensive empirical research.

The prisoners themselves, of course, do not represent a cross section of an entire societal population, but may be drawn disproportionately from racial, ethnic, religious, or regional minorities. Whether the prisoners are members of groups of higher than marginal status on the outside will partly determine the parameters of the conditions and policies of confinement. What penal deprivations are defined as legitimate substantially depends on the social, economic, and political status of those who are imprisoned.

Almost one hundred and fifty years ago de Beaumont and de Tocqueville observed that the egalitarianism of American society prevented social status from being recognized inside the penitentiary. This situation sharply contrasted with French penal institutions, where a prisoner with sufficient wealth could supplement substantially his diet and living conditions. The issue of whether social class differences are explicitly or implicitly recognized in prison continues to be important. It is reported that Mexican prisoners can rely on their personal resources to purchase better food and other benefits (*New York Times*, May 23, 1976:22). The same is true in Pakistan, where the laws prescribe different entitlements for prisoners drawn from different social strata. Prisoners in the higher tax brackets and those with higher education are provided "better class" accommodations. Social class penetrates the prison more indirectly in Colombia, which designates separate penal facilities for violators of traffic laws (including vehicular homicide), who are drawn disproportionately from the members of the urban sector, including chauffeurs.

The Prisoner and the Rights of Citizenship

The definition of who is a member of the community and what rights and obligations membership entails are central issues for understanding the emergence of mass society and the welfare state. In his seminal lectures "Citizenship and Social Class," T. H. Marshall (1964) distinguished three aspects of citizenship — civil, political, and social. Civil citizenship meant "the rights necessary for individual freedom — liberty of person, freedom of speech, thought and faith, the right to own property and to conclude valid contracts and the rights to justice." Also included was the right to bargain collectively over the conditions of employment. He defined political citizenship as "the right to participate in the exercise of political power, as a member of a body invested with political authority or as an elector of the members of such a body." Social citizenship designated "the whole range from the right to a modicum of economic welfare and security to the right to share to the full in the social heritage and to live the life of a civilized being according to standards prevailing in the society." All three aspects of citizenship are problematic for those convicted and punished for violating the criminal laws (*see* Cohen and Rivkin 1971). How modern societies have accommodated notions of citizenship with criminal jurisprudence is an important distinguishing characteristic of different types of contemporary regimes.

Civil Rights of Citizenship

In *Miller v. Twomey* (1973) Judge (now Justice) John Paul Stevens wrote for the seventh Circuit Court of Appeals:

> Liberty protected by the due process clause may — indeed must to some extent — coexist with legal custody pursuant to conviction. The deprivation of liberty following an adjudication of guilt is partial, not total. A residuum of constitutionally protected rights remains. . . . The view once held that an inmate is a mere slave of the state is now totally rejected. The restraints and the punishment which a criminal conviction entails do not place a citizen beyond the ethical tradition that accords respect to the dignity and intrinsic worth of every individual. Liberty and custody are not mutually exclusive concepts.

[23]

Precisely this question, whether imprisonment is necessarily incompatible with the rights and obligations of society's members-in-good-standing leads us to compare the juridical systems of different modern states. In those societies not ensuring freedom of speech and religion to members-in-good-standing, of course, there is no need to inquire whether those liberties are held by felons. What is important is to identify the rights of citizenship withdrawn from the convicted criminal. Does the prisoner lose the rights to contract, marry, divorce, inherit property, and use the courts?

In Argentina, for example, an individual sentenced to three years of imprisonment or more suffers *inhabilitación* (absolute disqualification), forfeiting paternal rights (*patria potestas*), the right of administering his estate, and the right of disposing of it by *inter vivos* transactions. He is placed under the creator-guardianship system of the civil code.

In the United States, much has been written about the extraordinary post - World War II legal changes extending the civil rights of citizenship to minorities, criminal defendants, servicemen, students, women, the mentally ill, and, more recently, the mentally retarded. The momentum generated by the expansion of civil rights and liberties inexorably penetrated the prison's wall. The same trend toward the extension of substantive and procedural rights to prisoners, although to a more limited extent, is evident also in Great Britain (*see* Williams 1975) and Canada. In West Germany and Japan recent legal developments have broadened the opportunity of prisoners to object formally to the way in which they are being treated.

The Scandanavian countries have gone furthest in providing that the rights of prisoners are coextensive with those of society's members-in-good standing. One recent student of the Swedish penal system (Solomon 1976) has observed:

> There is a sense of oneness of community, that pervades Swedish society. Perhaps best expressed by the former Swedish prime minister, Per Albin Hansson, "the nation was seen as a home — folkhemmet — with its citizens as members of a single family." In terms of crime, *Swedes regard convicted persons as citizens who have broken the law, but nonetheless as citizens*. [Emphasis added.]

In Denmark and Sweden the governments have recognized prisoners' unions and have bargained over living conditions, wages, and prison policy (Ward 1972). What limits there are on how fully prisoners can enjoy the rights of civil citizenship without sacrificing the moral component of criminal jurisprudence is a crucial sociolegal problem for the modern welfare state.

That there are limits is suggested by recent shifts in public opinion in the direction of more punitive attitudes toward those who break the law. In addition, at some point the assertion of individual rights and liberties by prisoners conflicts with the administrative discretion required to manage successfully such volatile institutions as prisons. The intrusion of juridical norms into Illinois's Stateville Penitentiary exposed the administrative deficiencies of the old authoritarian regime that operated according to tradition rather than by written rules and regulations. For example, the authoritarian regime was unable to justify in court why it treated Black Muslims differently from members of traditional religions, despite the prison leadership's certainty that First Amendment claims were only a facade for "troublemakers" intent on their own self-aggrandizement.

By demanding some form of rational decision-making process, the courts hastened the demise of Stateville's old regime. But the professional, treatment-oriented administrators who next assumed command were only marginally more capable of fending off the increased legal challenges of prisoners and their public interest counsel. For a system of a decision making based upon custom and tradition, the professional, treatment-oriented administrators substituted a system based on "professional" judgment and discretion. State laws, court decisions, and the central department's own regulations were not followed consistently.

A breakdown of control and of the provision of basic services finally led to the emergence of a more rational legal bureaucracy, whose leaders were explicitly committed to modern management and to making visible the processes and justifications for institutional decision making. But the strain caused by the intrusion of juridical norms has not dissipated entirely. While the actual substance of the federal court decisions has generally not directly attacked the basic needs of prison administration, the recognition of prisoners' constitutional rights continues to have important indirect effects. The fear of being sued, and particularly of being held personally and financially liable, has demoralized the staff. The substantial administrative burden of responding to lawsuits and providing "due process" (hearings, appeals, and so forth) strains an organization chronically short of resources and constantly facing the threat of individual and collective violence.

Political Prisoners

In many countries, the civil as well as the political and social rights to which a prisoner is entitled depend upon whether he is defined as a political prisoner. It is an open question how political prisoners will be treated. They are not universally granted fewer rights than common criminals. Political prisoners can be separate but equal, separate but unequal, or integrated on an equal or unequal basis with common criminals. In political systems in which the change of leadership is fluid, the imprisonment of political opponents may be a regular part of the political process, and the conditions of such prisons may not be as repressive as those housing run-of-the-mill offenders. Adolf Hitler, for example,

[25]

wrote *Mein Kampf* while serving a prison term in the Landsberg fortress, a special facility for political prisoners, to which he was sentenced after the abortive Beer Hall Putsch of 1923. During the struggle for independence on the Indian subcontinent, such political prisoners as Gandhi and Nehru were treated like dignitaries. As the struggle expanded and demonstrators began to flood the prisons, the government decided to treat lesser political prisoners the same as common criminals in the hope of deterring them (Barker 1944).

American law does not recognize political crimes, although other Western democracies such as France have explicit designations for political crimes and special prisons for political prisoners (La Santé in Paris). In the United States it is assumed that the political institutions of society are flexible enough to resolve all legitimate political conflict. This is not to say that there have not always been American prisoners who have preferred to define themselves and have been defined by their fellow prisoners as political (*e.g.*, Jackson 1970, 1972; Flynn 1972; Wright 1973). The prison in the Anglo-American system is not explicitly defined as a *political* institution. The prisoners are not defined as enemies of the state and as offenders against the political order, but rather as actors opposing the social order. Perhaps as a result, the political system can more easily accommodate reform efforts aimed at "helping" the prisoners and justify the prison as an institution of rehabilitation.

Either explicitly to recognize or to deny the prison's political purpose has important implications for the day-to-day treatment of those who are confined. Where, as in the Soviet Union, the prisons are used to enforce political and economic orthodoxy, one would expect the relationship of the staff to the prisoners to be quite different from what it is in those societies in which the prisoners are offenders against life and property but are seen as victims of the system. Because political prisoners in the Soviet Union are enemies of the state, the officials need not be accountable for their survival (Cressey and Krassowski 1958; Solzhenitsyn 1973, 1975). No interest groups exist committed to protecting the rights of political prisoners aside from the few with an international reputation. In the Soviet labor camps the common criminals are offered some advantages in exchange for their repression of the political prisoners. Another extreme example is the Nazi concentration camp, where the inmates were granted no rights of citizenship whatsoever, having been placed beyond the bounds of the political community (Kogon 1966).

One danger in explicitly recognizing "political crime" and separating political prisoners from other types of offenders is that they will reinforce each other's opposition to the regime. Consider the case of the well-known sociologist Gino Germani, who was imprisoned for political activity in fascist Italy during the 1930s.

He learned two specific lessons from the prison experience. First that working-class culture had a coherence and vitality of its own. (His own lower-middle-class background had not exposed him to the true proletarian culture before.) For example, there were songs and codes for sending messages through the jail walls that originated in social protest movements a century earlier; all workers knew them and were astonished that Germani did not. Second, he was exposed to both Marxism and the Communist Party. Many radical intellectuals, "some of the best people in Italy" were on the prison island, as were many leaders of the party. [Kahl 1976]

Of course, mixing political (or politicized) prisoners with garden-variety offenders raises the risk of politicizing the entire prisoner population, particularly if certain social definitions (such as ethnicity) link them together.

Political Rights of Citizenship

In *Reynolds v. Simms* (1964), one of the great reapportionment cases of the 1960s, Chief Justice Earl Warren wrote, "The right to vote freely for the candidate of one's choice is of the essence of a democratic society, and any restrictions on that right strikes at the heart of representative government." The chief justice also pointed out that "history has seen a continuing expansion of the scope of the right to suffrage in this country." Given the centrality of the franchise to the meaning of citizenship, one of the most poignant indications of what conviction of crime means is the disenfranchisement accompanying it. Indeed, in many states in the United States, an individual convicted of a serious crime loses the right to vote forever, unless pardoned by the chief executive.

The drive toward equality which gained momentum throughout the decade of the 1960s led to the passage of the Voting Rights Act and judicial decisions striking down various restrictions on suffrage which prevented minorities from participating in the political process. One might have thought it only a matter of time before the disenfranchisement of prisoners and ex-prisoners would be struck down as well. This proved not to be the case, although the state's interest in disenfranchising felons was not entirely clear (*see Stanford Law Review* 1973). Even in a Western democracy such as Australia, where voting is an obligation (failure to vote is punishable by a fine), individuals serving a sentence for a crime carrying a penalty of one year or more of imprisonment are denied the vote.

Rejecting a prisoner's challenge to the New York law, Judge Henry Friendly of the second U.S. Circuit Court of Appeals put forth the following justification for placing the convict outside the bounds of the political community.

[27]

The early exclusion of felons from franchise by many states could well have rested on Locke's concept ... that by entering into society every man authorizes the society ... to make laws for him as the public good of the society shall require. A man who breaks the laws he has authorized his agent to make for his own governance could fairly have been thought to have abandoned the right to participate in further administering the compact. [*Green v. Board of Elections* 1967]

In 1974 the U.S. Supreme Court upheld California's voting law disenfranchising ex-felons, thereby putting to rest the legal efforts to extend suffrage to prisoners and ex-prisoners. Writing for the unanimous court Justice William Rehnquist said:

Pressed upon us by the respondents, and by amici curiae, are contentions that these notions are outmoded, and that the more modern view is that it is essential to the process of rehabilitating the ex-felon that he be returned to his role in society as a fully participating citizen when he has completed serving his term. . . .But it is not for us to choose one set of values over another. If respondents are correct, and the view which they advocate is indeed the more enlightened and sensible one, presumably the people of the State of California will utimately come around to that view. And if they do not do so, their failure is some evidence, at least, of the fact that there are two sides to the argument. [*Richardson v. Ramirez* 1974]

In West Germany the court has the discretion to deprive the convicted criminal of the right to seek office or to vote if the criminal law specifically provides for this penalty. The laws that do provide for disenfranchisement are those proscribing breaches of the peace, high treason, and endangering the democratic constitutional state. Thus, common criminals are typically permitted to vote by absentee ballot.

In Sweden, also, prisoners are permitted to exercise the franchise. A prisoner's union was formed in Sweden in 1966, and in 1968 its efforts succeeded in changing the law to allow prisoners to vote in general elections. The right of Swedish prisoners to vote and to bargain collectively with the state over wages, hours and conditions of work marks the furthest extension of the definition of citizenship to prisoners in a Western democracy.

Loss of the right to vote is not the only forfeiture of the political rights of citizenship attached to criminal conviction. The prohibition on holding public office, the ban against service in the armed forces, and exclusion from jury service should also be considered in the same context. The extent to which such political rights are taken away and for how long should be an important issue for those carrying out comparative macrosociological research.

Social Rights of Citizenship

In many modern societies the state takes responsibility for assuring the citizen-in-good-standing some minimum standard of living and certain other social and economic benefits and protections. For example, the welfare state provides compensation to those who are unemployed, welfare to those who cannot support themselves, disability payments to those injured on the job. Public education is provided without charge.

At issue for our purposes here is the extent to which these benefits are forfeited once an individual is convicted of crime and committed to prison. Does the social welfare system extend behind the walls? In the United States and England, to take two well-known examples, education is widely available to prisoners. The rules governing the English prison system even provide that illiterates may attend to their schooling instead of working, and almost every prison with which I am familiar in the United States has some sort of educational program. Illinois law provides that the state prisons constitute a separate school district on a par with all others in the state. Basic education seems almost to have achieved the status of a right for prisoners in Great Britain and the United States. In addition, social work services, psychological therapy, and job counseling are typical aspects of the American prison regime.

During the 1970s medical care for American prisoners vastly improved. In no small part this trend may be attributed to the Supreme Court's decision in *Estelle v. Gamble* (1976), which holds that "deliberate indifference to serious medical needs of prisoners" is a violation of the Eighth Amendment. The American Medical Association has promulgated a set of standards for prison medical care which embodies the principle that those who are incarcerated are no less deserving of adequate health care than free citizens.

Job training, counseling, and placement services for prisoners and ex-offenders proliferated since the mid-1960s under the stimulation of the federal Manpower Development and Training Act (1964) and the Comprehensive Employment and Training Act (1973). Both of these massive federal employment initiatives designated prisoners as a targeted group with special labor market problems and needs. The Department of Labor has been deeply involved in experiments, research, and evaluation in the area of crime and employment since the days of the "great society" programs. In short, it is a worthy hypothesis that over the 1960s and 1970s the prison and its inmates have been incorporated into the American welfare state.

Although the welfare state extends to prisoners, its coverage is only partial. Typically, in the United States workers' compensation does not apply to prisoners who are injured in the course of institutional labor. Social security continues to be paid to prisoners, except to those convicted of espionage and similar crimes, who may in the discretion of the court have their social security forfeited forever. The possiblity of prisoners receiving disability payments was virtually eliminated by 1980 amendments to the Social Security law. (Pub. L. No. 96-473). In Argentina, *inhabilitación* includes the suspension of state pensions and social security benefits.

One should also consider here the significant deprivations on the right to work which are imposed upon ex-prisoners. In the United States hundreds of occupations are closed to those with a felony record. Where such restrictions on the pursuit of a calling are placed upon ex-prisoners, the society has reinforced the definition of the prisoner as a noncitizen, almost a pariah.

Moral Status of the Prisoner in Mass Society

Since World War II strong evidence suggests that in the United States, and elsewhere in the West, there has occurred a transition in the prisoner's status. Whereas previously the prisoner had been a pariah, totally separated from the mainstream society, its central institutions and moral community, that status has attenuated as ties have proliferated between outside forces (interest groups, volunteers, courts, media, and so forth) and those incarcerated for crime. It would be interesting to explore the question of whether the prisoner is more "acceptable" in American society today.

There is also some indication that a heightened sensitivity to the humanness of the prisoner is occurring in other countries as well. In survey of correctional practices around the world, John Conrad (1965) found a remarkably "modern" consensus among top prison officials in capitalist and socialist countries alike. The consensus is stated in five postulates: (1) offenders are social deviates; something is wrong with them; (2) punishment exacted by the system is futile; commitment to the prison system is punishment enough; (3) during the period of commitment the correctional agency has an obligation to administer a regime which will equip offenders to "lead a good and useful life on discharge"; (4) because the treatment required by the offender varies from individual to individual in accordance with what is "wrong" with each, the duration and circumstances of the commitment must also vary; (5) all correctional agencies have an obligation to maintain control over committed offenders.

Even if Conrad's observations were and remain accurate, one cannot say, of course, that actual practice always follows the ideology put out for public consumption. It is an important empirical task to chart the "fit" between law, ideology, and social reality. Still, what seems significant is the strong sense among contemporary prison "professionals" that national and international opinion (embodied in the United Nation's *Standard Minimum Rules for the Treatment of Criminals*) expects a benign and rehabilitative stance toward the prisoner.

Given such developments, it would be most interesting to test Edward Shils's (1962) controversial theory of "mass society" by examining the penal systems of various societies. The key characteristic of "mass society," according to Shils's specialized use of that term, is the heightened sensitivity of the elite to the dignity, moral worth, and humanity of the masses. Whether or not the political and moral aspects of "modernization" have led to a redefinition of the criminal's moral status is a question that might shed light on the growth and elaboration of the welfare state in at least several democratic states. The mass society conception seems less appealing when we look at the moral status of the prisoner in authoritarian (leftist or rightist) societies in which torture, at least of a significant number of "political prisoners," continues (*e.g.*, Laber, 1976). Ideology may be more useful in seeking to explain the differential treatment of prisoners in various industrialized societies. Nevertheless, Shils's point is worth pursuing: does "development," at least under certain circumstances, lead to a greater appreciation of the prisoner's moral worth?

Recourse to Coercive Sanctions

One key indicator of the prisoner's moral status is the coercive measures that prison officials are permitted to use to maintain order and discipline. At the time that de Beaumont and de Tocqueville toured the American penitentiaries, use of corporal punishment was widespread. In the decades that followed it was utilized on an even greater scale. As was the case with capital punishment, the use of corporal punishment in the United States tapered off in the decades following World War II. For example, in 1968 the last state prison system using the whip to maintain discipline was held to be violating the Eighth Amendment's proscription against cruel and unusual punishment (*Jackson v. Bishop* 1968). Heightened sensitivity to the dignity and moral worth of the prisoner has also led courts to strike down many other practices and conditions. The list includes aversive conditioning, excessive overcrowding, sensory deprivation, use of Thorazine, poor medical care, and poor diet. In several cases, not merely prison practices but the prison (or jail) itself has been declared violative of "evolving standards of decency which are the mark of a civilized society."

Recent exposés of conditions in French prisons have led to the establishment of a cabinet-level minister in charge of penal facilities in that country. In England, according to Conrad (1965:13), the reintroduction of capital punishment is "massively blocked by the unwillingness of any public agency, especially the Prison

[31]

Commission, to administer it. It is as though the correctional administrator, having shed the role of turnkey, finds his new role too attractive to return to the old ways."

Of course, abuses persist in prisons and, for that matter, in schools, courts, hospitals, old age homes, and welfare bureaucracies. Nothing that has been said necessitates the conclusion that prison conditions will continue to improve unilinearly. It may be that, the drive toward redefining the moral status of the prisoner having temporarily reached its limits, there is now a countertrend that re-emphasizes the threat of criminality and the necessity of punishment.

Comparative macrosociological inquiry might profitably focus upon the kinds of coercive sanctions permitted in various societies. Which countries, for example, allow corporal punishment, deprivation of food, electric shock, torture, and killing? To what extent are the prison administrators held accountable for the lives and well-being of their prisoners? Are records kept? Are investigations pursued? Are prison officials and lower-echelon personnel ever held liable before the criminal and civil law for abuses in their treatment of prisoners?

Conclusion

I began this chapter by noting that prison scholarship is dominated by micro-level analyses of the attitudes, values, and roles of prisoners and staff. I hope to have shown that the findings of these many studies could be enriched by paying more attention to the shifting role of the prison in modern society. Both longitudinal and comparative cross-sectional studies might illuminate which trends in the larger society are most responsible for the organization that develops behind the walls.

Beyond shedding light on the operation of the prison, however, the types of macrosciological research on which I have touched should be pursued because they may add much to our basic knowledge of the dynamics of total societies. Imprisonment is the keystone of coercive control in modern society. How the prison and its segments articulate with the larger society will increase our understanding of society's distribution of power, stratification, and system of legal rights and obligations.

[2]

The Prisoners' Rights Movement
and Its Impacts

During the past two decades prisoners have besieged the federal courts with civil rights suits challenging every aspect of prison programs and practices. It is as if the courts had become a battlefield where prisoners and prison administrators, led by their respective legal champions, engage in mortal combat. Although the war has dragged on for almost twenty years, and shows no sign of abating, strangely enough there seems to be no agreement on which side is winning.

It frequently appears that both sides are trying to convince the public and themselves that their own defeat is imminent. Prison officials complain that the demands of litigation and court orders have pressed their beleagured staffs and limited resources to the verge of collapse; they decry the naiveté of judges who cannot see the deadly struggle for power which lies behind the disingenuous facade of legal petitions that ask "only" for "humane treatment" and "basic civil rights." Even worse, from the perspective of prison officials, judges have not been content merely to resolve limited conflicts, but have made Herculean efforts, by use of structural injunctions (*see* Fiss 1978, 1979), special masters (*see, e.g.*, Nathan 1979), and citizens' visiting committees, to restructure and reorganize prisons according to their own value preferences. Legal attacks and judicial interference have, according to some prison officials, fatally undermined these officials' capacity to administer their institutions and to maintain basic order and discipline.

Activist prisoners and their advocates are equally despondent. Each victory seems to accentuate how far their cause still has to go to attain its goals. And unfavorable court rulings, especially those of the Supreme Court, seem to har-

Reprinted in slightly different form from Norval Morris and Michael Tonry, eds., *Crime and Justice: An Annual Review of Research*, vol. 2. (Chicago: Univ. of Chicago Press, 1980).

binger the final demise of all prisoners' rights. One decision heralded as apocalyptic is *Bell v. Wolfish* (1979). The Supreme Court, in an opinion by Justice William Rehnquist, reversed a sweeping injunction condemning a multitude of conditions and practices at the Federal Bureau of Prisons' Metropolitan Correctional Center in New York City. The Court rejected the Court of Appeals standard for review of jail conditions, under which pretrial detainees could "be subjected to only those 'restrictions and privations' which inhere in their confinement itself or which are justified by compelling necessities of jail administration." Instead, the majority required only a showing that jail practices are reasonably related to a legitimate governmental objective. Applying this less restrictive standard, the Court upheld a prohibition on receiving books and magazines from any source other than the publisher as well as a restriction on receipt of packages, double-bunking, unannounced cell searches, and mandatory visual inspection of body cavities.

With both sides claiming defeat, who is the real winner and who the real loser in the war over prisoners' rights? So put, the question is too simplistic to be useful. What is needed is a holistic understanding of the role of litigation and law reform in creating and sustaining a prisoners' rights movement, which includes prison reform efforts of all sorts, by prisoners and others.

Unfortunately, research has not been directed to this level of analysis. While the *Index to Legal Periodicals* lists more than 850 articles on prisoners' rights since 1963, most merely summarize recent legal developments or dissect judicial opinions. Strinkingly absent are efforts to place the changing legal status of prisoners in a larger sociopolitical context and empirical studies on the impact of legal change on prisons, prisoners' lives, and the drive for prison reform. The social science literature is even less helpful.

This chapter seeks to chart a course for holistic analysis of the prisoners' rights movement. The first section sketches the origins and development of the movement and identifies the key actors, agencies, and institutions whose activities would have to be carefully studied and related to one another before the full story of the prisoners' rights movement could be told. The second section presents a critique of those who see the prisoners' rights movement as an example of judicial failure and suggests a strategy for evaluating the impacts of the prisoners' rights movement.

Prisoners' Rights as a Sociopolitical Movement

In speaking of the prisoners' rights movement I refer to far more than the sum total of court decisions affecting prisoners. We are dealing with a broad-scale effort to redefine the status (moral, political, economic, as well as legal) of prisoners in a democratic society. The prisoner's rights movement, like other social movements — the civil rights movement, the women's movement, the student movement — includes a variety of more or less organized groups and activities; there is also wide variation in the extent and intensity of individual participation. What is decisive, however, is a shared sense of grievance and the commitment to enhanced rights and entitlements for prisoners.

The prisoners' rights movement must be understood in the context of a "fundamental democratization" (Mannheim 1940) that has transformed American society since World War II, and particularly since 1960. Starting with the black civil rights movement in the mid-1950s, one marginal group after another — blacks, poor people, welfare mothers, mental patients, women, children, aliens, gays, and the handicapped — has pressed for admission into the societal mainstream. While each group has its own history and a special character, the general trend has been to extend citizenship rights to a greater proportion of the total population by recognizing the existence and legitimacy of group grievances.

Prisoners, a majority of whom are now black and poor, have identified themselves and their struggle with other "victimized minorities," and pressed their claims with vigor and not a little moral indignation. Various segments of the free society linked the prisoners' cause to the plight of other powerless groups. To a considerable extent the legal system, especially the federal district courts, accepted the legitimacy of prisoners' claims.

To recognize the prisoners' rights movement as part of a larger mosaic of social change is not to deny this movement's own sociopolitical history. The drive to extend citizenship rights to prisoners must be placed in the context of two hundred years of effort at prison reform. The issues being argued today in constitutional terms have previously been debated on religious and utilitarian grounds (*see, e.g.*, Rothman 1980). Reformers of earlier generations did not pursue their objectives in the courts because, until recently, the courts were unreceptive to such complaints. The rule of law did not apply to prisoners; their status placed them "beyond the ken of the courts" (*Yale Law Journal* 1963).

Before the 1960s prisoners were a legal caste whose status was poignantly captured in the expression "slaves of the state" (*Ruffin v. Commonwealth* 1871). Like slaves, prisoners had no constitutional rights and no forum for presenting their grievances. But unlike slaves, prisoners were invisible, except perhaps for occasional riots, when they captured public attention.

Until the 1960s the federal judiciary adhered to a "hands off" attitude toward prison cases out of concern for federalism and separation of powers and a fear that judicial review of administrative decisions would undermine prison security and discipline. A prisoner who complained about arbitrary, corrupt, brutal, or illegal treatment did so at his peril. Until recently, protest to the outside world was severely repressed (Hirschkop and Millemann 1969). Prisoners were, therefore, isolated from the rest of society; the possibility of forming alliances with groups outside prison was very limited. The precondition for the emergence of a prisoners' rights movement in the United States was the recognition by the federal courts that prisoners are persons with cognizable constitutional rights. Just by opening a forum in which prisoners' grievances could be heard, the federal courts destroyed the custodians' absolute power and the prisoners' isolation from the larger society. And the litigation in itself heightened prisoners' consciousness and politicized them.

The new era of prisoners' rights began in the early 1960s in the wake of the civil rights movement. In prisons, it was the Black Muslims who carried the torch of black protest. The Muslims succeeded with the assistance of jailhouse lawyers, and in turn provided an example for using law to challenge officialdom. A rights movement clearly had appeal for a generation of minority youth that had become highly conscious of its rights and entitlements. But the movement was not comprised solely of prisoners. It depended heavily on the involvement and efforts of free citizens, particularly lawyers and reinvigorated prison reform groups. Of course, the prisoners' rights movement would not have been possible without activism in the federal judiciary and some stamp of approval by the justices of the United States Supreme Court. Nor is prison reform the sole prerogative of courts; a complete sociopolitical history of the prisoners' rights movement would have to take federal and state legislative and administrative activity into account.

The Black Muslims and the Religious Freedom Controversy

A high priority for building a body of research on prisoners' rights is to document fully the activities of the Black Muslims in American prisons and jails. The Black Muslims filed lawsuits throughout the country in the early 1960s asserting denial of racial and religious equality. (By my count, there were sixty-six reported federal courts decisions pertaining to the Muslims between 1961 and 1978.) The issues raised by the Muslims were timely and likely to appeal to federal judges. The legitimacy of demands by blacks for equal protection under the law in other contexts was becoming well established. The rights asserted — to read religious literature and to worship as one wishes — are fundamental in American values and constitutional history and difficult to deny. The only posture available to prison officials was to deny the Muslims' sincerity. Prison officials often disputed the Muslims' claim to religious legitimacy, but the result was to strengthen Muslim resolve and intensify their struggle.

The Supreme Court's first modern prisoners' rights case, *Cooper v. Pate* (1964), was an appeal from a lower court ruling upholding the discretion of prison officials to refuse Muslim prisoners their Korans and all opportunities for worship. The Supreme Court's decision was narrow: the Muslim prisoners had standing to challenge religious discrimination under Section 1983 of the resurrected Civil Rights Act of 1871. But for the prisoners' movement it was not the breadth of the decision that mattered but the Supreme Court's determination that prisoners have constitutional rights; prison officials were not free to do with prisoners as they pleased. And the federal courts were permitted, indeed obligated, to provide a forum where prisoners could challenge and confront prison officials. Whatever the outcome of such confrontations, they spelled the end of the authoritarian regime in American penology.

Once disputes between prisoners and prison officials were seen by outsiders to be religious controversies and not simply struggles for institutional control, the result was inevitable (Rothman 1973). The success of the Muslims on the constitutional issue of free exercise of religious rights brought the federal courts into the prisons. The abominable conditions in American prisons kept them there. Prisoners and their advocates presented their grievances in constitutional terms and federal courts became more deeply involved in disputes over prison practices, policies, and conditions.

The Black Muslims are undoubtedly the best organized and most solidary group to exist for any length of time in American prisons. They set an example for other prisoners, who soon began organizing themselves in groups and blocks, in contrast to the cliques of former times (Clemmer 1958; Irwin 1980). In place of the subcultural norm "do your own time," the Muslims introduced a new morality — group time (*see* Jacobs 1976). They showed how, through legal activism, prisoner groups could achieve solidarity and some tangible successes.

The issue of religious freedom was picked up by diverse prisoner groups, who saw the opportunity to formulate as a religious controversy their objections to prison life and their opposition to prison officials. The most dramatic example was the Church of the New Song, a "religion" begun by federal prisoners in Marion, Illinois, which soon spread to other federal and state facilities. The church earned nationwide media attention: its leader proclaimed himself the Bishop of Tellus, prophesied in the Book of Revelations; its "liturgy" required porterhouse steaks and Harvey's Bristol Cream; its agenda called for the wholesale destruction of the American prison system. The status of the Church of the New Song was vigorously litigated in the Fifth and Eighth federal judicial circuits; the prisoners achieved several legal victories requiring correction departments to afford them the same opportunities and prerogatives as traditional religions. (*See, e.g.,* Theriault *v.* Silber 1977; Remmers *v.* Brewer 1976.)

[37]

Jailhouse Lawyers and Access to the Courts

The traditional role of the jailhouse lawyer had been to assist fellow prisoners in preparing postconviction petitions asserting defects in their prosecution or conviction. Prison officials often were hostile to jailhouse lawyers because of their status among, and influence over, fellow inmates (*Washington and Lee Law Review* 1968). There were also not unwarranted fears that jailhouse lawyers might abuse their power over other prisoners (Brierley 1971). It was not uncommon for prison rules to prohibit giving legal assistance of any kind; punishments could be very severe. Consequently, jailhouse lawyers often functioned "underground." Official hostility to jailhouse lawyers intensified as prisoners' rights actions succeeded and as the jailhouse lawyers became judicially recognized adversaries.

The Supreme Court's decision in *Johnson v. Avery* (1969) ushered in a new age in jailhouse lawyering (Wexler 1971). The Court held that when prison officials are not providing prisoners with adequate legal services, prisoners cannot be punished for providing legal assistance to one another. The decision marked another triumph for a class of prisoners whom the officials disliked and feared. More victories followed. In 1972, the Court held, in *Haines v. Kerner* (1972) that prisoners' *in forma pauperis* petitions had to be treated in a manner most advantageous to prisoners; where there was a glimmer of a federal cause of action in the complaint, the case could not be dismissed. *Wolff v. McDonnell* (1974) extended the jailhouse lawyer's authority of representation to civil rights suits attacking institutional conditions and policies. The Court went even further in *Bounds v. Smith* (1977), holding that the constitution imposed upon the states an affirmative obligation to provide prisoners with either adequate law libraries or adequate assistance from persons trained in the law. These decisions have established the jailhouse lawyer as an institutionalized adversary and have undoubtedly contributed to the popularity of litigation as a prisoner avocation.

Prisoners

By the late 1950s and early 1960s blacks constituted a majority of the prisoners in many northern prisons and in some states. Their consciousness aroused by the civil rights movement, it was only natural that this generation of minority prisoners would demand its rights even behind bars; it was not about to accept being invisible. By the late 1960s some black prisoners, such as Eldridge Cleaver, George Jackson, and Martin Sostre, had achieved extraordinary prominence. Their ties to outside groups, and to batteries of lawyers, could not be severed. And they may well have politicized their lawyers as much as their lawyers politicized them. Riots and law reform were paths to political change in the larger society during this period and the same phenomena became increasingly evident in the prisons.

The Prisoners' Rights Bar

A platoon, eventually a phalanx, of prisoners' rights lawyers, supported by federal and foundation funding, soon appeared and pressed other-than-religious constitutional claims. They initiated, and won, prisoners' rights cases that implicated every aspect of prison governance. In many cases the prisoners' attorneys were more dedicated and effective than the overburdened and inexperienced government attorneys who represented the prison officials (Bershad 1977, quoting Supreme Court Justice Lewis Powell).

Many of the leading prisoners' rights lawyers had earlier gained considerable experience working for black civil rights (Bronstein 1977). Herman Schwartz, a professor at the State University of New York at Buffalo, Alvin Bronstein of the American Civil Liberties Union's National Prison Project, William Bennett Turner and Stanely Bass of the NAACP Legal Defense Fund, and others brought both national perspective and some minimal coordination to the prisoners' rights litigation.

Notwithstanding the role played by a few national prisoners' rights groups and institutions, day-to-day advocacy has been carried on by hundreds of lawyers and paralegals on the state or local level. Many of these groups were founded and supported under the auspices of OEO Legal Services (*see, e.g.,* Welch 1979). Prisoner Legal Services in Illinois, begun in the early 1970s by a nonlawyer activist, had nine full-time attorneys, several social workers, and a staff of forty by the mid-1970s, and was a potent force in the life of northern Illinois prisons. Prison administrators viewed the organization as a powerful and omnipresent watchdog. Consideration of policy decisions always involved some attention to the likely reaction of the Legal Services staff. A number of prisoners' rights projects were established in law schools (Cardarelli and Finkelstein 1974) and contributed to the flow of outside legal actors into the closed prison world. A 1973 report by the Council on Legal Education for Professional Responsibility listed sixty-three law schools as providing some form of legal assistance to prisoners.

Many of these law students and prisoners' advocates identified strongly with the prisoners' interests, thereby building up the prisoners' hopes and encouraging their protests. In turn, the prisoners gave these legal personnel a "cause" and strong personal reinforcement. At times legal services personnel went well beyond even far-reaching class actions and worked on such "political" tasks as establishing prisoner unions (*e.g.*, *Jones v. North Carolina Prisoners' Union* 1977). Many lawyers began to see themselves no longer as technicians but instead as prisoners' rights advocates working for the reform or abolition of the prison system. The most extreme example was a small but influential group of radical lawyers and law collectives.

The American Bar Association gave the prisoners' movement the imprimatur of the established legal community. It created in 1970 the Commission on Correctional Facilities and Services for the purpose of advancing correctional reform. With Ford Foundation funding, the comission opened full-time offices in Washington. Its Resource Center for Correctional Law and Legal Services was a central clearinghouse for information and coordinated effort and resources among prisoners' rights groups and litigators. Legal periodicals on prisoners' rights were established, including one published for an ABA section. At least seven sections of the ABA later formed prisoners' rights committees, and, as of 1974, twenty-four state bar associations had special committees working on prison reform (American Bar Association, Commission on Correctional Facilities and Services 1975). The most active ABA Committee is the Joint Committee on the Legal Status of Prisoners. Its *Tentative Draft of Standards Relating to the Legal Status of Prisoners* (1977) prescribes, among other things the minimum wage for prisoner laborers, a right to form prisoner organizations, and a limited right to privacy. While not yet adopted by the ABA, that such standards are being seriously considered is an indication of the degree of legitimacy which the prisoners' rights movement has attained (*see also* U.S. Dept. of Justice 1978; National Council on Crime and Delinquency 1966, 1972).

Federal funding for prisoner legal services has lately become more difficult to obtain, in part because of the displacement of OEO Legal Services by the Legal Services Corporation. The ABA Resource Center for Correctional Law and Legal Services ran out of money in mid-1978. Illinois Prisoner Legal Services for all practical purposes went out of existence because of lack of funds at about the same time. Increasingly, those government grants that are available prohibit civil rights suits and class actions (American Bar Association, Resource Center on Correctional Law and Legal Services 1974:407).

The luster of the prisoners' rights movement may also be fading. The image of the prisoner as hero, revolutionary, and victim is disappearing. Other minority rights movements, such as that associated with the handicapped, are increasingly attracting resources and the energies of young attorneys. The pathbreaking prisoners' rights litigation is behind us. The nitty-gritty of more routine legal services may be less attractive to young lawyers with reformist aspirations. Whether a viable prisoners' rights movement at the grass roots level can survive funding cutbacks, judicial retrenchment, and other social and political change is unclear.

[40]

It would be wrong, however, to conclude that the prisoners' rights movement is dying. Increasing numbers of cases are filed each year; 11,195 prisoners' rights petitions were filed in federal district courts in the year ending June 30, 1979, a 451.5 percent increase since 1970 and a 15 percent increase over 1978 (U.S. Administrative Office of the United States Courts 1979; *see also* McCormack 1975). The vast majority of these cases are filed *pro se*, without legal representation. Most of the cases are dismissed at the pleading stage or on summary judgement (Turner 1979), but if only a small percentage survive, the number of litigated cases will continue to be substantial.

Fewer prisoners' rights lawyers are now available, but many of those are experienced and highly skilled. The ACLU's National Prison Project has only seven full-time attorneys but carries on major litigation across the country, often supporting cases originally brought by a local ACLU chapter. The project effectively employs the services of a cadre of expert witnesses including such ex-correctional officials as David Fogel and John Conrad. The experience that this litigation team has accumulated over years in lawsuits around the country makes it a formidable opponent. The project's director, Alvin Bronstein, exerts influence in many ways beside litigation: for example, by lobbying, accepting speaking engagements, and maintaining a high profile at national meetings and conferences.

It is possible that the U.S. Department of Justice will emerge as a crucial force in the reconstituted prisoners' movement of the 1980s. The Special Litigation Section has intervened in a number of important cases in the last few years, most notably a massive challenge to the Texas Department of Corrections. The Civil Rights of Institutionalized Persons Act, passed by Congress in 1980, clarifies and broadens the Justice Department's authority to represent prisoners in institutional litigation.

The Supreme Court

Any analysis of the prisoners' rights movement must acknowledge the crucial role of the United States Supreme Court. The prisoners' rights movement required at least the passive acquiescence of the Court. The movement also needed the symbolic energizing that *Brown v. Board of Education* provided to the civil rights movement. The crucial prison case was *Cooper v. Pate* (1964). Although a *per curiam* opinion, lacking the powerful language of *Brown v. Board of Education*, it left no doubt that prisoners have rights that must be respected.

Many legal victories followed after *Cooper v. Pate*. Each contributed to the strength, self-confidence, and momentum of the prisoners' rights movement. A high-water mark was reached in *Wolff v. McDonnell* (1974), which raised issues about the procedural protections to which prisoners are entitled at disciplinary hearings. The Supreme Court finally provided the kind of clarion statement that could serve as a rallying call for prisoners' rights advocates. Speaking for the Court, Justice Byron White said:

[The State of Nebraska] asserts that the procedure for disciplining prison inmates for serious misconduct is a matter of policy raising no constitutional issue. If the position implies that prisoners in state institutions are wholly without the protections of the Constitution and the Due Process Clause, it is plainly untenable. Lawful imprisonment necessarily makes unavailable many rights and privileges of the ordinary citizen, a 'retraction justified by the considerations underlying our penal system' [citations omitted]. But though his rights may be diminished by the needs and exigencies of the institutional environment, a prisoner is not wholly stripped of constitutional protections when he is imprisoned for crime. There is no iron curtain drawn between the Constitution and the prisons of this country.

Since *Wolff,* prisoners have won several important victories in the Supreme Court — *e.g., Estelle v. Gamble* (1976) (deliberate indifference to serious medical needs constitutes cruel and unusual punishment); *Hutto v. Finney* (1978) (approving a wide-ranging structural injunction against certain practices and conditions in the Arkansas prisons) — but none equals *Wolff* for eloquence.

I stress the symbolic importance of Supreme Court prisoners' rights decisions, not to belittle the holdings, but to emphasize that from a sociopolitical perspective what is critical is the psychological impact of court decisions, the feeling of those in the field, in this case prisoners' advocates, prison officials, and their respective lawyers, that the Supreme Court and the Constitution are for them or against them. The negative impact of court decisions on morale is nicely captured in a case study of protracted litigation involving Louisiana's Jefferson Parish Prison (Harris and Spiller 1977:213-14):

The one negative factor that unquestionably did flow from the suit involved the aggravation and adverse personal effects associated with it. Overall, it appears that the worst effects of the judicial intervention may have been psychological ones. It was psychologically very difficult for the defendants to accept that what they had been doing was wrong or inadequate when they believed that they were doing a decent job. It was psychologically very difficult for the defendants to accept that a federal judge who had never operated a correctional facility could dictate what would be done. It was psychologically very difficult for defendants to have their job performances criticized by persons who were not believed to understand their problems. It was psychologically very difficult for the defendants to accept blame for defects for which they saw others as being responsible. Acceptance of all of these things was made even more difficult by the fact that they were imposed publicly.

[42]

The positive impact of court decisions on movements such as the prisoners' is more sharply grasped by Stuart Scheingold (1974:131) than by any other writer with whom I am familiar:

> Regardless of the problems of implementation, rights can be useful political tools. It is possible to capitalize on the perceptions of entitlement associated with rights to initiate and nurture political mobilization — a dual process of activating a quiescent citizenry and *organizing* groups into effective political units. Political mobilization can in its fashion build support for interests that have been excluded in existing allocations of values and thus promote a realignment of political forces. . . . Since rights carry with them connotations of entitlement, a declaration of rights tends to politicize needs by changing the way people think about their discontent.

The symbolic and psychological significance of being "vindicated" or "repudiated" by a court explains wildly exaggerated reactions to court decisions — exaggerated, that is, when viewed through the lawyer's detached lens. But once the potential of court decisions and even litigation itself to power a movement or to demoralize its opposition is understood, then the relationship of courts to sociopolitical movements becomes much more complicated than simply looking at the "holding" of each new judicial decision.

It is hardly surprising that such decisions as *Bell v. Wolfish* (1979) and *Rhodes v. Chapman* (1981) are being heralded by prisoners' rights advocates as a fatal blow to the movement and by prison officials as a vindication of their authority and competence. What makes *Wolfish* more than just another case is Justice Rehnquist's rhetoric: for example, his quip that the Constitution embodies no "one man, one cell" principle and his repeated emphasis on the need for judicial deference to prison officials.

> The deplorable conditions and draconian restrictions of our Nation's prisons are too well known to require recounting here, and the federal courts rightly have condemned these sordid aspects of our prison systems. But many of these same courts have, in the name of the Constitution, become increasingly enmeshed in the minutiae of prison operations. Judges, after all, are human. They, no less than others in our society, have a natural tendency to believe that their individual solutions to often intractable problems are better and more workable than those of the persons who are actually charged with the running of the particular institution under examination. But under the Constitution, the first question to be answered is not whose plan is best, but in what branch of the Government is lodged the authority to initially devise the plan. This does not mean that constitutional rights are not to be scrupulously observed. It does mean, however, the the inquiry of federal courts into prison management must be limited to the issue of whether a particular system

violates any prohibition of the Constitution, or in the case of a federal prison, a statute. The wide range of "judgment calls" that meet constitutional and statutory requirements are confided to officials outside the Judiciary Branch of Government.

Neither prison officials nor prisoners' rights lawyers are much impressed by the facts that *Wolfish* is only one case, that it can be distinguished from many prison cases on its facts, that it is arguably applicable only to modern jails like the Metropolitan Correctional Center, or that a later case, such as *Vitek v. Jones* (1980), scores a victory for prisoners by establishing a right to a hearing before transfer to a mental health facility.

This Supreme Court has demonstrated its concern that the prisoners' rights movement, or more specifically, the involvement of federal courts in matters of state prison administration, not go too far. The Court has not signaled a return to the "hands off" doctrine or a redefinition of prisoners as nonpersons. But prisoners' rights activists should not in the foreseeable future expect highly dramatic decisions that will mobilize social and political energies on behalf of prisoners. If there is to be a stimulus for further momentum in the prisoners' rights movement it probably will not come from the Supreme Court. Having liberated prisoners from being slaves of the state, this Court seems unwilling to establish them as citizens behind bars.

The Lower Federal Courts

The significance of Supreme Court decisions notwithstanding, it would be a grave error, as Jerome Frank admonished three decades ago, to rely too heavily on appellate decisions as indicators of what lower courts are doing. Frank (1949) spoke of "the myth that upper courts are the heart of the courthouse government." Frank was right. Most legal analysts of the prisoners' rights movement are transfixed by Supreme Court decisions. Each new decision generates intense examination of the opinion's language, new doctrinal syntheses, and unending critiques of judicial logic. Hardly any attention is paid to what the trial courts are doing in prisoners' rights cases (*but see* Turner 1979).

Prisoners' rights cases are won and lost on the record. The Supreme Court has not effectively hemmed-in activist federal judges (Frankel 1976). Most complaints deal with access to lawyers and legal materials, property loss or damage, brutality, censorship of mail, and medical care (Turner 1979). All of these fall within the ambit of recognized constitutional violations or are controlled by state law or previous consent decrees. Many prisoners' complaints can be redressed without breaking new ground.

Justice Brennan pointed out in *Rhodes v. Chapman* (1981:353) that "Individual prisons or entire prison systems in at least 24 states have been declared unconstitutional under the Eighth and Fourteenth Amendments, with litigation underway in many others." *Bell v. Wolfish* failed to prevent major judicial interventions into the operation of state prisons, such as *Ramos v. Lamm* (1979), which shut down "old Max," Colorado's Canon Correctional Facility, and *Ruiz v. Estelle* (1980), which declared the entire Texas prison system to be in violation of the Constitution. And even a cursory glance through the *Criminal Law Reporter* will bolster the spirits of those who fear that the prisoners' rights movement is dead. Consider *Cooper v. Morin* (1979), a post-*Wolfish* decision by New York's highest court, which held that while *Wolfish* forecloses the argument by pretrial detainees that they have a federal constitutional right to "contact visits" with family and friends, such a right is guaranteed by the state constitution's due process clause.

Many prisoners' rights cases are not decided in the courts. Settlements are negotiated, sometimes with the approval and even the collusion of reform-minded administrators. These administrators are not averse to admitting that facilities are dilapidated and poorly maintained, or that medical care is inadequate; a court-approved consent decree on such matters may greatly improve their leverage in the executive budget competition and with the legislature (Herman Schwartz 1972:791; Harris and Spiller 1977:92 - 96). Furthermore, rules and practices can be liberalized and then blamed on the courts, thereby blunting criticism from rank-and-file guards.

Legislatures

The federal courts have been the most important redefiners of the legal status of marginal groups, with lawyers and federal judges the key implementers. However, to focus only on litigation would be too limited. Legislatures and executive agencies have also had key roles to play. Correctional politics is as much a legislative as a judicial game. Prisoners' rights advocates have frequently encountered intransigence and hostility among legislators, but they have also sometimes won support for important new programs. Increased legal activism focuses attention on prisoners and on prisons and may bring some legislators to the realization "that something must be done."

Some states moved to codify the basic requirements set forth in the landmark cases. The Illinois legislature, in 1973, enacted a comprehensive Unified Code of Corrections, addressing issues ranging from procedures for disciplinary action to availability of radios, televisions, and legal materials, and the treatment of prisoners with mental health problems (Illinois Ann. Stat. Ch. 38 § 1001-1-1 et seq. [1973]).

Other states, while continuing to delegate their rule-making authority for prisons to their correctional agencies, adopted strict rule-making procedures, including provisions for public input and court review. California law, for example, until 1975 permitted the director of corrections to prescribe rules and

[45]

regulations for the administration of the prison system and change them at his pleasure. Under the current statute he may promulgate new rules only in accordance with California's Government Code, which requires notice and public hearing prior to an exercise of rule-making authority. Furthermore, copies of proposed rules must be posted in the state's penal institutions (Ca. Penal Code § 5058 [1970 and 1979 Supp.]). Until 1968, California Law (Penal Code § 2800) provided that a sentence to prison suspended an individual's civil rights. The section was amended in 1968 to provide what has come to be called an inmate bill of rights (*U.C.L.A. Law Review* 1973:481).

In many states, legislation was necessary to establish halfway houses, work release programs, home furloughs, and grievance procedures (*see, e.g.*, N.Y. Correc. Law §§ 22-A, 22-B, 26, 139 [McKinney's Supp. 1978]). To take another example, the Minnesota legislature established an ombudsman for the department of corrections in 1973. The point is that a preoccupation with the courts should not blind us to the role of legislatures in both stimulating and impeding the goals of prisoners' rights advocates and their allies.

Departments of Corrections

When the federal courts began to involve themselves in prison disputes, some officials realized that written, uniform, and, most important, reasonable rules would reduce charges of unfairness, and reduce the chance of judicial intervention. Today, for example, because of a decision by a federal district judge, every rule of the Arizona Department of Corrections must be approved by the federal court (*Harris v. Cardwell* 1977). The court-approved rules cover every aspect of prison operations.

Connecticut's rules and regulations run to more than four hundred pages. Some regulations track Supreme Court or lower federal court decisions, others go substantially beyond the courts. For example, prisoners are entitled to a hearing and an appeal in cases of disciplinary transfer from a minimum to a maximum security prison, despite a 1976 Supreme Court decision, *Meacham v. Fano* (1976), holding that the Constitution does not require such procedures. And despite approval in *Bell v. Wolfish* for rectal and genital searches whenever pretrial detainees meet visitors in person, Connecticut rules limit such searches to admissions from outside the institution and instances where officials have probable cause to believe that a prisoner is hiding contraband in a body cavity. *Bell v. Wolfish* itself noted that during the pendency of the case the Federal Bureau of Prisons liberalized one of the policies in dispute in the lawsuit, regarding receipt of books and magazines from sources other than the publisher. I suspect that litigation has frequently led to agency reconsideration and liberalization of policies and rules, even when not constitutionally compelled.

[46]

National Institute of Corrections; American Correctional Association

The National Institute of Corrections (NIC), a federal agency, has, in the past few years, played an increasingly important role in the prisoners' rights movement. NIC has sponsored research, conferences, and training programs of all sorts to institutionalize progressive legal reforms. For example, in conjunction with the Center for Community Justice, NIC provides training and technical assistance in the development and implementation of inmate grievance procedures. Recently it launched an ambitious project to train special masters to carry out more effectively their role of monitoring court decrees in prison cases.

It is not far-fetched to consider prison officials' key professional association, the American Correctional Association (ACA) as playing a role in the prisoners' rights movement, at least now. The ACA leadership and permanent staff are fully aware of legal developments, and through a variety of activities help to disseminate and clarify the legal requirements of prison officials. From 1977 to 1981, for example, with funding from the National Institute of Corrections, ACA sponsored a Corrections Law Project, which exposed prison officials and state attorneys general from all over the United States to legal scholars and practicing attorneys who specialize in prisoners' rights. More important is the ACA's substantial accreditation project (*see* American Correctional Association 1978), which attempts to hold state and local prisons and jails to comprehensive and progressive confinement conditions and practices.

Identifying and Evaluating the Impacts of the Prisoners' Rights Movement

The prisoners' rights movement is controversial. Some critics are deeply troubled by what they view as excessive judicial meddling in matters that would best be left to state legislatures and executive agencies (Glazer 1975). Other critics, or at least "doubters," are themselves prisoners' rights activists, but they judge reform through litigation to be torturously slow and often ineffective. In order to assess the validity of these criticisms, and to understand the intellectual and political millieu in which prisoners' rights activity is now being evaluated, it is necessary to sample the larger controversy over judicial involvement in reform of complex institutions like prisons, mental institutions, and school systems.

Some criticism of the role of courts in "institutional litigation" derives from objections rooted in political philosophy. Since the founding of the Republic there has been controversy over the proper role of the Supreme Court and the inferior federal courts. Those who favor majoritarian rule have always been

[47]

troubled by the power of American courts to impose their value judgments on the society and to overrule other branches of government (*see, e.g.*, Bickel 1962). They have also opposed federal court "supervision" of state institutions on federalism grounds. Of course, a powerful case can and has been made for the opposite position (*see, e.g.*, Fiss 1979). My concern is not to debate political philosophy but merely to stress that the perceptions of various observers and commentators regarding the success of institutional litigation are colored by their underlying philosophical views.

Those who decry judicial activism as politically suspect are also likely to brand judicial efforts to resolve controversies in prison as misguided and counterproductive. Critics of judicial involvement in institutional litigation point to the inherent unsuitability of adjudication to resolve such controversies. Drawing upon Fuller's classic article "The Forms and Limits of Adjudication" (1978), these critics may argue that the "social logic" of courts makes their primary role the adjudication of clear-cut two-party disputes. The further courts stray from their traditional adjudicatory function, according to this view, the less effective they are. And this especially holds true for "polycentric" disputes, a category not clearly defined by Fuller, but undoubtedly embracing complicated institutional litigation involving multiple and interrelated interests and issues.

In what is sure to become a classic article, Owen Fiss (1979) directly challenges Fuller's contention that dispute resolution is the primary function of courts. While Fiss's argument is a systematic assault on Fuller's model, for my purposes it is enough to note that for Fiss "courts exist to give meaning to our public values." Thus, there is nothing odd, unusual, or "parasitic" (to use Fuller's term) about courts attempting to vindicate rights threatened by public bureaucracies. What has changed, in Fiss's view, is not the function of courts, but the form of adjudication. The emergence of a society dominated by large-scale organizations requires that courts shape their procedures to a new reality.

> The structural suit is one in which a judge, confronting a state bureaucracy over values of constitutional dimension, undertakes to restructure the organization to eliminate a threat to those values posed by the present institutional arrangement. The injunction is the means by which these reconstructive directives are transmitted. [Fiss 1979:2]

The political or normative criticism of court intervention in institutional disputes is supplemented by an instrumental criticism — courts are not competent to adjudicate disputes involving complicated institutional policies, procedures, resources, and styles of administration. Perhaps the most sophisticated version of this criticism has been made by Donald Horowitz (1977). He argues that the following attributes of adjudication make it unsuitable for resolving complicated social problems: (1) adjudication is focused (the emphasis on rights implies disregard of costs); (2) adjudication is piecemeal; (3) courts must act when litigants call; (4) fact finding in adjudication is ill adapted to the ascertainment of social facts; (5) adjudication makes no provision for policy review.

This is not the appropriate place for a rebuttal to Horowitz (*but see* Fiss 1979; Eisenberg and Yeazell 1980). Adjudication does have limitations in resolving certain kinds of controversies, but legislatures and administrative agencies, as he recognizes, also have their limitations. Their failures are easily as numerous as judicial failures. And despite their limitations, courts have certain institutional advantages in dealing with "public law litigation." Courts have some insulation from political pressures. They can tailor solutions to particular situations, involve parties who otherwise might be left out, and generate useful information that will not be filtered through the rigid structures and the preconceptions of bureaucracies. Courts provide an effective mechanism for registering and responding to grievances generated by the operation of public programs in a regulatory state and can fashion solutions flexibly, without a bureaucratic straitjacket (*see* Chayes 1976:1308).

Not only the opponents of institutional litigation see court intervention as ineffectual. So vigorous a prison reform advocate as Leonard Orland (1975:63) writes despairingly that "in the last analysis, the judicial struggle is an almost hopeless one; moreover, it carries enormous cost to prisoner, correctional administrator and court alike." And the director of the ACLU's National Prison Project concludes that "most prisons are so diseased and bankrupt that [litigation] achievements represent only the smallest and earliest steps of a very long journey" (Bronstein 1977). "Movement lawyers," even as they continue to struggle for prison reform in the courts, complain that judges are basically conservative and wedded to the status quo (*e.g.*, Lottman 1976).

One can understand the frustration. Reform through litigation is time-consuming, frustrating, and often unsuccessful; of course, so are efforts to solve intractable social problems through comprehensive legislation or agency activism. Litigation moves slowly. Progress oftentimes is measured in years. Judicial proceedings are expensive and time-consuming. Plaintiffs are paroled, or die, or lose interest. The career structures of prisoners' rights lawyers are unstable: funding is uncertain and career progressions are ambiguous. Lawyers for the state and for agency personnel come and go. Election outcomes bring new political regimes, and lawsuits can often be disrupted by the disappearance of prison administrators. When cases are resolved and injunctions are issued, compliance is not always obtained: sometimes because of willful obstructionism, sometimes because of bureaucratic incapacity to make changes, and sometimes because of political problems and inadequate resources.

[49]

Judicial decrees are not self-executing. Sometimes the persistent efforts of lawyers are needed to prevent the case from being only a hollow victory. Sometimes even those efforts are not enough. Although judges have the power to hold noncomplying administrators in contempt, they are reluctant to take such drastic remedial action. In complicated "totality of conditions" cases, federal judges have sometimes turned to special masters to help monitor compliance, gather information, and resolve ongoing disputes between the parties. But the special master is not an institutional panacea either. If the master lacks a full-time appointment and a staff, which is usually the case, he may simply not possess the capacity to see that a structural injunction is fully implemented (*see Yale Law Journal* 1975; *Harvard Law Review* 1977; Nathan 1979). Even under the best of circumstances, the special master or other court appointed monitor (for example, citizens' committee) must depend upon the institution's staff for information as to whether a decree is being followed.

Notwithstanding these problems, I think it would be hard for anyone who studies America's prisons and jails not to conclude that enormous changes have occurred in the last two decades. For example, the editors of the *U.C.L.A. Law Review* (1973:502), in their survey of judicial intervention in California prisons, found that "all of the administrators responding to the questionnaire agreed that some changes in correctional procedures, regulations, and facilities have come about specifically because administrators have anticipated what courts might do and have acted accordingly." Likewise, Lawrence Bershad, former legal adviser to the District of Columbia Department of Corrections, observes (1977:60) that "agency heads in most of the large cities and states find themselves having to anticipate the persuasive impact that a major prison law decision made elsewhere will have on their jurisdictions. As corrections move sharply toward a legal due process model and away from the familiar and untrammelled authority inherent in the correctional chain of command, subject only to the dictates of the governor and the legislature, most wardens and administrators find themselves in the position of reacting to and coping with court decisions." William Bennett Turner (1979:639), an experienced litigator on behalf of prisoners, reaches much the same conclusion after an exhaustive nationwide study of prisoners' civil rights suits from 1973 to 1977: "Nearly everyone we interviewed believed that the cases have had great impact. Many have pointed out that even losing cases have resulted in reform." And finally, Allen Breed, former head of California's Youth Authority and subsequently the director of the National Institute of Corrections, remarked that "the role of courts over the past fifteen years in acting as a catalyst for much needed change in our nation's prisons cannot be overemphasized." My own observations and interviews with prisoners nd prison officials around the country lead me to the same conclusion. Perhaps the discrepancy between those who think the prisoners' rights movement has been ineffective and those who see it as the crucial influence on prison reform may be explained by the absence of a methodology for identifying impacts and the absence of criteria for judging their importance.

The Problem of Identifying Impacts

I argued earlier that two decades of effort to transform the legal status of prisoners should be viewed as a sociopolitical movement. It will not do to describe or analyze the prisoners' rights movement in terms of the breadth or narrowness of particular court holdings, or even in terms of administrative compliance with court orders. Some of the most important effects of the prisoners' rights movement include the organization of prisoners, citizen and interest-group mobilization, legislative and administrative budget-making decisions and law-making, professional standard-setting, and the redistribution of power inside the prisons (*see* Jacobs 1977). Narrow impact studies do not deal with these secondary effects. They focus, almost always, on the ability of courts to achieve compliance with their decrees. But even this subject is fraught with conceptual and methodological difficulties, as I hope to show.

The Problem of the Worst Case

Almost all critics of the propriety or effectiveness of judicial activism in reform of complex institutions have based their conclusions on a few "worst cases," such as South Boston High School (school desegregation), Partlow Hospital in Alabama (institutions for the mentally ill and retarded), and Cummings and Tucker prison farms in Arkansas (prisons). Critics point out that, in cases like these, litigation dragged on for years, "communities" became polarized, and the courts were never entirely successful in achieving their goals; sometimes, unintended secondary effects such as "white flight" defeated the goals of reform.

It is difficult, as I will argue below, to know what "success" is in cases such as these. Surely it would be naive to imagine that the worst, most neglected, prisons in America could be renovated overnight to resemble the best facilities anywhere. At this point, however, I want to emphasize that for every instance of protracted institutional litigation like that involving the Arkansas prisons, there exist a dozen run-of-the-mill cases and consent decrees in which constitutional violations are remedied without such high drama.

To be fair, I must admit that the preceding assertion is only my impression. To be systematic we should examine as comprehensively as possible the responses over time to prisoner demands for greater rights and entitlements in a representative sample of jails and prisons throughout the country. While no such comprehensive survey has yet been carried out, it would likely find enormous variations in almost everything having to do with jails and prisons. Some prisons and jails have been the focus of a great deal more legal activity than others. This variation may be accounted for by such factors as particularly bad conditions, the presence of politicized prisoners, the existence of outside legal resources, the fortuity of a "liberal" federal district judge, or some combination of these. In a real sense, there is no "typical" American jail or prison. Enormous variation exists across regions, and even among states in the same region, and jurisdictions within the same state. Thus, to evaluate fully the impact of the prisoners' rights movement requires a more precise understanding of the extent of variance among federal district courts and among penal facilities.

Some prison officials welcome judicial intervention and have used the courts to obtain resources that otherwise would have been unobtainable (H. Schwartz 1972:791). Shrewd reform-oriented administrators can sign consent decrees and blame change on the courts — as a tactic for overcoming anticipated staff opposition. In some prisons, top officials cannot implement changes even when they desire to do so, because of administrative ineffectiveness, poor morale, and incomplete bureaucratization. Of course, compliance often depends upon the cooperation of other state officials, including the governor and legislature. We need to follow a cohort of cases through the federal courts to see how the "typical case" is resolved (*see* Turner 1979). Short of that, we must rely on impressions drawn from a few extraordinary cases that receive disproportionate attention and surely distort our perception of the amount of conflict produced by legal change and the amount of institutional resistance to change.

The Difficulty of Defining Success

How can one tell whether the judicial resolution of a particular controversy has been successfully implemented? If the mark of success is a restructured institution where all interests have been harmonized, and where the original intent of the court has not only been followed to the letter but has produced no dysfunctions, even years later, no institutional litigation will ever succeed. A perceptive student comment in the *Harvard Law Review* (1977:434) puts the matter bluntly, and in my view correctly:

> Yet failure is a function of expectations: we tend to expect complete protection of all legal rights by someone — either legislator, administrator, or judge. However, given intense conflicts of interest, lack of cooperation among necessary parties, shortage of resources, and the complexities of control and unresponsiveness that characterize organizations, the probability of full implementation of reform policies is likely to be quite low.

Prison and mental health bureaucracies are large and complicated. They are frequently racked by conflicting goals and competing staff factions. Needless to say, prisons rarely function "smoothly." Perhaps the question should not be whether a particular court intervention on behalf of prisoners was "successful," but whether it made a positive contribution to prisoners' lives or to prison administration. Even to answer this question, however, will be difficult, particularly when there will be disagreement about which organizational changes — for example, improved programs, freer correspondence policy, a better warden, lower guard morale — can be attributed to a particular court intervention, to the more active role of courts generally, or to the prisoners' rights movement broadly defined. And how will we judge the net effect of changes that point in opposite directions — for example, fewer severe and fewer arbitrary punishments, but more inmate-on-inmate aggressions? I do not pretend to have a methodology for evaluating impacts; in this chapter I will be content to point out the complexity of the problem. (Recent writing on the impact of prisoners' rights litigation includes Champagne and Haas 1976; Calhoun 1978; Hawkins 1976; Rubin 1974; on the general subject of legal impact studies, *see* Brown and Crowley 1979.)

The Problem of Assessing Compliance

Simply to measure the extent to which a particular prison administration complies with a particular court decision is not a satisfactory way to assess the impacts of the prisoners' rights movement on institutions; the most important impacts may operate indirectly. But even in measuring compliance with court decrees we encounter substantial conceptual difficulty. How can one tell whether an injunction has been complied with? Initially one needs to know what the decision required. But many declaratory judgments, consent decrees, and injunctions in prison cases are ambiguous. Many details are deliberately left to the parties to resolve. The court may retain jurisdiction for several years. What is required is often not apparent for some time after the initial decision. Reasonable persons may differ sharply on what a decree "really means."

Neither is it clear when compliance should be measured. Immediately following a decree there may be confusion, limited resources, and lack of organizational skill. Considerable time must pass before we can know whether inactivity is merely the temporary product of inefficiency and turmoil or is instead a "failure of compliance." As time passes, however, intervening variables emerge to confound evaluation. Initial compliance may quickly be eradicated by new events. No directed social change can be expected to persist in perpetuity. That more lawsuits are later necessary to vindicate previously declared rights or to establish new ones need not mean that the original court intervention "failed."

[53]

Hypotheses on the Impacts of the Prisoners' Rights Movement

One way to think about the impacts of the prisoners' rights movement is to determine the extent to which changing legal norms have been implemented. Another way is to consider how the changing legal status of prisoners is reflected in social, political, and organizational change. This second approach requires a good deal of speculation and imagination, even intuition, but in the end it may provide a more profound understanding of the prisoners' rights movement. Based on my own reading and research, the following hypotheses suggest the kinds of empirical research and theory building which need to go on if we are to increase our understanding of the impact of legal change on prisons.

1. *The prisoners' rights movement has contributed to the bureaucratization of the prison.* As Max Weber (1954) pointed out, there is a close relationship between law and bureaucracy. Until recently, prisons operated as traditional, nonbureaucratic institutions. There were no written rules and regulations, and daily operating procedures were passed down from one generation to the next. Wardens spoke of prison administration as an "art"; they operated by intuition. The ability of the administration to act as it pleased reinforced its almost total dominance of the inmates.

Early lawsuits revealed the inability of prison officials to justify or even to explain their procedures. The courts increasingly demanded rational decision-making processes and written rules and regulations; sometimes they even demanded better security procedures. The prisons required more support staff to meet the increasing demand for "documentation." New bureaucratic offices and practices began to appear. Lawrence Bershad (1977:58) notes: "Court-imposed due process requirements have made extensive and time consuming documentation a necessity." Harris and Spiller (1977:24) draw the following conclusion from their comprehensive study of four cases of protracted jail and prison litigation:

> By focusing attention on the severe deficiencies of the correctional system, the litigation created pressure for management reforms. Contemporaneously with the litigation, or soon thereafter, a broad range of important changes occurred. Those changes assumed different forms — new organizational structure, increased funding, new administrators, changes in personnel policies, new facilities, additional personnel, improved management procedures, etc. These changes were generally considered beneficial.

(*See also* Jacobs 1977: chs.5 and 6.)

2. *The prisoners' rights movement has produced a new generation of administrators.* Litigation created pressures to establish rational operating procedures, to clarify lines of authority, and to focus responsibility. Wardens were required to testify in court. Their rules and practices were subject to blistering

cross-examination. The despotic wardens of the old regime were neither temperamentally nor administratively suited to operate in the more complex environment fostered by court judgments and gradually have been replaced by a new administrative elite, which is better educated and more bureaucratically minded (Alexander 1978).

3. *The prisoners' rights movement expanded the procedural protections available to prisoners.* The Supreme Court, in *Wolff v. McDonnell* (1974), ruled that prisoners were entitled to rudimentary procedural protections when faced with forfeiture of good time or with special punitive confinement. The extension of procedural due process to prisoners continues, despite setbacks (*see, e.g., Meacham v. Fano* 1976). *Vitek v. Jones* (1980), affirms the prisoner's right to a hearing before transfer to a mental hospital.

Many legislatures and administrative agencies responsible for operating prisons also mandated more procedures in a variety of decision-making contexts. Many corrections departments have instituted prison grievance procedures that provide a formal and orderly mechanism for dispute resolution; some provide for final step arbitration by a neutral outsider (Breed 1976; Breed and Voss 1978; Singer and Keating 1973; Keating 1975, 1976). Federal legislation now requires the attorney general to promulgate "minimum standards" for inmate grievance procedings and to certify whether the states are in substantial compliance.

4. *The prisoners' rights movement has heightened public awareness of prison conditions.* Prison cases are increasingly brought to the attention of the public through the mass media. In 1976 the *New York Times* reported on prisoners' rights litigation on seventy-eight different occasions, accounting for 16 percent of its total prison coverage. Prisoners' rights cases made the CBS national news on eight separate occasions (*see* Chapter 5). Prison litigation may be the peaceful equivalent of a riot, in bringing prisoners' grievances to public attention and in mobilizing political support for change. On this point the observations of Harris and Spiller (1977:26) are instructive:

> The litigation sensitized public officials and public servants to correctional deficiencies and increased responsiveness to correctional needs. Legislative, regulatory, and supervisory bodies adopted rules, provided funds, and took other actions that facilitated correctional improvements. Changes were initiated that had not been ordered by the courts. In each jurisdiction, progressive administrators were able to take advantage of the general climate change that accompanied the litigation. In a sense, the court was used as a "scapegoat" and the court orders as a tool for improving correctional programs.

5. *The prisoners' rights movement has politicized prisoners and heightened their expectations.* The availability of judicial forums encouraged prisoners to believe that their grievances would be redressed. But it is not clear that the

movement has assuaged prisoners' discontent; to the contrary, it may have intensified it. Indeed, it would be surprising in light of historical experience if rising expectations did not outpace the realities of reform. A high level of prisoner pressures for continued improvements in prison conditions is accompanied by a high level of frustration and tensions. Fred Cohen (1973:864) provides the following insight on the prisoners' rights movement's psychological impact on prisoners:

> In my own experience in visiting and talking with numerous inmates (adult and juvenile) and parolees, there can be no doubt that their self-image has been dramatically altered. Where two or three years ago the questions asked of me would be almost exclusively concerned with defects in the conviction or, with regard to prison conditions, loss of good time and the vagaries of detainers, now the discussion focuses on *rights....Advances that are not attributed to prison rebellions seem most closely linked to successful litigation.* That this may prove to be dangerously romantic and disillusioning is the one point that I hope remains with the reader. [Emphasis added.]

6. *The prisoners' right movement has demoralized prison staff.* There is some basis to believe that today's correctional officers are more insecure, both morally and legally, about their position vis-a-vis inmates (see Chapter 6) than were their predecessors. Staff resent the inmates' access to the courts (*U.C.L.A. Law Review* 1973:494). They resent even more the impression that courts believe the prisoners and "favor them" over the guards. Leo Carroll's (1974:54) research at Rhode Island's maximum security prison led him to observe:

> The result of these [judicial] intrusions upon the coercive powers of the custodians has not only been normlessness in the area of job performance, but also a deterioration of the working relationships among the custodians. Like the police in the case of the Miranda decision, the officers view the court decisions as placing the law and the courts on the side of the inmate and in opposition to them. By extending legal rights to inmates, restricting the power of the officers and placing the institution on eighteen months probation, the decision makes the prisoners the "good guys." In short, the officers feel themselves betrayed and "sold out" by agencies that should support their authority. These agencies are not only the courts but the Department of Corrections itself. The nature of the court ruling was in the form of a consent decree, a compromise agreement between counsel for the plaintiffs and the Department of Corrections. The officers interpret this action as a betrayal by their own superiors.

Not only the officers but the top administrators also may resent being "second guessed" by the courts. It takes a high degree of professionalism to accept that courts have their job to do and must test administrative practice against statutory and constitutional requirements. Thus, Lawrence Bershad (1977:61) notes:

Courts define correctional staff consistently as defendants — a startling role change for people who entered prison work ostensibly for a combination of law enforcement and social work reasons. Correctional administrators no longer live in obscurity; rather their thoughts are memorialized in court transcripts and their careers become the subject of debate in the media.

Added to the psychological impact of frequent publicity is the consistent failure to persuade the courts of the wisdom and 'rightness' of correctional methodology. Thus, frustration, bitterness, confusion, and demoralization inevitably result, although usually without public expression.

7. *The prisoners' rights movement had made it more difficult to maintain control over prisoners.* The prisoners' rights movement has brought about significant limitations on the punishments that can be used against prisoners. Starvation, whipping, standing at attention, and exposure to freezing temperatures have been eliminated. There are also restrictions on the reasons for which a prisoner can be punished. Guard brutality may also have been deterred (although hardly stamped out) by the threat of liability for money damages in a suit for prisoner abuse. The net result is that prisoners are harder to control. More staff may be necessary to maintain order. Less punitive but possibly more intrusive mechanisms of control are now becoming more popular — closed-circuit televisions, more frequent use of tear gas, sophisticated locking systems, and unit management that seeks to limit inmate movement and contact.

8. *The prisoners' rights movement has contributed to a professional movement within corrections to establish national standards.* At least among the top correctional leadership, there is a strong desire to avoid the embarrassment of judicial scrutiny and denunciation. These officials do not want to be rebuked in federal court for poor administration and maintenance of inhumane institutions. Like workers generally, they place a high value on autonomy — they would strongly prefer to run the prisons without outside intervention. There is a growing feeling that good administrators stay "ahead of the courts." Professional rule making and standard setting is seen as an opportunity to increase correctional resources, improve conditions, and shield the profession from scathing outside criticism. The American Correctional Association, the professional organization of American prison officials, has recently embarked upon a concerted accrediting process, based upon rigorous standards covering almost all aspects of prison management (American Correctional Association 1978). If, as appears likely, most states voluntarily agree to subject their penal facilities to accreditation review, the process could have an enormous influence on corrections in the next decade.

[57]

Assessing the Significance of the Prisoners' Rights Movement

Many prison observers, including lawyers, express misgivings over the benefits brought by the prisoners' rights movement. Perhaps some prisoners' rights advocates hoped that the recognition and vindication of constitutional rights would dismantle the entire American prison system. To their disappointment, the same facilities and many traditional problems remain; even the best run, most benign prison remains an institution of punishment. They have therefore concluded that expansion of prisoners' rights and judicial reform will not significantly change the "system."

The indirect effects of the prisoners' rights movement are difficulty to identify and difficult to evaluate. Is it better or worse that today's prison is more fully bureaucratized than the prison of a decade ago? Some of the autocratic wardens may have been rooted out of corrections, but excessive bureaucratization has its own dysfunctions. Prisoners may find something insensitive and inhuman about administration by the book. While bureaucratization was a response to an earlier form of organization which could not justify its decisions or focus responsibility, excessive bureaucratization may lead to the same result: a mass of offices and office holders insulated from effective outside scrutiny.

Closely related to the advent of bureaucratization is the proliferation of due process. Here, too, one can legitimately question whether more and better procedures have led to higher quality and better outcomes. The Harvard Center for Criminal Justice (1972) found positive prisoner reaction to the disciplinary procedures implemented by *Morris v. Travisono* (1970), although the researchers themselves doubted the significance of the procedural changes. My Stateville study (Jacobs 1977) revealed no change in the numbers of prisoners sent to disciplinary confinement or in the offenses charged after the establishment of disciplinary due process. That the same personnel continued to make the decisions under the new rules undercut the value of the improved procedures. But the involvement of the central office of the Illinois Corrections Department in final-step grievance resolution has produced a credible administrative vehicle for dealing with complaints. While the "justice model" (Fogel 1975) remains to be fully elaborated and tested, it is yet an intriguing possibility for a new organizational model built upon the rule of law.

It is a speculation worth pursuing that the prisoners' rights movement has made the provision of welfare benefits to prisoners more logical and legitimate (*see, e.g., New York University Law Review* 1976). A study by Abt Associates documents the large increase of noncustodial service-type personnel in American prisons since 1950, especially in the past decade. Therapists, teachers, counselors, and medical technicians have become visible members of the prison regime. Schooling has almost achieved the status of a right. The prisons constitute school districts in some states (*see* Miller 1978). Availability of a school education seems to be nearly universal. Tuition-free programs in which prisoners can earn college credits are also common (Seashore and Haberfeld 1976). At Attica one-sixth of the prisoners are enrolled in college or junior college programs.

In the last several years, and particularly since the Supreme Court's decision in *Estelle v. Gamble* (1976), there has been substantial improvement in prison medical services (Neisser 1977). In 1975, at Stateville, there was only a handful of medical personnel. In 1979 the Illinois Department of Corrections and Prison Legal Services signed a consent decree that called for a medical staff of forty-eight persons (*Cook v. Rowe* 1979). Care is to be provided around the clock and includes the services of medical technicians stationed in each cell house, fully qualified nurses, a half-dozen dentists, several doctors, a physical therapist, and an X-ray technician. The American Medical Association sponsors an influential prison medical services project and publications program to improve medical care and health services in correctional institutions. As in other prison areas, suits over medical care have spurred the development of American Correctional Association accreditation standards.

The direct effects of the prisoners' rights movement are easier to identify, if difficult to quantify. In practically every prison in the United States one could point to concrete improvements in administrative practices and living conditions directly attributable to the prisoners' rights movement. Inmates who previously were not permitted to have the Koran, religious medallions, political and sociological monographs, and law books now possess them. Inmates once afraid to complain to relatives and public officials about their treatment are now less afraid. Censorship of outgoing mail has been all but eliminated. Censorship of incoming mail is less thorough and intrusive, increasing the privacy of written communication. Prisoners in isolation, segregation, and other disciplinary confinement suffer less from brutal punishments, cold, hunger, infested and filthy cells, and boredom. In some cases, Arkansas, for example, unspeakable tortures have been stopped. In some jails and penitentiaries, prisoners are spared the misery of greater overcrowding than already exists because court decrees limit the number of inmates. In numerous institutions major advances in the quality and delivery of medical services can be directly attributed to court decisions.

None of this denies the considerable suffering still imposed upon those who are incarcerated in the United States. The question is whether the prisoners' rights movement has made things significantly better. One's answer depends upon one's definition of "significantly" and some standard of reform against which current efforts can be compared. An exploration of the legal rights of prisoners inevitably leads to philosophical questions about the nature of imprisonment in a democratic society. To what extent must it be punitive and impose suffering? In my opinion, neither the extension of the rights of citizenship to

[59]

prisoners nor judicial scrutiny of prison conditions and practices will alter the punitive reality of imprisonment any more than expansion of the franchise and passage of equal employment legislation will alter the reality of the ghetto. In neither case am I ready to conclude that legal reform is not significant or important, although, to be sure, one must recognize the limits of legal reform. The prisoners' rights movement has not transformed the American prison into a utopian institution and will not.

Prisons are too often dilapidated, overcrowded, underfunded, and poorly governed. Still, the impact of prisoners' rights must be judged in light of social and political realities, and in my view, seen in that light, the movement has contributed greatly to the reduction of brutality and degradation, the enhancement of decency and dignity, and the promotion of rational governance.

[3]

Race Relations and
the Prisoner Subculture

Blacks, Mexicans, Puerto Ricans and members of other racial minorities now constitute the majority of American prisoners.[1] Behind the walls, white, black and Spanish-speaking inmates exist in separate conflict-ridden social worlds. While the racial composition of American prisons is often reported by the media[2] and is obvious to prison employees, inmates, and visitors, most sociologists who have studied prisons have ignored race relations entirely.

The core prisoner-subculture tradition in sociology can be traced to Donald Clemmer's (1958) *The Prison Community*, first published in 1940. Clemmer's classic study of the prisoner subculture at the southern Illinois maximum security prison at Menard did not mention prevailing racial etiquette and norms, despite his intent to describe the prisoners' social organization and culture. The oversight is curious in light of Clemmer's decision to report the percentage of blacks in the prison population (22–28 percent) and to dichotomize several tables (for example, intelligence, family background, recidivism) by race. Clemmer did point out that two of fourteen prisoner leaders were Negroes, but he did not say whether leadership bridged racial lines, neither are we told whether blacks were proportionately represented in the prisoners' class system or whether primary groups were racially heterogeneous.

Reprinted in slightly different form from Norval Morris and Michael Tonry, eds., *Crime and Justice. An Annual Review of Research*, vol. 1 (Chicago: Univ. of Chicago Press, 1979).

[1] Figures for 1973 show 48.1 percent of state prisoners recorded as black (Law Enforcement Assistance Administration, U.S. Dept. of Justice, Census of Prisoners in State Correctional Facilities 1973 (1976)). By 1979 the nationwide incarceration rate was 600 per 100,000 for blacks and 70.8 for whites (Christianson 1980). This disparity will become even greater in the next two decades (*see* Blumstein, Cohen, and Miller 1980). The authors' extrapolations indicate that nonwhites will constitute 55 percent of American prisoners by the year 2000.

[2] The *New York Times*, for example, printed 120 articles on race relations in prison between 1968 and 1977. Taken together they illuminate a situation of tension, strain, and conflict among prisoners and between prisoners and staff.

The generation of prison scholars which followed Clemmer did not build on his investigation of prisoners' social backgrounds. For the most part, this generation pursued Clemmer's analysis of "the inmate code" (prisoners' special norms), "argot roles" (prisoners' unique social roles related to "the primary axes of prison life"), and the process of "prisonization" (the socialization of new inmates). The works of Gresham Sykes marked the pinnacle of this body of research. In *Society of Captives* (1958) he presented an elaborate description of inmate argot roles (rats, center men, gorillas, merchants, wolves, punks, fags, ball busters, real men, toughs, and hipsters) and argued that they were functionally adapted to conditions of maximum security confinement and that they could be accounted for by the unique economic, social, and psychological deprivations imposed by imprisonment. Sykes and a co-author (Sykes and Messinger 1960) extended this descriptive and theoretical analysis of prisoner subculture, identifying and explaining the tenets of the inmate code by use of structural/functional analysis. They classified the tenets of the inmate code into five major groups: (1) Don't interfere with inmate interests; be loyal to your class — the cons. (2) Don't lose your head; play it cool and do your own time. (3) Don't exploit inmates; be right. (4) Don't weaken; be a man. (5) Don't be a sucker; be sharp.

The tradition that Sykes enriched and stimulated came to be known as the "indigenous origin" model of prisoner subculture. Those who followed Sykes continued to discover new argot roles and to test commitment to the inmate code, but no important new conceptualizations were made. Some policy-oriented scholars attempted to explain recidivism in terms of prisoners' commitment to the code and argot role playing. None of these studies, however, considered the importance of race for the society of prisoners. Even though 50 percent of New Jersey's prisoners were black when Sykes studied Rahway Prison, his work contained no explicit reference to race relations. He did mention in passing that "the inmate population is shot through with a variety of ethnic and social cleavages which sharply reduce the possibility of continued mass action" (Sykes 1958:81). Other scholars during this period continued the color-blind approach.

In 1962 John Irwin and Donald Cressey published their influential article "Thieves, Convicts and the Inmate Culture," which directly attacked the dominant structural/functional model of the prisoner subculture. While their article did not mention race, their argument (now known as the "importation hypothesis") that prisoner subculture is rooted in criminal and conventional subcultures outside the prison encouraged later researchers, including Irwin himself (1970), to focus on racial groupings. Since 1970 a small number of important studies on prisons have dealt explicitly with prisoners' race relations. This chapter attempts to develop the race relations perspective suggested by these studies, thereby pointing to new directions for prisoner subculture research. The first section sketches the history of race relations in American prisons. The second explores the implications of this social history for the core tradition of prisoner subculture research. The third section suggests how the race relations perspective could enrich future research on the prisoner subculture.

A Capsule History of Prison Race Relations

Prisons in every section of the United States have long been characterized by racial segregation and discrimination.[3] In their seminal criminology text, Harry Barnes and Negley Teeters (1959:466) state:

Negroes have been segregated from whites in most prisons where they appear in appreciable numbers. Negroes make up the bulk of the population of southern prison camps. Few northern prisons exercise the courage and social insight to break with outmoded customs of racial segregation.

(*See also* Sutherland and Cressey 1974:499.)

State laws in the south often required that prisoners, especially juveniles, be incarcerated in racially homogeneous facilities. In some states, particularly those where prison officials controlled vast plantations, black and white adult offenders were assigned to separate camps. In Arkansas, for example, Tucker Prison Farm housed white inmates and Cummings mostly blacks. In states with only a single penitentiary, or where racially heterogeneous prisons were maintained, segregation was enforced by cell and work assignments, and in all "extracurricular" activities. Consider the following description of prison race relations in Oklahoma in the early 1970s (*Battle v. Anderson* 1974):

Prior to the July [1973] riot, the policy and practice at the Oklahoma State Penitentiary was to maintain a prison system segregated by race and by means of which black inmates were subjected to discriminatory and unequal treatment. Except for the maximum security unit, . . . all inmates were routinely assigned to housing units on the basis of race. The reception center, the mess hall, the recreation yard and barber facilities were racially segregated. Black inmates were discriminated against in job assignments and were subjected to more frequent and disparate punishment than white inmates.

---

[3] It is a mistake to speak of prisons and prisoner subcultures as if only a single type existed throughout the United States. The distinctive features of each region's social structure and culture are found in prisons as well as in other political institutions. A comprehensive history of prison race relations would examine each region (and subregion). No such history has yet been written, and my reading of the record is likely to blur important regional and state variations.

The situation in Okalahoma was not unique; between 1963 and 1974 various courts declared racially segregated penal facilities to be unconstitutional in Alabama, Arkansas, the District of Columbia, Georgia, Louisiana, Maryland, Mississippi, and Nebraska.[4]

Racial segregation, or a racial caste system based upon pervasive discrimination against blacks, also characterized northern prisons. The New York State Special Commission on Attica (1972:80) reported that Attica had been administered on a segregated basis until the mid-1960s. "There were black and white sports teams, different barbers for blacks and whites, and separate ice buckets for black and white inmates on July 4." Likewise, in the wake of serious racial protests at Pendleton Reformatory, the Indiana State Committee to the U.S. Commission on Civil Rights (1971) found that state to have had "a very segregated prison system" and extensive racial discrimination.

Prisoners' race relations cannot be divorced from prison race relations, the racial context in which all the actors in the prison organization relate to one another. Until recently, and in all regions of the country, there were few, if any, members of racial minorities on the staffs of prisons. Until 1963 only thirty blacks had ever been appointed to guard positions in Statesville and Joliet prisons in Illinois (Jacobs 1977:184). The New York State Special Commission on Attica (1974:24) observed that: "In September 1971, there were over 500 people who were free to leave Attica every day: the Superintendent, two Deputy Superintendents, a uniformed correctional staff of 398 (supervisors and officers), and 145 civilians. There was one black civilian teacher, no black correction officers, and one Puerto Rican correction officer." To the extent that race mattered at all, the preferences, biases, and values of individual whites predominated. An account of the prisoner subculture, past or present, that did not consider the influence of the racially dominant group among the staff in structuring the patterns of interaction and opportunities (licit and illicit) among the prisoners would be hopelessly incomplete.

Unfortunately, little research has been done on the social backgrounds and values of white prison officials and, more particularly, on their attitudes toward blacks and other racial minorities. A working assumption could reasonably be made that most wardens shared the biases of the rural white populations of the areas where prisons were located and from which prison guards and other officials were drawn. In these areas, as in American society generally, at

---

[4] Cases declaring prison segregation unconstitutional are: Alabama — *Washington v. Lee* (1966); Arkansas — *Board of Managers of the Ark. Training School for Boys at Wrightsville et al. v. George* (1967); District of Columbia — *Dixon v. Duncan* (1963); *Bolden v. Pegelow* (1964); Georgia — *Wilson v. Kelley* (1968); Louisiana — *Major v. Sowers* (1969); Maryland — *State Bd. of Public Welfare v. Meyers* (1961); Mississippi — *Gates v. Collier* (1972); Nebraska — *McClelland v. Sigler* (1971); Oklahoma — *Battle v. Anderson* (1974). *See also Singleton v. Board of Comm'rs of State Insts. et al.* (1966) (remanding challenge to Florida statute requiring racial segregation of male juveniles).

least until recently, blacks were viewed as a lower racial caste. This assumption is supported at Stateville Penitentiary in Illinois. The warden who served from 1936 to 1961, and the guards whom he recruited to serve with him, came from rural southern Illinois. While the regime was not vulgarly racist, it simply expected black prisoners to accept their lower caste status.

In the late 1950s blacks began to protest segregation and discrimination in prisons as in other sectors of the society. Their vehicle of protest was the Black Muslim movement, and in this sense the prison situation is unique. The Black Muslims actively proselytized black prisoners, preaching a doctrine of black superiority. They imported the spirit of "black nationalism" into the prisons, catalyzed the frustration and bitterness of black prisoners, and provided organizational and ideological tools for challenging the authority of white prison officials. Prison officials saw in the Muslims not only a threat to prison authority but also a broader revolutionary challenge to American society (*see* Jacobs 1977:ch. 3). Until the mid-1960s, and sometimes later, they did everything in their power to crush the Muslims. Paradoxically, this may have contributed to the vigor and success of the Muslims' efforts. In any case, the modern "crisis in corrections" is attributable to the changing pattern of race relations which began with the Muslim protests.

At the 1960 convention of the American Correctional Association, Donald Clemmer, head of the District of Columbia Department of Corrections (and author of *The Prison Community*), reported that the Black Muslims in D.C. prisons were a seriously disruptive force. "The disturbing phenomena of the Muslims in prison are their nonconformance and their bitter racial attitudes" (Clemmer and Wilson 1960:153). Clemmer explained that the Black Muslims preached racial hatred and defied authority by actively proselytizing other black prisoners and by congregating in the prison yard for meetings and prayer. He responded by locking the "cult" in punitive segregation, not to punish them for their religious beliefs, but for "direct violation of standard rules" (154). The American Correctional Association subsequently passed a resolution denouncing the Black Muslims, and rejecting their claim to be a bona fide religion. Two years after Clemmer's talk at the American Correctional Association convention, a federal court ordered him to stop treating the Muslims differently from other religious groups (*Fulwood v. Clemmer* 1962).

At Stateville Penitentiary in Illinois an internal memorandum of March 23, 1960, reported that fifty-eight Negro prisoners were affiliated with the Muslims (Jacobs 1977:ch. 3). In July 1960 the first collective disturbance at Stateville in more than a decade occurred when the Muslims demonstrated in the segregation unit where they had been placed as punishment for congregating in the yard. Four years later, the Muslims became the first prisoners in Stateville's history to present written demands to the administration. They called for an end to interference with Muslim religious practices and to racial discrimination. Illinois officials resisted every demand, including opportunities for group prayer, reading of the Koran, contact with ministers, and access to *Muhammad Speaks*, the official Black Muslim newspaper.

When C. Eric Lincoln published his history of the Black Muslims in 1961, there were already three Muslim temples behind the walls. Claude Brown (1965), Malcolm X [Little] (1965), Eldridge Cleaver (1968), and George Jackson (1970,1972) all pointed in their writings to the significance of the Black Muslims in the prisons during the late 1950s and early 1960s. These authors, except Claude Brown, were themselves politicized through their contacts with the Black Muslims in prison.[5]

The ideology of black superiority, preached by Elijah Muhammad and his followers, appealed to many black inmates. It provided a vehicle for venting frustration and hostility against the prison officials who had assigned blacks to second-class status in an institution that already denied its inhabitants the rights of citizenship. The Muslims claimed that American blacks had been repressed and degraded by white society and blamed white prison officials for continuing that repression.

As the numbers of Muslims increased and their influence grew, the social organization of the prison underwent profound changes. Through the Muslims black nationalism penetrated the prison and politicized the minority prisoners. First, the Muslims directly and successfully challenged the caste system that assigned blacks to a subservient position. Second, the Muslims challenged a basic tenet of penal administration — that every prisoner "must do his own time." Like the Jehovah's Witnesses who had been incarcerated en masse in the federal prisons for draft resistance during World War II (Sibley and Wardlaw 1945), the Muslims wanted to be recognized not as individuals but as a group with its own authority structure and communal interests. Thus, the Muslims contributed to the Balkanization of prisoner society, a salient characteristic of prisoner subculture ever since. Third, the Muslims initiated litigation that resulted in federal court intervention in prison administration. In hundreds of lawsuits the Muslims protested censorship, disciplinary practices, and, or course, religious discrimination. The Muslims won most of the opportunities for religious worship enjoyed by members of conventional religions, although full equality has yet to be achieved. Few prisons, for example, hire Muslim ministers on the same basis as Catholic and Protestant chap-

---

[5] In a "random sample" of seventy-one wardens and superintendents of federal and state prisons, Caldwell (1968) found that 31 percent claimed "substantial Muslim activity." Another 21 percent reported "some or limited Muslim activity." According to the author, "those who reported no Muslim activity came from states with relatively small Negro populations and small percentages of Negroes in prison."

lains. Pork-free diets, Arabic Korans, religious medallions, and opportunities for daily prayer continue to be litigated. Still, the Muslims are responsible for a new era of federal court involvement in prison administration. David Rothman points out (1973:14—15):

> When Black Muslims in 1961 pressed the cause of religious freedom in prison, judges found the right too traditional, the request too reasonable, and the implications of intervention ostensibly so limited that they had to act. They ruled that inmates should be allowed to attend services and to talk with ministers without fear of penalty. "Whatever may be the view with regard to ordinary problems of prison discipline," declared the court in *Pierce v. LaVallee* (1961), "we think that a charge of religious persecution falls into quite a different category." That the litigants were black, at a time when courts were growing accustomed to protecting blacks from discrimination, made the intervention all the more logical.

No studies were made of the impact of the Black Muslims on the prisoners' informal network of social relations. The Muslims appear to have heightened tensions between black and white prisoners. While the Muslims were more antagonistic to white officials than to white prisoners, white prisoners often complained of racist talk and behavior by blacks (Jacobs 1977:ch. 3). Undoubtedly members of the dominant white caste were made uncomfortable by the Muslims. By achieving such a high degree of solidarity the Muslims probably strengthened the positions of individual members in the prisoner subculture and perhaps increased their opportunities for economic gain within the prisoner economy. Ironically, after their religious grievances were redressed, the Muslims became a quiescent and stabilizing force in many prisons, which began to be rocked by new cohorts of violent and disorganized ghetto youth (*see, e.g.*, Glaser 1964:152—54; New York State Special Commission on Attica 1972:112).

By 1970 racial avoidance and conflict had become the most salient aspect of the prisoner subculture. John Irwin (1970:80) now supplemented the earlier Irwin-Cressey (1962) "importation hypothesis" with explicit attention to the subject of race:

> For quite some time in California prisons, hostility and distance between three segments of the population — white, Negroes and Mexicans — have increased. For several years the Negroes have assumed a more militant and ethnocentric posture, and recently the Mexicans — already ethnocentric and aggressive — have followed with a more organized, militant stance. Correspondingly, there is a growing trend among these two segments to establish, reestablish or enhance racial-ethnic pride and identity. Many "Blacks" and "Chicanos" are supplanting their criminal identity with a racial-ethnic one.

[67]

The prisons were an especially ripe arena for protest and conflict because of their long history of segregation and discrimination. Once again, the findings of the New York State Special Commission on Attica (1972:4) are illuminating:

> Above all, for both inmates and officers, "correction" meant an atmosphere charged with racism. Racism was manifested in job assignments, discipline, self-segregation in the inmate mess halls, and in the daily interaction of inmate and officer and among the inmates themselves. There was no escape within the walls from the growing mistrust between white middle America and the residents of urban ghettos. Indeed, at Attica, racial polarity and mistrust were magnified by the constant reminder that the keepers were white and the kept were largely black and Spanish-speaking. The young black inmate tended to see the white officer as the symbol of a racist, oppressive system which put him behind bars.

By 1974 a nationwide census of penal facilities revealed that 47 percent of all prisoners were black (Gottfredson, Hindelang, and Parisi 1978). In many state prisons blacks were in the majority.[6] The numbers of Puerto Ricans and Mexicans also increased, but nationwide figures are unavailable since statistics in most states still make no distinction between Spanish-speaking and "white" prisoners.[7] In a few north central states, native Americans in the prisons emerged as an increasingly militant group.[8] Race relations are characterized by avoidance, strain, tension, and conflict.[9] The most publicized racial polarization has occurred in California, where Chicanos, blacks, and whites compete for power and dominance (Minton 1971; Irwin 1970; Pell 1972; Yee 1973; Wright 1973; Davidson 1974; Irwin 1977). Each racial block promotes its own culture and values, and attains what supremacy can be achieved at the expense of the others. A disaffected San Quentin staff member describes the prisoner subculture in the early 1970s in the following terms:

[6] In 1973 the states with a majority or near majority of black prisoners were Alabama (62 percent), Arkansas (48 percent), Delaware (60 percent), Florida (49 percent), Georgia (64 percent), Illinois (58 percent), Louisiana (71 percent), Maryland (74 percent), Michigan (58 percent), Mississippi (63 percent), New Jersey (50 percent), New York (58 percent), North Carolina (54 percent), Ohio (46 percent), Pennsylvania (57 percent), South Carolina (59 percent), and Virginia (59 percent) (U.S. Department of Justice 1976).

[7] In 1973 Arizona reported 25 percent Mexicans. Theodore Davidson (1974) reports that 18 percent of the prisoners at San Quentin were Mexican at the time of his study, 1966–68.

[8] North Dakota and Minnesota are two states with a visible native American presence in prison. One Minnesota official told me that one cell house wing at the Stillwater maximum security unit is known as "the reservation." Minnesota listed 10 percent of its prisoner population as "other" in 1973 and North Dakota 15 percent (*see* U.S. Department of Justice 1976).

[9] Vernon Fox (1972:14) points out that the first prison race riot in American history occurred in Virginia in 1962. In a survey using the *New York Times* Index, the South Carolina Department of Corrections (1973) identified race as at least one of the causes of eleven different riots between 1969 and 1971. A survey of the *New York Times* Index for 1972–78 reveals scores of conflicts in which race is named as a contributing factor. Of course many other collective disturbances may not have come to the attention of the *Times*, or may not have been reported.

The dining hall continued to be segregated, and any man sitting out of his racially determined place was risking his life. The television viewing room in each living unit was segregated, proximity to the TV set being determined by which racial group possessed the greatest power at any particular time. Within the living units, any man who became too friendly with a man of another race would be visited by representatives of his own racial group and pressured into maintaining segregation. If he did not, he would be ostracized from his group and would run the risk of physical attack or even death at the hands of his own race. [Rundle 1973:167−68]

A Soledad prisoner writes:

CTF Central at Soledad, California, is a prison under the control of the California Department of Corrections.... However, by the 1960s the prison had earned the label of "Gladiator School"; this was primarily because of the never-ending race wars and general personal violence which destroyed any illusions about CTF Central being an institution of rehabilitation.... Two of the wings — O and X — are operated under maximum custody under the care of armed guards. There is no conflict between policy, reality and intent here: These are the specially segregated areas where murder, insanity and the destruction of men is accepted as a daily way of life. It is within these wings that the race wars become the most irrational; where the atmosphere of paranoia and loneliness congeal to create day-to-day existence composed of terror. [Minton 1971:84]

And in an interesting and thoughtful account of racial violence in Soledad and San Quentin, journalist Minn Yee (1973) traces a macabre series of events which began when three black prisoners were fatally shot by a white guard in a Soledad exercise yard in early 1970. A white guard was reputedly murdered in retaliation. George Jackson and two other "Soledad Brothers" were charged with the crime. Jonathan Jackson's attempt to free the Soledad Brothers in a guerrilla-style attack on the Marin County Court House led to his own death, that of a judge, and several others. A few months later, six prisoners and guards, and George Jackson himself, were killed in a bizarre "escape attempt" at San Quentin.

Racial polarization was reinforced by the proliferation of formal organizations built around racial symbolism and ideology. The Black Guerrilla Family emerged as an umbrella organization for blacks, and the Aryan Brotherhood, a neo-Nazi organization, served to organize whites, particularly rural "okies" and "bikers" (motorcycle gang members). Race relations deteriorated to such an extent that California officials felt compelled to segregate their maximum security "adjustment centers" to avoid bloodshed.

California's Chicano prisoners have also attracted a great deal of attention, probably because of the murderous feud that has for several years raged between two factions, La Familia and Mexican Mafia (Park 1976). Theodore

[69]

Davidson (1974), an anthropologist, studied the organization of La Familia at San Quentin before the internal feuding began. He pointed out that La Familia emerged in response to staff racism and the Chicanos' own feeling of cultural isolation. La Familia's organization and code of secrecy are rooted in the barrio culture and the creed of *machismo*.

Numerous killings and knifings (58 deaths and 268 stabbings in 1971–73), largely attributable to the feud between the two Chicano groups, have led to official attempts to separate La Familia and Mafia in different prisons. Since it has not been possible to identify all members accurately, the violence continues. The real and imaginary structure and activities of the two organizations have captured the imagination of many California prison officials and prisoners (Park 1976:93–94).

Racial polarization is also evident in California's juvenile institutions. Norman Dishotsky and Adolph Pfefferbaum (1978:4) report that

> the ordinary events of everyday life at Northern California Youth Center, like those at the maximum security penitentiaries, were dictated by a code of ethnic separation. Afro-American, Caucasian-American and Mexican-American inmates lived side by side but maintained three distinct adolescent ethnic cultures by selected ingroup relatedness and outgroup avoidance. Inmates did not eat at the same table, share food, drinks, cigarettes or bathroom facilities with individuals of other ethnic groups. They would not sit in the same row while viewing television or even talk for more than brief interchanges with members of a different ethnic group. These customs were enforced by the power faction within each ethnic group.

Members of "white power," "black power," and "Mexican power" factions are hard-core racists:

> Symbols of ethnic group and power subgroup identification were a prominent feature of adolescent inmate culture. Body tattoos were indelible symbols of group identification. Among Mexican-American youths, the tattoos were ethnic group symbols — such as "La Raza," and the hometown barrio. Among Caucasians the tattoos were subgroup symbols such as "White Power," the swastika and NSWPP, the initials of the National Socialist White Peoples Party — a derivative of the American Nazi Party. [Dishotsky and Pfefferbaum 1978:6]

Leo Carroll (1974) found the same pattern of racial separatism, albeit with less violence, at Rhode Island's maximum security prison in 1970–71. He found that, despite efforts by the administration to integrate the facility, the prisoners voluntarily segregated themselves in all facets of the daily round. Black and white prisoners lived and worked next to each other, but their interaction was limited. Each group organized its own social and economic systems. Despite their shared status as prisoners, the gap between blacks and whites was unbridgeable. The cultural world of black prisoners revolved around "soul" and "black nationalism." Blacks defined whites as weak and exploitable; they related to each other as "brothers" and "partners." To the extent that divisions existed among the black prisoners, it was on the basis of politicization; Carroll distinguished "revolutionaries," "half-steppers," and "toms."

Francis Ianni's research on New York State prisons led him to conclude that ethnic segregation is the first rule of inmate social organization (1974:162). A study of an Ohio juvenile facility with equal numbers of blacks and whites further supports the claim that today's prisoner subculture is dominated by racial polarization and conflict (Bartollas, Miller, and Dinitz 1976). Lower-class blacks are the dominant group, followed by middle-class blacks, lower-class whites, and middle-class whites. Inmate norms for blacks are: exploit whites, do not force sex on blacks, and defend your brother. In contrast, whites' norms include: do not trust anyone and each man for himself.

My own study of Stateville Penitentiary (Jacobs 1977) also reveals a prisoner subculture divided along racial lines. The blacks are the dominant group, although divided into three warring "super gangs" that have been transported from Chicago's streets. The "Latinos" define themselves as separate from blacks and whites. They voluntarily interact only with other Spanish-speaking inmates and have achieved some solidarity through the Latin Kings, a Chicago street gang. The whites constitute a weak minority (except for an Italian clique associated with the Mafia), lacking any organization or cohesion; white prisoners are highly vulnerable to exploitation.

The prisoner subculture at Stateville is an extension of gang life in the ghetto. Inside the prison interracial hostilities intensify because intraracial peer groups completely dominate the lives of the prisoners. Few, if any, other activities or interests compete for a prisoner's energies. Inmates live as if in fish tanks where behavior is continually scrutinized. Under such circumstances "hardline" racist norms are easy for leaders to enforce and difficult for individual prisoners to ignore.

By the mid-1970s the dominance of racial cleavages in American prisons was evident to growing numbers of observers, including scholars. In every region of the country, race is the most important determinant of an individual's prison experience. Explicit discrimination by staff members may have decreased over the past decade, but racial polarization and conflict among prisoners have intensified. And staff members have been charged with exacerbating and manipulating interprisoner racial hostilities as a means of maintaining control (*see, e.g.*, Ianni 1974:171; Yee 1973).

The status and opportunity structures of prisoners and of their culture are now, in many prisons, dominated by blacks and Spanish-speaking inmates. The prison, like the urban school, has undergone a massive demographic transition. As in the case of the school, the influx of urban blacks and other minorities has

[71]

had enormous effect on the "client culture" and the formal organization.

One of the most striking facts about contemporary prison race relations is the dominance of the black prisoners. Francis Ianni (1974:178) contrasts the positions of a typical black and a typical white prisoner in one of New York State's penal facilities:

> Hicks is typical of the young, black inmate from the urban ghetto whose posture toward the authorities has become offensive rather than smiling-at-the-man-while-picking-his-pocket. He operates on an awareness that, in terms of sheer presence, the black inmates are the largest, and because of their numbers the most influential group in prison. McChesney [a white prisoner] is more typical of traditional inmate attitudes of "doing your own time" which include attitudes of guilt and submissiveness toward the authorities. His cloak-and-dagger schemes are the result of his sense of isolation and his fearful outlook.

Even in prisons where blacks constitute less than a majority, they exercise dominion. At the Rhode Island Adult Correctional Institution, where blacks were only 25 percent of the prisoner population, Leo Carroll found that 75 percent of the homosexual rapes involved black aggressors and white victims (1974:182). There were no cases of white aggressors and black victims (*see also* Davis 1968; Scacco 175:4). As one black prisoner told Carroll:

> "Every can I been in that's the way it is . . . It's gettin' even I guess . . . You guys been cuttin' our b——s off ever since we been in this country. Now we're just gettin' even" (1974:184).

The black prisoners completely dominated whites in an Ohio juvenile institution studied by Clemens Bartollas, Stuart Miller, and Simon Dinitz (1976). The inmate leaders, except one, were black, even though almost 50 percent of the inmates were white. The white prisoners were unable to organize. Consequently, they were highly vulnerable to exploitation.

> The exploitation matrix typically consists of four groups, and the form of exploitation found in each is fairly clear cut. At the top normally is a black leader called a "heavy." He is followed closely by three or four black lieutenants. The third group, a mixture of eight to sixteen black and white youths, do the bidding of those at the top. This group is divided into a top half of mostly blacks, known as "alright guys," with the bottom half comprised mostly of whites, designated as "chumps." One or two white scapegoats make up the fourth group in each cottage. These scapegoats become the sexual victims of the first three groups. [Bartollas, Miller, and Dinitz 1976:72]

The black prisoners not only wielded physical power, but "through their prevailing position, blacks control[led] the music played, the television programs watched, the kinds of food eaten, the style of clothing worn, and the language employed" (Bartollas, Miller, and Dinitz 1976:61). White youths seeking to improve their status adopt black language, mannerisms, and clothing styles.

Several research studies have shown that interracial rapes in prison are predominantly perpetrated by blacks against whites (*see* Carroll, 1974; Scacco, 1975; Davis, 1968). This finding has been most recently confirmed in Daniel Lockwood's study of prison sexual violence in New York State (1980:28):

> About half of the whites in the random sample were targets [of sexual aggression] at one time, compared to about a fifth of the blacks and Hispanics. If we look only at whites interviewed in the youth prison, the rate is even higher (71 percent), indicating the problem is most severe among white youths. Looking at the race of aggressors in incidents described by targets, we find that most are black (80 percent), some are Hispanic (14 percent), and a few are white (6 percent). The percentages are almost reversed when we examine the ethnicity of targets in incidents: Most incidents had white targets (83%), some had Black targets (16%), and a few had Hispanic targets (2%). Other studies parallel our finding with respect to the tendency of targets to be white and aggressors to be black.

Numbers will not fully explain the hegemony of black and other minority prisoners, even when the dominant group is also a majority. The key to black dominance is their greater solidarity and ability to intimidate whites. As the distinct minority in the larger society, blacks have long experienced racial discrimination. They have necessarily defined themselves in terms of their racial identity and have linked their opportunities in the larger society to the fate of their race. Whites, especially outside the South, have had almost no experience in grouping together on the basis of being white. Ethnicity has been a more important basis for social interaction, although even ethnicity has been a weaker basis of collective action for whites than race for blacks. "Whiteness" simply possesses no ideological or cultural significance in American society, except for racist fringe groups. Consequently, whites face imprisonment alone or in small cliques based on outside friendships, neighborhood, or ethnic background.

Aside from Italian cliques clothed in the Mafia mystique (*see* Carroll 1974:67-68; Jacobs 1977:159), white cliques are too weak to offer individuals any protection in the predatory prisoner subculture. Only in California does it appear that white prisoners have been able to achieve a strong enough organization to protect themselves. It is significant that such organization has been achieved by groups that already had some sense of group consciousness ("okies" and "bikers"), and only then by an extreme emphasis upon white racism. Neo-Nazi prisoner movements have also appeared in Illinois, especially at Menard, and may in the long run be the basis on which white prisoners achieve solidarity.

This picture of intense racial polarization, perhaps leading toward extreme racism on all sides, poses tremendous challenges to prison officials.[10] Unfortunately, the challenge comes at a time when prison officials have lost confidence in themselves owing to the repudiation of both punishment and rehabilitation as justifications for imprisonment. Authority has also been lost to the courts and to outside agencies, including centralized correctional bureaucracies. In addition, the legitimacy of prison regimes has been sharply questioned on racial grounds. Several national commissions, academic critics, and numerous prisoner petitions have attacked the hegemony of whites in elite as well as staff positions in the prisons. Affirmative action efforts have slowly increased the number of minorities (*see* American Bar Association 1973), but it is questionable whether this change has increased the legitimacy of prison regimes in the eyes of the prisoners. Furthermore, the politics of race have created intrastaff tensions, with some white guards doubting the loyalty of black employees. Lawsuits have been brought by both black and white guards charging discrimination, and patterns of racial self-segregation are now evident among prison staff as well as among the prisoners.

Prison Race Relations and the Core Tradition of Sociological Prison Research

Despite the importance of race relations for staff-prisoner, prisoner-prisoner, and staff-staff relations and for stimulating the intervention of the courts into prison administration, few studies of prison race relations were carried out before 1970. It is beyond the scope of this chapter to explain why prison

[10] In his fictional account of maximum security prison life based upon his own experience in California prisons, Edward Bunker (1977:42) has the wife of a San Quentin prisoner describe her husband's drift toward organized racial hatred: "He did not use to be prejudiced but now he hates blacks. He and some other white friends formed an American Nationalist Socialist group which I guess is a Nazi group because they hate blacks so much." Sociologist John Irwin (1980:182), probably the most penetrating observer of the California prison system over the past quarter century notes that "the races, particularly black and white, are divided and hate each other . . . white prisoners, whether or not they were racially hostile before prison, tend to become so after experiencing prison racial frictions . . . whites hate, and, when they are not organized to resist, fear black prisoners." Psychiatrist Norman Dishotsky and Adolph Pfefferbaum (1979) provide a provocative theoretical analysis to explain why and how prisons are a breeding ground for racism.

scholars of the 1950s and 1960s failed to include race in their descriptions and analyses of prisoner subcultures. One might ask why researchers in many disciplines for so long ignored the roles of women and blacks. Perhaps an intellectual history of research on prisoner subcultures will reveal that white sociologists simply were not sensititive to the pains and affronts of the prison's racial caste system. We should not forget that many studies were carried out at a time when race relations throughout American society were characterized by *de jure* segregation and pervasive discrimination. It may even be that race relations in some prisons were more "progressive" than in other social contexts. At least in such prisons as Stateville, blacks and whites lived and worked in close physical proximity.

Another possible explanation lies in the intellectual history of sociology itself. As John Irwin (1977) has noted, prison sociology historically has followed the discipline's dominant concepts and theories. Such sociologists as Donald Clemmer sought to apply concepts such as "primary group" and "culture." Sociologists in the 1950s and 1960s strove to fit prison research into the structural/functional paradigm. Later, as conflict theory became popular, some sociologists (*e.g.*, Wright 1973) began to view the prison in a more political light, especially emphasizing the fact that blacks and other minorities were overrepresented in prisoner populations by five times and more.

A theory, or even an intellectual tradition, can be criticized for internal inconsistencies or for failing to account for observable phenomena that the theory purports to explain. However, a theory cannot fairly be criticized for failing to explain what it does not purport to explain. The core tradition of prisoner subculture research has been subjected to extensive criticism on grounds of internal consistency, methodology, and inability to find confirmation in empirical studies. Indeed, "reviews of the literature" themselves are increasing so rapidly that a "review of the reviews" will soon be in order (*see, e.g.*, Hawkins 1976; Thomas and Petersen 1977; Bowker 1977). These internal criticisms will not be repeated here. Instead, we may inquire whether data about prison race relations invalidate the model of prisoner subculture based upon an inclusive inmate code and a functionally interlocking system of argot roles.

One may ask whether there ever existed an inmate code that was known by all prisoners and that commanded their lip service. If such a code did exist, in what sense did it provide standards by which members of prisoner society evaluated their own actions and those of fellow prisoners? In light of what is known about prison race relations through the mid-1960s and assuming the existence of an inmate code, it seems implausible that black and white prisoners were equally committed to each of its tenets or that members of each racial group applied the code uniformly to themselves and to members of the other group. The tenet requiring class solidarity among prisoners seems particularly vulnerable in light of the systematic discrimination against black

[75]

officials and white prisoners. Likewise, members of the Black Muslims explicitly rejected the notion that all prisoners should be treated the same and that all prisoners should do their own time.

The second strand of the core tradition's description of the prisoner community was a system of functionally interlocking argot roles, unique to prison life. The number and types of argot roles and their definitions varied from study to study. The race relations perspective does not deny the existence of such roles; it does suggest that argot roles, like other roles, are differentially available to different segments of a population according to salient background characteristics, particularly race. Sykes's research, and that of other prison scholars, would have been enriched by an analysis of the racial distribution of the various argot roles. Where whites were established as the dominant caste it seems unlikely that the argot roles organized around illicit economic transactions (for example, merchants) would have been equally available to blacks and whites. If so, it surely undermines the validity of the conceptualization of the prisoner social system as a system of functionally interlocking roles.

Whether one focuses on the normative (inmate code) or action (argot role) components of prisoner subculture as depicted in the core tradition, integration and consensus appear to have been overemphasized at the expense of factionalism and conflict. This does not mean, however, that the prisoner subculture would more adequately have been described as two cultures — one black and one white — any more than American society as a whole would be best described in such dualistic terms. It is possible both to speak of prisoners as a class or group and, at the same time, to recognize this class to be internally fragmented.

The only social science journal article on race relations covering the period of officially sanctioned racial segregation in prison supports this view. Nathan Kantrowitz, a staff sociologist at Stateville, studied prisoner vocabulary during the late 1950s and early 1960s (Kantrowitz 1969). He found that black and white prisoners lived in two separate linguistic worlds. Of 114 words used by prisoners to connote race, only 8 were used by both blacks and whites; Negro prisoners had 56 words referring to race, which they alone used; whites had 50 unique words. With respect to other aspects of prison life (for example, drugs, sex, religion) common vocabulary far exceeded separate vocabularies. Thus, Kantrowitz concluded: "Among convicts, the worlds of black men and white men are separate and in conflict. But each of their — ironically, separate but equal — worlds contains an 'inmate culture' almost identical with the other" (1969:32).

The prisoner subculture can be analyzed in abstract holistic terms or it can be studied more concretely with stress on its strains and divisions. At different times, in different regions, and in different prisons either the inclusive or divisive aspects of the prisoner subculture may appear more salient. Beginning in the late 1950s racial divisions in prison came closer to the surface. Racial protests and even race riots were soon reported by the press. Since that time the core tradition has seemed less useful in explaining what is happening in American prisons. Although Lee Bowker (1977) devotes only two pages to race and ethnic group relations in his book-length review of prisoner subculture research, he offers this curious conclusion: "In surveying the literature on prisoner subcultures, we find that the more contemporary the study, the less likely the unitary subculture model is to be consistent with the data collected. Wherever minority groups begin to gain numbers, multiple subcultures arise" (1977:126). His view reflects the gropings of many contemporary prison scholars. The old prisoner subculture research seems to be exhausted; there is a pressing need for new descriptions and conceptualization.

Race Relations and Future Prisoner Subculture Research

Future research should focus on the racial composition of various prisoner subcultures. Do prisoner populations with a black majority, or large minority, behave differently from the way prisoner populations act where blacks comprise a smaller percentage of the total? To what extent are prisoner subcultures that consist of three or more racial groups different from prisoner subcultures where there are only two racial groups? And in the multiracial group prisons do the same interracial group alliances always form? Studies along these lines must correct the long-standing tendency to ignore regional differences. It should make a difference whether prisons are located in the Southwest, with its large Mexican-American population, in the north central states, where native American movements are becoming significant, or in the South, with its distinctive history of paternalistic race relations. Few, if any, of the prisoner subculture studies reported in the literature have been conducted in these regions.

The prison is but one setting, albeit with very special characteristics, in which relationships among the races in American society are undergoing change. How race relations in prison differ from race relations in other societal contexts should be a prime issue for research, the answer to which will reveal much about the nature of prison and the functioning of the contemporary prisoner subculture.

Unfortunately, no systematic study of race relations in prisons has yet appeared. However, the studies discussed in the first part of this chapter suggest a situation of avoidance, self-segregation, and interracial conflict. It is crucial to compare the degree of avoidance, self-segregation, and conflict in the prisoner subculture with that in other settings, such as housing projects, schools, and the military where members of different racial groups are involuntarily thrown together.

It is hard to imagine a setting that would be less conducive to accommodative race relations than the prison. Its inmate population is recruited from the least successful and most unstable elements of both majority and minority racial groups. Prisoners are disproportionately representative of the more violence-prone members of society. As a result of crowding, idleness, boredom, sexual deprivation, and constant surveillance prisons produce enormous interpersonal tension.

Future prisoner subculture research needs to consider what factors serve to stabilize prisoners' race relations. Leo Carroll (1974) points out that a group of white Mafia in the Rhode Island prison exerted their influence to prevent prison race relations from further deterioration. In California, despite an extraordinary amount of violence, an uneasy power balance exists between three racial blocs, with groups of Chicanos allied with both blacks and whites. At Stateville, Latinos protected themselves through a high degree of solidarity and the strength of the Latin Kings, a well-organized street gang that posed a credible threat of retaliation for assaults on Latino prisoners. Prison officials provided some protection for whites by placing them in jobs where they would not be vulnerable. Throughout the 1970s, whites increasingly sought protection by having themselves assigned to "protective custody" — twenty-four-hour-a-day confinement in special tiers (Conrad and Dinitz 1977). In many prisons as much as 25 percent of the inmate population is assigned to protective custody; usually the vast majority of this population is white. How prevalent and how effective each of these social control mechanisms is for preventing racial conflict in the prisoner subculture are questions which can be answered only by extensive empirical research.

Do prisoner race relations differ according to levels of security? My own observations at Vienna, a model minimum security unit in Illinois (*see* Chapter 5) indicated a prisoner subculture highly polarized along racial lines, although the level of violence was very low. The two studies of male juvenile institutions discussed earlier in this essay (Dishotsky and Pfefferbaum 1978; Bartollas, Miller, and Dinitz 1976) suggest that prisoner race relations in juvenile institutions are quite similar to adult male prisons. Perhaps the race relations perspective will lead to integration of prisoner subculture research on adult, juvenile, and women's institutions.

Conclusion

The view of the prison as a primitive society, governed by its own norms and inhabited by its own distinctive social types, was always somewhat exaggerated. Racial divisions are not the only cleavages that exist within the prisoner subculture, but in many contemporary prisons racial politics set the background against which all prisoner activities are played out. Taking race relations into account will help correct the overemphasis on the uniqueness of prisons and will lead to a fuller understanding of the prison's role as an institution of social control. No prison study of any kind can afford to overlook the fact that minorities are overrepresented in the prisoner population by a factor of five, and that prison, ironically, may be the one institution in American society which blacks "control."

[4]

The Limits of
Racial Integration

Notwithstanding the salience of race relations for all segments of the prison community, academic commentators, like prison officials themselves, have shied away from studying and commenting on the patterns of racial conflict within prisons. In the public school context, segregation, integration, tracking, busing, and white flight have produced mountains of print. But similar issues in the prison context have failed to stimulate interest or analysis. This lack of interest is curious, to say the least, in light of the magnitude of racial problems in prisons and the large number of court decisions on the legality of racially conscious policies of assigning prisoners to particular institutions, housing units, cells, and jobs.[1]

These court decisions have almost invariably held that the Fourteenth Amendment requires "complete desegregation" in prisons for the same reasons that *Brown v. Board of Education* (1954) requires it in schools. Indeed, in several prison cases, courts have imposed an affirmative duty of achieving "racially balanced" housing and work units, although it is not clear whether this was thought necessary to remedy past discrimination or to promote integration.

Reprinted in slightly different form from *Criminal Law Bulletin* 18, no. 2 (March-April 1982):117–53.

[1] In spring 1981 attention was drawn to racial problems in New York City's jails when Mayor Edward Koch criticized a judge who refused to send a white, middle-class student to Rikers Island because he might be homosexually raped. "We take judicial notice of the defendant's slight build, his mannerisms, dress, color, and ethnic background," said Judge Stanley Gartenstein. "Ross would be immediately subject to homosexual rape and sodomy and to brutalities from prisoners such as make the imagination recoil in horror" (*New York Times*, April 9, 1981:B-5, col. 1).

This chapter questions the unreflective application of school desegregation law to prisons in light of the racial warfare that engulfs prisons and jails, the differing purposes of schools and penal facilities, and the differences in the rights and interests that are at stake. With our racially polarized, conflict-ridden prisons, the time has come to assay the rights and values that are affected by various prison policies that require or condone racial segregation.

Lest these introductory paragraphs suggest or advocate racially segregated prisons, let me emphasize that I approach the topic not as a penologist, but as a legal scholar concerned with the proper role of the federal courts in protecting individual rights. I do not know whether concentrating or dispersing racial groups within cell houses, tiers, and cells will make the greater contribution to safety, security, and decency. My impression is that prison administrators differ in their judgment on this question. There is surely too much variation in overcrowding, administrative capacity, and prisoner subculture to expect a single rule of thumb to suffice. Even if prisons were identical in all of these respects, the fact that some contain prisoner populations with nearly equal numbers of blacks and whites, while others have a single race overwhelmingly in the majority, suggests that there will be different patterns of racial conflict and different strategies for control. It need hardly be added that courts must closely scrutinize such strategies to ensure that they are not a subterfuge for discrimination, but are motivated by bona fide and demonstrable security considerations.

Involuntary segregation by cell house, tier, and cell assignments is one thing, but merely permitting prisoners some choice in cell partners, even if it reflects racial prejudice, is another. I do not believe that prison officials have an affirmative constitutional duty to integrate prisoners to the maximum extent feasible. An administrative policy that recognizes inmates' cellmate preferences, while not constitutionally required, should not be held unconstitutional.

Race Relations and the American Prison

After 1970 prison observers and scholars finally recognized that race was the most important factor in the prison subculture, determining more than anything else how one "did time" in most of the nation's major prisons. Not only was race a factor in cell and job assignments, it was decisive for one's place in the prison society, determining opportunity for illegal dealings and vulnerability to assault by other inmates. Racial conflict, including extreme violence and riots, is a reality of institutional life in prisons around the country.

The 1970s began with blacks comprising a near majority of prisoners nation-wide and a clear majority in many states. In some of the metropolitan jails and in some of the state prisons the population is 80 — 90 percent black. In some of the northeastern and mountain states, the percentages of blacks and whites are just the reverse. Under such circumstances, meaningful integration is not an option. The issue is whether the Constitution requires the random dispersion of the white or black minority throughout all of the cell houses and tiers.

Prison officials are at a loss as to how to handle interracial conflict; the matter is particularly complicated by society's sensitivity to race questions. Like leaders in the military, industry, and education, prison administrators rarely go public with their race relations problems. It is not difficult to under-stand their reluctance to admit that efforts to establish harmonious race rela-tions in prisons have failed (*see* Morris and Tonry 1981). They also fear that any such admission might invalidate certain of their administrative practices.

Prison officials face two main problems — the threat of conflict among well-entrenched groups of blacks, whites, and hispanics and the threat of indi-vidual acts of predatory behavior by members of the strongest group against members of the weakest group. To cope with these problems, officials resort to several strategies, none of which they like to talk about and none of which has been approved by the judiciary.

Prison officials sometimes use explicit segregation within prisons. My im-pression is that California attempts to keep its highly racist groups separate from each other and has operated its disciplinary units on a segregated basis for a number of years.[2] In many prisons, officials explicitly consider race in mak-ing work and cell assignments in order to keep certain groups apart or, in some cases, to achieve racial balance. But most officials are frightened to admit that they act in this way; they fear that the courts would find their practices uncon-stitutional. A safer practice is to make informal assignments of different races to different institutions, cell houses, and tiers by using such surrogate variables as residence, dangerousness, or gang affiliation. Thus, for example, Pennsyl-vania's Grateford prison near Philadelphia is almost completely black, while the State Correctional Institution at Pittsburgh is almost half white. Similarly, in Illinois, the Joliet prisons near Chicago are almost completely black, while the department maintains a large white population at Menard, in the southern part of the state.

Another administrative practice with great significance for prison segrega-tion is protective custody, that is, providing around-the-clock confinement for prisoners afraid to mix with the general population. The explosive growth over

---

[2] Gangs are also separated on other grounds than race. In California, for example, members of rival Chicano gangs are kept apart from one another by being placed in different prisons.

the past decade of protective custody has led to a good deal of racial separation, as protective custody units are usually populated predominately by whites.[3] It is an interesting question whether a state could have an entire prison for protective custody cases if a prison population composed almost completely of whites were the result.

Not all separatism among prison inmates is involuntarily imposed by the officials; there are powerful motivations and strong peer pressures among the prisoners to segregate themselves. As Norval Morris and Michael Tonry (1981) have conjectured, "if secret votes were taken among prison administrators, prison staff, all prisoners, and each minority group of prisoners, overall and within each category, they would vote overwhelmingly for racially segregated institutions."

Prison officials have been more than happy to accede to prisoners' wishes for self-segregation. In dining rooms, recreation fields, and television rooms, the common pattern is for white, black, and hispanic prisoners to separate themselves in racially homogeneous and carefully demarcated sections and rows. In prisons with multiple celling, the typical practice is to assign prisoners cellmates of their own race, a practice that almost always corresponds to prisoners' preferences. To the officials, this is common sense; it would be the height of absurdity to assign cell partners randomly if the result was to force individuals with strong racial prejudices to spend eighteen hours or more per day with members of a race they hated or distrusted.

How then will a prison system fare when it is challenged with maintaining individual penal facilities whose racial compositions vary substantially from one to another? Will courts someday be willing to follow school desegregation cases to their logical conclusion and require busing to maintain racially balanced prisons within an overall prison system? Will such "neutral" classificatory variables as residence, dangerousness, and gang affiliation pass constitutional muster when explicit racial classifications would be held illegal? If one pushes the school analogy far enough, these questions must be confronted.

---

[3] The Report of the Special Committee appointed by Governor Milliken to investigate the causes of the disturbances at several Michigan prisons in May 1981 provides the following observations on racial tension and administrative strategies to deal with the problem: "Racial tension between black and white prisoners is evident. When the riots began at the Michigan Reformatory, white prisoners, for their safety, fled the cellblock and took refuge on the roof of a prison building, refusing to leave unless assured of protection by the State Police and prison officials. Further hostility between the prisoners is reflected in those prisoners requesting and receiving protective custody who fear for their safety in the general population. Seventy-five percent of those seeking such protection are whites [although whites make up less than 40 percent of the prisoner population]. In addition, there is pronounced, self imposed segregation of the races in the dining rooms and other activities."

The Duty to Desegregate

American prisons were substantially segregated before 1954, the year in which the Supreme Court decided *Brown v. Board of Education*. Throughout the South, state laws required prisoners to be separated on the basis of race as well as sex. These laws did not reflect the judgment of prison officials that blacks and whites could not be integrated without jeopardizing safety and security, but a "societal" and legislative judgment that blacks and whites should not share the same facilities. Racial segregation in the South, like all other pre-1954 segregation, was part of the total sociopolitical system whose aim was to keep blacks separated, subordinated, and exploited.

For the most part, neither southern nor northern prisons desegregated voluntarily after *Brown*; a wait-and-see attitude prevailed.[4] Lawsuits, frequently supported by the ACLU and the NAACP, began in the South. The lower federal courts found in favor of the plaintiffs; they explicitly rejected the argument of prison officials, and sometimes of black and white inmates (*e.g., Rentfrow v. Carter* 1968), that segregation was necessary to prevent racial conflict and violence (*e.g., Wilson v. Kelly* 1968). The federal judges were well aware of the overall mosaic of invidious racial discrimination of which segregated prisons were only one tile. Genuine security concerns did not explain the legislatively mandated policy of keeping blacks and whites separate in prisons.

Only one of these lower court segregation cases ever reached the Supreme Court. *Washington v. Lee* arose out of a challenge to Alabama laws that provided that:

> [In the state's penal institutions] there shall be proper separation . . . whites from blacks . . . [and that] white and colored convicts [be not] chained together or allowed to sleep together . . . [and that] arrangements shall be made for keeping white and colored convicts at separate prisons and they shall not be allowed to be kept at the same place [and that with regard to the county jails] sheriffs and jailers and other keepers of town and city jails must keep white and negro prisoners separate or be guilty of a misdemeanor [and that] each county jail or city prison must contain separate compartments for whites and negroes and racially segregate both facilities. [1940 Ala. Code, Tit. 45, §§4, 52, 121–123, 172, 183 (*recomp.* 1958) (*held unconstitutional* 1966)]

---

[4] In the District of Columbia, prison integration was accomplished by an order of July 17, 1962 (*see Dixon v. Duncan* (1963)). At trial in *Washington v. Lee* (1966), plaintiff's expert witness, John Boone, testified that the Federal Bureau of Prison's Atlanta prison was desegregated in stages from 1954 to 1965. It is not clear whether Mr. Boone was describing a Federal Bureau of Prison Policy or an administrative practice at Atlanta. In any case, the director of the Federal Bureau issued the following statement on February 7, 1966: "The policy of non-discrimination and full integration in Bureau of Prisons institutions is clear and of long standing. The policy applies to all aspects of institutional management relating to inmates and personnel" (Bureau of Prisons, Bulletin 1001.1 (1966)).

The Alabama defendants did not present evidence of racial violence at trial, probably because strict segregation left little opportunity for racial conflict. The trial itself consisted of the opinion testimony of an expert witness for plaintiffs and the opinions of the defendants. While the defendants expressed concern for the security implications of integration, their case rested largely on procedural points and the theory that prisoners have no rights. They also assumed that in the event the law mandating segregation were struck down, they would retain administrative discretion to segregate as required for safety and security.

The three-judge district court, in an opinion authored by Judge Frank Johnson, disposed of the defendant's case in a few conclusory paragraphs, relying on *Brown*:

> Since *Brown v. Board of Education*, . . . and the numerous cases implementing that decision, it is unmistakably clear that racial discrimination by governmental authorities in the use of public facilities cannot be tolerated . . .
> [T]his Court can conceive of no consideration of prison security or discipline which will sustain the constitutionality of state statutes that on their face require complete and permanent segregation in all the Alabama penal facilities. We recognize that there is merit in the contention that in some isolated instances prison security and discipline necessitates segregation of the races for a limited period. However, recognition of such instances does nothing to bolster the statutes or the general practice that requires or permits prison or jail officials to separate the races arbitrarily. Such statutes and practices must be declared unconstitutional in light of the clear principles controlling.[*Washington v. Lee* 1966:331]

Judge Johnson ordered the "complete desegregation" of the state's prisons and jails. He did not, however, offer any definition of "complete desegregation," a concept that was already generating a good deal of controversy in school desegregation.[5] No distinction was drawn between separating races in different prisons and separation within the same prison by cell house, dormitory, tier, or cell. It is important to emphasize that the court did not say that racial segregation would never be permissible; rather, it denounced racial discrimination and legislatively mandated permanent segregation — policies that could only be designed to perpetuate racial segregation for its own sake. In other words, it is one thing for the legislature to require segregated prison facilities and another thing for prison officials to segregate temporarily on the

---

[5] In the school context, complete desegregation came to mean the elimination of racially identifiable schools, at least in those districts with a history of state-imposed segregation (*Green v. County School Bd.* 1968; *Swann v. Charlotte-Mecklenburg Bd. of Educ.* 1971). Complete desegregation in the prison context, however, has usually focused on the administration of a single institution containing blacks and whites. The parallel in the school context is the "tracking" issue (*see, e.g., Hobson v. Hanson* 1967).

basis of particular exigencies. Of course, the court had no occasion to consider the permissibility of a state policy respecting a prisoner's preference for a cell partner of the same race.

Had the case been one in which prison officials desired to separate races because of bona fide fear of serious racial violence, the Supreme Court might have had to explicate further the core rationale of *Brown* and to confront the differences between schools and penal facilities. "Separate but equal" is not so inherently unequal when it comes to cell houses and tiers in a single maximum security prison.

It is not by accident that the Supreme Court decision that struck down the South's apartheid system arose out of a dispute over state education. Education is an important benefit. The entire *Brown* decision is permeated by statements about the importance of education for an individual's self-concept, intellectual growth, occupational opportunities, and citizenship participation. Segregated schooling was pernicious because black children stood to lose those benefits.

In the decade following *Brown*, the Supreme Court struck down the segregation of the races in a variety of contexts (*see, e.g., Mayor of Baltimore v. Dawson* 1955 [beaches]; *Gayle v. Browder* 1956 [buses]; *Holmes v. City of Atlanta* 1955 [golf courses]; *New Orleans City Park Improvement Ass'n v. Detiege* 1958 [parks]). All of these cases must be understood in terms of the Court's effort to dismantle the total system of southern segregation, which was established and sustained to subordinate blacks. The laws that supported this system could not seriously be explained as having any purpose other than the perpetuation of the racial caste system.

In prisons there are few if any benefits at stake. Whereas parents pin their hopes and dreams for their children on educational achievement, the only hope in prison is for survival. The goal of rehabilitation has not been realized. Prison is an institution whose very purpose is the imposition of burden and stigma (Lipton, Martinson, and Wilks 1975; Morris 1975).

Fear, conflict, and violence exist in prisons on a different order of magnitude than in the schools. Although conflict and violence do occur in schools, school children do not very frequently kill one another and their teachers, perpetuate brutal assaults and homosexual rapes, or destroy their school buildings during riots. It is precisely these kinds of threats that set the atmosphere in our prisons.

Legal analysis of prison race relations has, from the beginning, been distorted by the school analogy. Prisons should not be equated with schools; they have different populations, different social functions, and different administrative problems. Behavior taken for granted in prisons would be considered aberrant in schools, indeed, probably in all other social contexts. No

[86]

other institution so thoroughly controls and regiments its inmates or clients, denying them privacy and freedom of choice. In no other institution are relations so fraught with violence. It is a serious mistake to believe that what makes sense in the educational environment is appropriate for prisons.

As Charles Black (1960) has so persuasively shown, it was central to the holdings in the school desegregation cases that segregation of white and black children was understood by southern whites and blacks as an insult to blacks. Blacks were separated in the schools, parks, movie theaters, even in the courts because they were considered inferior and held in contempt by a white society committed to a racial caste system that subordinated blacks.

The situation in today's prisons is different. Blacks are frequently the majority, not the minority, and administrative methods for controlling race conflict do not bespeak contempt for either blacks or whites. While the insult to blacks intended by the South's racist system was clear to anyone, black or white, the meaning of certain racially conscious administrative practices in today's prisons is hardly to be understood in the same way. Just as it is the case with affirmative action that there are legitimate reasons for treating people as members of a racial group, so too in prisons there may be good reasons for taking race into account.

The *Lee* case, as it came to the Supreme Court, hardly stimulated thought about whether race classifications in prisons should be handled differently from the way racial classifications in the other public services that the Court had dealt with while dismantling southern segregation are. The Alabama laws mandating penal segregation gave the Court no difficulty, and deeming Judge Johnson's opinion "unexceptional," the justices affirmed the lower court in a three-sentence *per curiam* opinion (*Washington v. Lee* 1968). A concurring opinion by Justices Hugo Black, John Harlan, and Potter Stewart did note the special problems of prison race relations and suggested that prisons presented a difficult case:

> In joining the opinion of the Court, we wish to make explicit something that is left to be gathered only by implication from the Court's opinion. This is that prison authorities have the right, acting in good faith and in particularized circumstances, to take into account racial tensions in maintaining security, discipline, and good order in prisons and jails. We are unwilling to assume that state or local prison authorities might mistakenly regard such an explicit pronouncement as evincing any dilution of this Court's firm commitment to the Fourteenth Amendment's prohibition of racial discrimination.

Unlike school desegregation, where dozens of Supreme Court decisions map the boundaries between permissible and impermissible administrative practices, the Supreme Court has not decided another prison desegregation case since *Lee*.[6] Many serious questions have been left unanswered. For example, what "particularized circumstances" short of a race riot will allow prison officials to consider race in maintaining security?[7] How long could prison officials use *Lee's* emergency rationale to maintain some racial separation? Can prison officials condone and cooperate with prisoners' efforts to segregate themselves? Or is there an affirmative duty to promote integration to the maximum extent feasible? In this chapter, my intent is not to attempt an exhaustive or definitive resolution of these knotty issues. I will try, however, to expose the superficiality of several lower federal court forays into these uncharted waters and suggest somes alternative lines of analysis.

Prison Racial Classifications in the Lower Federal Courts

None of the reported decisions on racial integration in prisons gives the subject anything like the thought and attention it deserves. For the most part these decisions reject the security concerns of prison officials and mandate maximum feasible integration, citing *Brown* and *Lee* as authority. Three of these opinions illustrate the tenor of the court opinions.

McClelland v. Sigler (1971)

Plaintiffs attacked the housing policy at the maximum security unit of the Nebraska Penal and Correctional Complex on equal protection grounds. Of the several institutions comprising the complex, only the maximum security unit, for security reasons, made assignments on the basis of race. There were two cell houses in this unit; blacks were excluded from one of them. West House held 115 blacks, 62 whites, 14 native Americans and 6 Mexicans — all in one-man cells. East House held 205 whites, 32 native Americans, and 8 Mexicans — in four-man and one-man cells. The black plaintiffs objected to being excluded from East House.

Judge Warren Urbom did not attempt a close reading of *Lee*, but dealt with the case as if it arose in any other social context. He began by quoting from Chief Justice Warren's eloquent condemnation of segregated schools in *Brown*: "The impact [of segregation] is greater when it has the sanction of law; for the

---

[6] In 1972 the Court did cite *Lee* for the proposition that "racial segregation, which is unconstitutional outside prisons, is unconstitutional within prisons, save for the necessities of prison security and discipline" (*Cruz v. Beto* 1972).

[7] In *Mickens v. Winston* (1978), the court held that a "generalized expectation of racial violence is insufficient" to justify segregation under the *Lee* period. However, the court did not elaborate on what "particularized circumstances" *would* be sufficient.

policy of separating the races is usually interpreted as denoting the inferiority of the negro group. A sense of inferiority affects the motivation of a child to learn." The judge found the rights of black prisoners to be violated, because, in his view, prisons, like schools, have an educational mission, [that is, rehabilitation]. That rehabilitation could be adversely affected by racial separation, presumably because of its negative effect on the capacity of black prisoners to learn.

Judge Urbom's analysis is flawed for several reasons. The fundamental sociological insight of *Brown* — that the southern racial caste system stigmatized and demoralized black school children, stunting their psychological and emotional development and their preparation for future careers — rings hollow when it comes to prisons. Prison rehabilitation has proven to be more myth than reality; in any case, it is hardly the equivalent of public schooling with respect to self-concept or career development. Even if rehabilitation could be analogized to public education, it does not follow that assigning blacks to East House would improve their performance or self-image. More logically, the school analogy would require integrated rehabilitation programs, not integrated housing units. However, it bears noting that, in *McClelland*, all of the black prisoners were already living in an integrated cell house. This case was not so much about "segregation" as about racial classifications.

The issue, therefore, is whether prison officials can, in the interests of security, make cell house assignments on the basis of race. Racial classifications in prisons, like all racial classifications, are "suspect" and will be subjected to "strict scrutiny." The state must be able to justify its policies with a constitutionally "compelling" reason and show that they are the most effective means of achieving these legitimate goals. In practice, states have almost never been able to shoulder this burden. In effect, the "compelling ends — perfect means" formula imposes a nearly irrebuttable presumption against the validity of racial classifications.

For the reasons discussed earlier, I think it makes sense to treat racial classifications in prisons somewhat differently from the way other racial classifications are treated. My preference is for a broad interpretation of *Lee* — one that recognizes that the unique problems posed by interracial prison violence could justify a racial classification that is substantially less than perfect, a racial classification that would be unconstitutional if used in schools or, indeed, in any other social setting.[8] This does not mean eliminating the burden on prison offi-

---

[8] *See Yale Law Journal* 1974. The author argues that the need to formulate an immediate classification would theoretically justify a segregative policy that would be impermissible elsewhere. Similarly, Paul Brest notes that the objective of preventing discrimination is accommodated with other concerns: "A flat prohibition of race-dependent decisions provides as much assurance as possible against discrimination, but at the cost of precluding what may be thought to be desirable uses of race — for example, the temporary segregation of prisoners during a race riot" (Brest 1976:15).

cials to demonstrate the legitimacy of their goal and their reasons for adopting a race-conscious means of achieving it. It does mean that prison officials should not face an almost conclusive presumption against the constitutionality of their efforts to prevent interracial violence.[9]

McClelland did involve discriminatory treatment of blacks. There was evidence that the living conditions in East House, from which blacks were excluded, were more desirable than those in West House. This fact alone warranted a decision in favor of the plaintiffs. However, the case should have been analyzed as one of discrimination with respect to living conditions. Racially motivated housing assignments are clearly unconstitutional if they are invidious (that is, impose a burden or deny a benefit out of contempt for members of a particular race).[10] While prison officials may or may not have had good reasons for imposing some racial segregation, doing so by excluding blacks from the more desirable cell house was highly suspect.

Suppose prison officials, continuing to be concerned about racial violence, had transferred the East House prisoners to West House and vice versa? In the context of a racially integrated prison, a short-term policy of separate cell houses could hardly be compared with the wholly separate school systems of the pre-1954 South. In this hypothetical variation on *McClelland*, there are no benefits or burdens at stake, unless one were to consider inmates stigmatized by such a policy. Prison officials could argue in good faith, however, that they are not making a judgment that one race is more dangerous than another but rather that the decision to segregate temporarily is motivated by an overall judgment concerning the special conflicts created by race relations in prisons. The plaintiff's race, they could argue, is not being treated contemptuously. The segregative policy is being implemented with equal regard for prisoners of all races. In any case, incarceration already stigmatizes prisoners as dangerous. The problem of a classification imposing stigma, so important in resolving school desegregation cases, is a lesser concern in

[9] Even under an expansive reading of *Lee*, the legality of a prison's racially conscious housing policies would depend upon whether the particular security concerns could justify the degree of racial segregation imposed. For example, a fight between a black and a white inmate obviously would not allow a policy of separate cell houses for blacks and whites, although it might support the temporary segregation of the tier on which the fight took place. On the other hand, a major conflict between black and white gangs, with other prisoners threatening to take sides along racial lines, would seem to justify temporary segregation by cell house.

[10] "By the end of the 1960s it was clear that the Court had finally accepted what seemed to be the correct original position: that the government could not classify persons by race to impose a burden on, or deny benefits to members of minority races" (Nowak, Rotunda, and Young 1978:558)).

a maximum security prison, which necessarily imposes stigma on all of its inmates.[11]

The dismissal of officials' security concerns is another major flaw in Judge Urbom's analysis. The prison complex's chief administrator, Warden Sigler, testified that he felt it unsafe to assign blacks to East House; he feared "uncontrollable trouble," pointing to the vulnerability of younger and weaker white prisoners to sexual assaults by a small number of violent black prisoners. He also feared the consequences of ordering fifty self-avowed white racists to live in an integrated setting. Racial tensions had been high in the unit for several years; to the warden, the cell house policy seemed a sensible way to make the best of a bad situation. Judge Urbom rejected these concerns:

> Racist attitudes evoke powerful responses in those who possess them. But powerful responses are also available to those who must strive to eliminate the effects of bigotry....
> Threats of recalcitrant prisoners whose racial prejudices are erected to defy the constitutional rights of black prisoners need to be quashed. The prisoners who threaten violence, rather than those who seek their right to nondiscriminatory treatment, should be the ones to feel the weight of the consequences of their overt bigotry. An image of the whole penal system of Nebraska being held at bay by fifty men is unacceptable.[*McClelland v. Sigler*, 1971:834]

This analysis does not recognize the gravity of the situation. While their ability to do so may be unacceptable, fifty extremists can in fact cause havoc in a prison where "troublemakers" cannot be simply expelled or arrested. Transferring these individuals to disciplinary units does not solve the problem either, since it is frequently within these units that the most extreme racial violence occurs. Perhaps the warden's fears were unfounded; perhaps they were a subterfuge for discrimination. Resolution of these factual issues, rather than obeisance to *Brown*, should have determined the case's resolution.[12]

[11] Justifying a segregative policy on this theory raises fresh problems. What answer could be given to a plaintiff inmate who objects to being placed with members of his own race, on the ground that they are more dangerous to him than members of another race? Would this individual be alleging the imposition of a burden on the basis of race? Would not individual determinations of dangerousness, a more perfect classification than race, be required?

[12] Nothing in this analysis contradicts *Cooper v. Aaron* (1958), the case in which the Supreme Court refused to allow fears of violence to delay a court-ordered school desegregation plan. In *Cooper*, the Court was reacting to years of "massive resistance" by the Arkansas legislature and Governor Faubus. That kind of effort to maintain segregation for its own sake hardly corresponds to the kind of good-faith effort to maintain prison security which we are considering in our hypothetical variation on *McClelland*.

Taylor v. Perini (1976,1977,1979)

In 1969 plaintiffs brought a class action challenging a number of policies, practices, and conditions of Ohio's Marion prison. In 1972 Federal District Judge Don Young entered an order based upon an agreement worked out between the prisoners and the department. Three years later, in late 1975, Judge Young appointed a special master to determine whether the department was in compliance. The portions of the 1972 order most relevant to racial discrimination stated:

> Within sixty (60) days of the entry of this Order, [the department will] prepare and submit to this Court a plan for rectifying the present effects of past discrimination in job assignment with respect to all office jobs, the plumbing shop [and several other prisoner assignments].
> Within sixty days of the entry of this order [the department will] prepare and submit to this Court a plan for the elimination of the present effects of past assignments of inmates to beds on the basis of racial criteria.

With respect to jobs, the special master apparently proceeded under the assumption that any deviation from the prisonwide racial percentages in any job category was a vestige, or perhaps itself proof of, illegal discrimination. Thus, the master was distressed to find that white prisoners constituted 43.5 percent of the population, but 58 percent of all office workers. Other evidence of discrimination was that "80% of the tractor and truck drivers on Coy's tractor gang are white, as are 89% of the 'where and if needed' employees in the hog lot. On the other hand, 100% of the ash crew and porters in the power plant are black, as are 100% of the 'labor' employees in the dairy barn." To eliminate such discrimination, he required that the proportion of black and white prisoners at each work assignment be equivalent to the proportion of blacks and whites in the entire prison population. The remedy went even further than this, however. According to the special master, racial balancing on work assignments would not purge the institution of discrimination if blacks and whites clustered in homogeneous work groups in the same shops: "Even in an employment unit which is reasonably balanced overall, disparities exist with respect to particular jobs. For example, all (5) wash tank workers and all (9) spray painters in the sheet metal shop are black; all (9) shears operators are white" (First Report of the Special Master, *Taylor v. Perini* 1976:245–46). Requiring the prison to assure racial balance on each job assignment probably goes further than the Constitution requires (*see Washington v. Davis* 1976) or even the most extreme remedies for employment discrimination outside of prison (*see Griggs v. Duke Power Co.* 1971), and also is likely to defeat the prisoners' own preference to work next to fellow inmates most like themselves.

The special master also sought racial balance in the dormitory housing units by outlawing deviation of more than 5 percent from the prison's overall racial composition, this despite the fact that the most desirable "honor dormitory" contained a disproportionate number of blacks (61.6 percent). Further, even racial balance was not conclusive proof of nondiscrimination in a dormitory if beds were arranged in racially identifiable rows or if, within the rows, members of the same race tended to cluster together: "The bed patterns within the honor dormitory continue to indicate improved racial distribution and the practice of maintaining segregated rows within the bays has ceased. There continue to be concentrations of black and white inmates within the rows, however, and efforts must be made to distribute inmates more evenly within the honor dormitory" (Fourth Report of the Special Master, *Taylor v. Perini* 1978:1216). It is difficult to believe that the Fourteenth Amendment could be stretched so far in any area of society, much less a maximum security prison (*see Pasadena City Bd. of Educ. v. Spangler* 1976). This order must be predicated on the belief that the Constitution requires governmental units to act affirmatively to achieve maximum feasible integration.

Thomas v. Pate (1974)

Plaintiffs Thomas and Miller, black prisoners incarcerated at the Illinois State Penitentiary, at Joliet, sued Illinois prison officials for, among other things, assigning cellmates on the basis of race. At the time of the trial, the prison population was 60.2 percent black, with whites and other minorities, including a substantial percentage of hispanics, making up the balance. The relationship among the races was riddled with conflict. Blacks were divided into three organizations corresponding to outside street gangs, as were the hispanic prisoners; by contrast, the whites were unorganized. They survived as best they could, frequently seeking transfers to prisons downstate with larger white populations or seeking protective custody (*see* Jacobs 1977). Notwithstanding this situation, plaintiffs alleged that the administrative policy of assigning inmates to "racially segregated cells" violated the Constitution. The district court dismissed the charge, but the Court of Appeals for the Seventh Circuit, by a 2-1 majority, sent the case back for trial to determine whether the maintenance of racially homogeneous cells was "intentional segregation." The court's opinion referred to black prisoners as being "stamped with a badge of inferiority":

> Because of the relatively small size of the prison community, its closed nature, and the numerous facets of prison life subject to regulation, any racially discriminatory action by prison officials is likely more effectively to create a badge of inferiority

for black inmates than would necessarily attach to minority residents of a city as a result of discriminatory action outside prison walls. [*Thomas v. Pate* 1974:163]

This statement presumes that the preferences of prisoners for same-race cell partners stamps the dominant black majority with a badge of inferiority, a view hardly consistent with the prisoners' own view of the situation. Similarly, and with equal unrealism, it suggests that randomly dispersing the white minority would contribute to equality for blacks.

While *Thomas* languished on remand, an independent suit was filed by the special litigation section of the Department of Justice (*United States v. Illinois* 1976). Negotiations produced a consent decree — one, however, with the same air of unreality as the Court of Appeal's decision:

> With regard to the housing of inmates, the defendants agree that any unofficial practice of routinely assigning black inmates to cells with other black inmates and white inmates to cells with other white inmates and any practice of permitting inmates or residents to choose their cellmates on a purely racial basis shall be prohibited. All assignments shall be made on the basis of rational, objective criteria and shall not be made on the basis of race. To achieve these goals the Affirmative Action Plan . . . shall provide. . . .
>
> 3. The racial composition of each housing unit to approximate the overall racial composition of the inmates committed to the institution and shall not deviate more than ten percent (10%) of total inmate population of that institution without reasonable justification . . . .
>
> 6. Illinois Department of Correction Regulation 867 shall be modified to exclude the following statement. . . .
>
> [T]he department shall not refuse to honor an incoming resident's preference on the sole ground that prospective roommates are of different racial or religious backgrounds.

One may wonder what "rational, objective criteria" the state could use to make cell assignments and whether these would achieve the same result as the race-conscious policy. If so, it is hard to see why such criteria would be any more legitimate. It is also interesting that no mention is made of hispanic inmates. Are they counted as whites or, consistent with the prison definition of the situation, defined as a third racial group?

The consent decree does not identify the legal rights that are infringed by permitting the prisoners their racial preferences for cellmates. The parties agreed to a color-blind standard of prison administration that has no counterpart in the rest of society. While the associational rights of prisoners of all races (assuming they survive imprisonment) would be infringed by a blanket refusal to permit members of different races to cell together, neither this right nor any other is violated by the officials' recognition of the prisoners' preferences, even if racially motivated, any more than the state is acting unconstitutionally when it honors the racial preferences of prospective adopting parents.

Competing Interests

Prisoners' Social Preferences

Attendance at public school, although a rather encompassing experience, is nowhere near as total and pervasive an experience as prison. The public school student returns home at the end of the day, frequently to a segregated neighborhood, almost always to a segregated home and family. Once at home the student is beyond the range of governmental policy and is free to organize the private details of life as he or she likes. School does not infringe upon a student's privacy or associational rights in anything like the degree that prison does.

There is no private refuge for prisoners. The degree of intimacy in two- or three-man cells with a shared toilet, sink, bureau, and standing room can hardly be imagined (*see Schwartz* 1972). Even if cellmates cared for each other, such confinement would be tense. Where cellmates fear or hate one another the tensions may be unbearable. The complete absence of privacy militates against the success of race relations. It is worth hypothesizing that race relations will be most successful in those public settings where relations are simple and at arm's length and where the individual is still left a substantial private life to manage as he or she sees fit, even on a racially prejudiced basis. It is understandable that prisoners typically prefer to share a cell with others most like themselves. When possible it would seem humane, as well as sensible administrative policy, to honor requests concerning cell partners, even if such requests reflect racial or religious prejudice.

The attack on segregation in this country rarely, if ever, intrudes on such personal matters as one's choice of roommates or eating companions. Even the 1968 Fair Housing Act provided an exemption for landlords who rent rooms in their homes (42 U.S.C. §3603(b)(2) (1976)). Individuals retain limited freedom to discriminate in their personal lives (for example, in the matter of adoptions). It is true that in prison, "state" action is theoretically universal; the state is implicated in almost everything that takes place behind bars. But prison officials should not be seen as "authorizing" all acts of prisoners, including their preference for cell partners. Some prisoner activities and choices should be defined as "private," even under conditions of total state control.[13] The

---

[13] *Cf. Flagg Bros. v. Brooks* (1978). In other social settings that involve state action, ratifying voluntary preferences for roommates, even if racially motivated, is perfectly acceptable. At Cornell University, for example, the 144-bed Ujama House is occupied almost exclusively by minority and third-world students who have elected to live there.

prison officials should not have an affirmative duty to promote integration in any manner possible and by any means, especially when it involves overriding prisoners' personal preferences. Certainly no such obligation has been imposed upon the states and their subdivisions in the larger society.

A related question is whether a large state correctional system could implement a freedom-of-choice plan that permits prisoners to designate their institutional preferences. If such institutions became "racially imbalanced," would the official be guilty of a constitutional violation? Assuming that the plan was not set up to promote segregation (that is, that the officials had a bona fide nonsegregative intent), I cannot see why such a plan would be unconstitutional. It would seem to be no different from a public housing authority's policy of honoring requests for placements in specific housing developments, or a pupil assignment plan based upon open enrollment.[14]

Another variation of the freedom-of-choice plan poses more difficulty. Imagine a department of corrections unable to mount an effective program for the small minority of hispanic offenders at each of its institutions. Could the department designate one prison for hispanics in order to concentrate its Spanish-speaking personnel and special programs for hispanic prisoners? If such a program were successful, could the department set up similar institutions for native Americans and blacks, again stressing programs especially relevant to these groups? And assume further that placement at one of these special institutions is voluntary. Such a plan is clearly racially conscious and promotes racially homogeneous institutions. But the department will argue that it is not imposing a burden or denying a benefit to anyone, and that its policy holds no racial group in contempt. To the contrary, it could argue that its policy represents a "benign racial classification" — an effort through affirmative action to address the special needs of minority offenders. The legality of such a plan might be sustained under the Supreme Court's opinions in *Board of Regents of the University of California v. Bakke* (1978) and *Fullilove v. Klutznick* (1980). Special ethnic programs that operate within a single prison pose another variation of this problem. Surely programs that were directed at meeting the special needs of Spanish-speaking and native American inmates would pass constitutional muster.

[14] It should not be thought that such a freedom-of-choice plan would be invalid under the rationale of the Supreme Court's seminal decision in *Green v. County School Bd.* (1968). There, the Court held that a freedom-of-choice plan that left the old pattern of de jure segregation intact was not consistent with the order in *Brown* to desegregate. In effect, the school officials were acting in bad faith and the freedom-of-choice plan was merely a means of perpetuating segregated schools.

Cruel and Unusual Punishment

The judicial expansion of the concept of cruel and unusual punishment, the concomitant whittling away of official immunity, and the greater willingness of federal and state courts to hold prison officials liable suggest we are dealing with a situation of rights in conflict. Prison officials, under some circumstances may well have a legal obligation not to assign prisoners to jobs and cells without taking their race into account.

During the 1970s, federal courts began to recognize that prisoners had a constitutional right to some protection from assaults by fellow inmates. (*Chicago-Kent Law Review* 1977). "Deliberate indifference" to violence and sexual assaults has been held to constitute the "unnecessary and wanton infliction of pain" and is "manifestly inconsistent with contemporary standards of decency," and hence violative of rights secured by the Eighth and Fourteenth amendments (*see Little v. Walker* 1977 citing *Estelle v. Gamble* 1976). Indeed, inadequate protection of inmates was a factor often cited by federal court decisions ordering the upgrading of entire state penal facilities. (*See, e.g., Gates v. Collier* 1974; *Holt v. Sarver* 1971; *Nadeau v. Helgmore* 1976).While a single assault due to simple negligence does not rise to constitutional significance, a "pattern of undisputed and unchecked violence" or "an egregious failure to provide security to a particular inmate" is cruel and unusual punishment (*e.g., Penn v. Oliver* 1972). It is not necessary for the inmate plaintiff actually to be attacked; incarceration in an institution "where violence and terror reign"[15] will state a claim for relief under 42 U.S.C. §1983.[16]

Prison officials may also be held accountable in tort for failure adequately to protect inmates. Even a single attack, if proximately caused by the negligence of officials or supervisory personnel, or even by the failure of officials to provide sufficient staff, will state a claim for relief (*Tulane Law Review* 1977). Unlike a Section 1983 action, tort claims against prison officials can be sustained by a showing of simple negligence.

In the past, prison officials have been accused of using integration as a form of punishment. George Jackson (1970:19-21) and others (e.g., Opo-

---

[15] *See Woodhouse v. Virginia* (1973). In *Little v. Walker* (1977), the Court of Appeals for the Seventh Circuit became the first federal court to allow a claim for damages, as opposed to purely injunctive relief, on the sole ground of failure adequately to protect inmates. The court held that the qualified immunity enjoyed by prison officials could be overcome by a showing of deliberate indifference, interpreted to mean either actual intent or objective recklessness.

[16] In 1980 two white inmate rape victims filed suit in the Northern District of Illinois alleging that the failure of Cook County Jail personnel to remove them from tiers predominantly populated by blacks, after they had been threatened, violated their Eighth Amendment rights (*see Daly v. County of Cook* 1980; *Sawinski v. Elrod* 1980; *Mayes v. Elrod* 1979).

towsky 1972:54), for example, charged prison officials in California with transferring "troublemakers" to areas of violent racial conflict in order to have them beaten or killed. Today, such cynical perverse manipulation of "integration" would easily rise to the level of actual intent to inflict cruel and unusual punishment. The more difficult case would be where prison officials randomly assign prisoners to cell houses, tiers, and cells without regard to the reality of interracial violence. Such a policy could be viewed as deliberate indifference, particularly if it were implemented over the objections of the inmate plaintiff. These types of problems merely reiterate the need to question what constitutional value is being vindicated by dispersing members of a white, black, or hispanic minority by cell house, tier, and cell. The price of such maximum feasible integration may well be the derogation of other constitutionally protected rights.

Conclusion

I sympathize with those who would repress this subject. To admit that we have failed to eradicate racial hatreds among prisoners is to pave the way for other admissions and to lay bare the vulnerability of our hopes as a society. It is precisely because prison provides a distorted but strangely powerful picture of the total society that it is so painful to confront this failure. I fear that if we recognize the necessity of separating races in prison it will be argued by some that such policies are just as beneficial in other contexts.

Yet, actions appropriate in one context may be wrong in another. It hardly needs pointing out that sexual segregation of prisoners is assumed to be normal and reasonable even though in almost any other context sexual segregation would be extraordinary and probably impermissible (*cf. Vorchheimer v. School Dist. of Philadelphia* 1976). Thousands of prisoners, black, white, and hispanic, live in greater danger and insecurity because of what the symbol of an integrated society means to people whose own lives and institutions are far less integrated than those of prisoners.

[5]

The Politics of Corrections

TOWN-PRISON RELATIONS AS A DETERMINANT OF REFORM

Vienna Correctional Center (VCC) has earned the distinction of being the most successful state prison in Illinois. Its campuslike atmosphere, extensive academic and vocational programs, and relatively harmonious inmate-staff relationships have made it the focus of nationwide attention. The National Advisory Commission on Criminal Justice Standards and Goals (1973:345) described VCC as "[a] remarkable minimum security correctional center. . . . Although a large facility, it approaches the quality of the non-penal institution. Buildings resembling garden apartments are built around a 'town square' complete with churches, schools, shops, and library. Paths lead off to 'neighborhoods' where 'homes' provide private rooms in small clusters. Extensive provision has been made for indoor and outdoor recreation. Academic, commercial, and vocational facilities equal or surpass those of many technical high schools."

At a time when the traditional thinking in corrections advocates small, secure institutions in close proximity to major population centers, the success of this completely open minimum security prison set in a rural, conservative, and economically depressed area of Illinois demonstrates that the peculiar problems of certain small rural communities may present a large public institution with sufficient leverage to pursue reform goals that would not be possible in the political and social context of the urban environment. Precisely because of the interdependency of town and prison there has emerged at VCC an equilibrium that allows the institution broad latitude in defining prison policy.

This section reprinted in slightly different form from *Social Service Review* 50, no. 4 (December 1976):623-31, by permission of The University of Chicago Press.

Located 350 miles south of Chicago, Vienna is a quiet town with a population of only 1,300. Both VCC employees and local citizens agree that when the prison was first proposed, and during its early years of construction, there was considerable fear and resistance.[1] That no organized opposition coalesced is widely attributed to the energies of the town's political and business elites. Despite being sparsely populated and economically depressed, Vienna is home for two of Illinois's most powerful state legislators. They and the town's leadership were convinced that a large public institution, such as a prison or a mental hospital, was a necessity if economic depression was to be reversed, and that a large public institution with a substantial payroll would increase the influence of the political elite through the expansion of patronage. The two legislators supplied the crucial lobbying that provided the opportunity to build a major state institution in Vienna.

The groundwork for community acceptance was laid by informally "talking it up" and by working through the traditional community organizations. From the beginning a scale model of the proposed institution was repeatedly presented, along with a speech on the advantages to be derived from the prison, to the Kiwanis, Chamber of Commerce, VFW, and numerous church organizations. This strategy of cultivating community acceptance was taken over after 1968 by the first warden, who redirected the public education campaign from the need for a public institution to the desirability of a progressive minimum security prison at the cutting edge of prison reform. There is hardly a citizen in Vienna who has not on one occasion or another toured VCC. When the final dedication of the institution took place in 1971, local businessmen served as hosts to scores of politicians and dignitaries from all over the state.

The consequence of the efforts by the warden to sell his program has been the wide diffusion of the prison reform ideology throughout the Vienna citizenry. While there are scattered criticisms about the "country club atmosphere" and especially about the recent decision to make the prison coed, the warden's political support, personal popularity, and unquestioned claim to professional expertise in corrections has insured widespread acceptance of a minimum security prison holding some of the most serious offenders in the Illinois prison system.

The VCC resident population does not differ significantly from the Illinois prisoner population as a whole with respect to offense. However, prisoners typically do not obtain transfers to VCC until they are close to parole. Inmates with poor disciplinary records in the maximum security prisons are ineligible

---

[1] The research upon which this section is based was conducted during the summer of 1974. Informal interviewing was carried out for several weeks on Vienna's main streets. Participant observation and formal interviews were conducted with inmates and staff on an almost daily basis at the institution.

for transfer to Vienna. Likewise, those at the minimum security facility have a strong incentive to follow the rules and regulations lest they be transferred back to the incomparably worse maximum security institutions, such as Stateville, Menard, and Pontiac. (*See* Steele and Jacobs 1977.)

The Economics of Interdependence

No resident of Vienna can be unmindful of the economic impact that VCC has had upon the town and county. The net assets of the county's three banks have steadily increased since the prison's inception. The greatest percentage growth in assets occurred between 1971 and 1972, corresponding to the final completion of VCC and to the augmentation of its payroll. One of the bank's officers estimated that 30 to 40 percent of the increase in assets can be attributed to the presence of VCC.

In addition to the multiplier effect generated from VCC employees' paychecks, the prison does a substantial amount of local purchasing. In fiscal 1973 VCC spent $35,232 in Vienna alone. The figure, of course, would be much larger if the county and its surrounding area were included. Inmates and their families shop in the local town as well. Several times per week a dozen or more VCC inmates are taken on a trip to town to purchase anything from TVs to art supplies. For the few small local establishments where inmates shop purchases may constitute a substantial (one store owner estimated 20 percent) part of the business. For the first six months of 1974, inmate expenditures in town averaged $2,500 per month; they were expected to increase.

Any doubt remaining as to the importance of VCC for the economy of the surrounding locale may be dispelled by noting that between 1960 and 1970 every other county in southern Illinois, except for one housing a large expanding state university, lost population while the county in which Vienna is located increased its population as well as its school enrollments (the latter by more than 18 percent).

The Social Context of Interdependence

The prison is by far the largest employer in the county and 61 percent of those who work at the prison are also county residents. This identity of occupational role and political citizenship is the strongest of the many interrelationships between the prison and the surrounding society. Not only are the majority of VCC employees residents of nearby towns, they include many local formal and informal leaders. When the research was conducted, the president of the Vienna Kiwanis was an employee, as was the president of the Chamber of

Commerce. Vienna's incumbent mayor was VCC's business manager. A former mayor was director of the ambulance program, and the mayor of a nearby town was a guard lieutenant. Many of the most deeply entrenched and powerful families in the local area are represented at the prison, thereby reinforcing the community's stake in the prison's continued success.

The importance of co-opting local community leadership was not lost upon the warden, himself born and raised in the local area. The warden's youthful administrative assistant grew up in Vienna and starred on the high school basketball team. He was given a job at VCC during each of the summers between college terms and was offered a full-time job as personnel director immediately after graduation. When he hesitated the warden insisted that the young man speak to Vienna's powerful state legislator before making a final decision. The story is not unique; one of the prison counselors, a local baseball star, was recruited in the same way.

The staff at VCC are friends and neighbors and need to cooperate at the prison in order to sustain small-town community life. What is most arresting about the staff world is the interlocking system of personal relationships. The director of the grade school program attributed the success of his department to the fact that he knew all of his teachers personally before he hired them ("except for one outsider from the East"). Staff call each other by first name. Tenure on the job is lengthy; turnover is almost nonexistent. Between July 1, 1973, and July 1, 1974, there were only thirteen openings for established positions and they resulted from death or retirement.

The identity of staff and citizenry has meant that an entire network of personal relationships has been imported into the prison. That there is so little of the traditional conflict between treatment and custody can be explained better by the fact that treatment and custody staffs are friends and neighbors than by focusing upon the functional consequences of administrative policy. Indeed, a distinctive southern Illinois style of life and culture (*see* Brownell 1958) pervades the prison. In conformity to the folkways of southern Illinois, staff members are reluctant to criticize one another directly, strongly preferring conciliation and compromise to open conflict. At VCC even a guard union conducts itself in a low-key manner in sharp contrast to the militance that has characterized the union locals in the northern part of the state.

The most fateful consequence of this relationship between prison staff and local citizenry is a widespread and strong commitment to the perpetuation of the institution. The abandonment or shake-up of the prison would threaten the security and vested interests of some of the community's leading citizens. On the other hand it should be pointed out that the nature of this equilibrium makes the institution vulnerable to community attitudes and sentiments. It is a widely held belief among the administrative elite at VCC that, should the attitude of the local political and business elites turn against the prison because of escape, scandal, or any other reason, the continued existence of VCC in its present form would become problematic. While the community's stake in the institution is great, its commitment to the specific reform program is much weaker. This commitment has been buoyed up by tying the reform programs themselves to needs of the community.

The Prison and the Grass Roots

The folkways of southern Illinois stress informality and personal trust. Throughout the 1970s, the relationship between the prison and the local community was personified in the relations between the then warden and various community leaders. The warden shared an informal personal relationship with political leaders from both parties and a working relationship that allowed some normalization of the patronage system. Local politicians would not force job seekers and campaign supporters on the warden against his wishes, although the latter was not likely to oppose or ignore consistently the strong feelings of the politicians.

The warden's personal friendship with the editor of Vienna's only newspaper (the two men were golfing partners) was another example of the personal ties between prison and community leaders which hold the institution's program together. Believing that it was his responsibility "to let some negative things about the prison pass and to stress what's good out there," the editor frequently carried articles about the value of new programs and the warden's philosophy of rehabilitation.

The relationship between the local junior college and the prison typified the mutual advantages to be gained through cooperation. When the warden was appointed in 1968, a large state university located fifty miles away held a sizable grant from the Department of Health, Education, and Welfare (DHEW) to administer vocational programs at the prison. Neither the warden nor the local political leadership was pleased with the university's performance; the warden complained of poor administration, the politicians objected to the fact that the giant educational empire needed to pay no deference to Vienna or VCC interests. What resulted was a struggle, carried on in Springfield and Washington, to wrest the grant away. Ultimately, the grant was withdrawn and reissued to the small community college nearest to Vienna. At the time of the research, 25 percent of this college's students were VCC inmates, and a substantial portion of its budget was spent on programs at VCC. In return the college benefits from favorable financial arrangements for reimbursements and the publicity that its prison programs attract.

The local citizenry was cultivated in many ways. An interesting example is the more than one hundred fishing permits per season which the warden issued to local sportsmen who wanted to try their luck in the prison's seventy-acre lake. Outsiders also enter the prison to participate in church services, Bible readings, and other events. In the winter of 1973 VCC hosted an invitational basketball tournament in its well-equipped modern gymnasium to which teams from all over southern Illinois were invited. In addition visitors as individuals or as members of groups are encouraged to come out to the prison for tours that are conducted by several of the prisoners most enthusiastic about the VCC program. (In all there averaged 658 noninmate-related visits to VCC each month between January and June 1974).

The prison also serves as a type of community center by providing key services to a locality lacking institutions usually taken for granted in a metropolitan environment. The local junior college offers an evening program at VCC which includes an assortment of vocational training courses. At the time the research was conducted, 132 local citizens were enrolled in evening classes conducted at the prison. The daytime vocational program was augmented by twenty "hard core unemployed" whom the Department of Labor assigned to the prison for job training; like the inmates, they were paid to go to school out of federal funds.

Not all the social services provided by VCC for the surrounding community are delivered at the prison. To the contrary, the prison has found in the community's need for services a reason to expand its own prison reform programs outward, beyond the boundaries of the prison. The best example is the Emergency Medical Technician Program, an ambulance service manned by eighteen trained inmates working twenty-four-hour shifts. A crisis in ambulance service occurred when new state licensing laws effectively removed undertakers from the business. There was no other means to provide ambulance service in the area. The prison quickly applied for and received a grant to train inmates as emergency medical technicians and to purchase ambulances. Between January 1, 1974, and June 30, 1974, the ambulance teams made 126 runs. They became well known in the local hospitals and were heartily accepted by the citizenry. One elderly Vienna citizen told me, "I don't know what we would have done without the prison."

The prison volunteered labor on several community projects. Perhaps the most auspicious was the little league field which the prisoners built and maintained for the city. When the city of Vienna was faced with a crisis over the closing down of its sanitary landfill by the Environmental Protection Agency, the prison permitted the city to use its landfill until a new one could be built according to legal specifications.

The provision of community services to the local citizenry by VCC has accustomed residents to the presence of convicted felons in their midst. The boundaries between VCC and the local community have become more amorphous and more permeable. Prisoners travel out to local communities for vocational field trips, speeches on prison reform, band concerts, and even to provide transactional analysis therapy for emotionally disturbed children in a nearby institution. In addition, VCC athletic teams participate in local leagues and travel to the various southern Illinois towns where the games are held. During the summer when this research was carried out, twenty-three prisoners (the majority of them black) served as umpires in Vienna's boys' and girls' softball leagues. The daily evening contests regularly found the young ball players crowding around their favorite umpires who are regarded as something of local heroes.

Policy Implications

The movement toward community-based corrections as an alternative to the maximum security megaprison raises important questions about the quality of the relationship between the community and the prison. It cannot be expected that all communities will welcome minimum security or work release facilities without any quid pro quo. Two controversies between the Department of Corrections and local communities in Illinois reinforce my observation that the foundation of community-based corrections must be delicately laid in the economic, political, and social environments of the proposed institutions. A VCC-like minimum security institution planned for a subdivision of Joliet, located roughly thirty miles from Chicago, had to be scuttled when a constellation of community interests mobilized popular support and political muscle to overwhelm the Illinois Department of Corrections. During the summer of 1975 the scenario repeated itself when residents of Chicago's New Town section forced the Illinois Department of Corrections to dismantle a women's work release center that the department had attempted to place in New Town without the prior approval of community groups. In both cases local residents saw no advantage in having open correctional institutions move into the neighborhood. In neither case were powerful local interests cultivated or co-opted.

Urban communities pose particular difficulties for those who wish to establish minimum security prisons, halfway houses, or work release centers. Fear of crime is already high in the urban areas, and community-based institutions raise concern about attracting more "deviants" to the neighborhood. While skid row areas and other disorganized sections of the inner city will probably be too powerless to prevent the state from imposing new agencies and institutions, those (often mixed) neighborhoods that still maintain some economic and political viability may define their situation as a struggle for existence; in such circumstances the presence of any type of prison facility will be defined as accelerating the deterioration of the community.

It must also be emphasized that local interests are not as easily identified or satisfied in an urban environment. While 200 jobs are enough to tie the entire county area to VCC, such is not the case in an urban area where populations are much greater and where friendship and familial networks are not nearly so deeply or extensively entrenched. A small institution has little to offer a densely populated, economically variegated, and politically pluralistic community. Under such circumstances it is not surprising that the department of corrections falls back upon abstract intellectual arguments aimed at mobilizing liberal sentiments of sympathy for the prisoner. Such a political strategy seems very unlikely to produce a stable social and political foundation for the establishment of community-based corrections. What is more likely is that these facilities, when they are established at all, will continue to be located only in the most disorganized and highest crime-rate areas of the city.

It is ironic and instructive that perhaps the best prospect for developing small, flexible, experimental, and humane prison facilities may be in the rural communities toward which criminologists have for so long expressed negative bias. In the unlikely milieu of rural southern Illinois a highly imaginative and highly successful prison has been established. The growth of VCC and the expansion of its reform program, highlighted by the continuous movement of local citizens into the prison and of prisoners out into the surrounding community, has occurred because of, not in spite of, the unique requirements of the surrounding environment.

THE MASS MEDIA AND PRISON NEWS
COAUTHOR HELEN A. BROOKS

Traditional penological thinking holds that the public is thoroughly ignorant of what goes on inside prisons and that the only kind of information which comes to its attention concerns riots and other sordid violence. It follows that because the public lacks knowledge about prison conditions and alternatives for change, there will be no public demand for, or even support of, reform. Despite the importance of this thesis, there exists no corpus of research on public knowledge and opinion concerning prisons. One strategy for studying this issue is to focus on the quantity and content of information about prisons which is disseminated by the mass media.

We conducted a content analysis of prison news coverage in newspapers, periodicals, and television for a single year, 1976. Two newspapers were chosen: the *New York Times* (daily readership 2,197,500) and the *New York Daily News* (daily readership 4,359,000), the nation's two largest dailies. All magazines indexed in the *Reader's Guide to Periodical Literature* were searched for articles about prisons, as were all CBS news programs (audience estimated to be 17,300,000 daily), through the use of transcripts obtained from computer files.

Of course, these sources do not exhaust all information disseminated by the media. We have not, for example, analyzed radio news or suburban newspapers, or other large urban papers. Still, an analysis of the chosen sources should give some indication of the amount and type of prison news which penetrates the environment, at least of New York City residents, and to some extent of the larger regional and national population.

The Extensiveness of Prison News

Not unexpectedly, the daily newspapers provided the largest number of stories about prisons (see Table 1). In 1976 the *New York Times* carried 495 articles, and the *Daily News* 361. Between them, prison-related news was reported every day of the year. Both papers printed front-page articles on prison issues: the *Times* on 10 occasions, and the *Daily News* on 58. During the same year, 46 prison-related articles appeared in a variety of magazines and journals. The magazines and journals that reported stories on the prison can be divided into three types: news magazines, such as *Time*, *Newsweek*, and the *U.S. News and World Report*; political commentaries, such as *Nation*, *New Republic*, and *Commentary*; and popular magazines, such as *Ebony*. About 98 percent of the 1976 prison articles appeared in the news and political commentary magazines. The largest number of articles (7) appeared in *Newsweek*; *Nation* carried 2, and *Time Magazine* 5.

We would expect to find fewer prison stories on television because of greater competition for less "space." However, 127 prison segments [2] were aired by CBS in 1976; prison-related news appeared at least once on 104 different days. And, on July 2, 1976, the CBS "Evening News" opened with a lengthy segment on prisoners' reactions to the Supreme Court's reinstatement of the death penalty.

These gross statistics seem to belie the assertion that the public is uninformed about prisons. Compared with other social issues — for example, nursing homes, mental health, and welfare, — the prisons fare well in the competition for news space. The *New York Times*'s prison news, for example, was double its coverage of nursing homes and mental health, and substantially more than its coverage of welfare. Similarly, magazines gave more coverage to prisons than to nursing homes, mental health, and welfare.[3] And on CBS, the coverage of prison news was substantially greater than coverage of these other

---

[2] A story repeated several times during the day was counted only once.

[3] In 1976 only two stories on nursing homes, 18 on mental health, and 12 on welfare were catalogued in *Reader's Guide to Periodical Literature*.

Table 1. Number and percent of items in selected media devoted to prison issues, by category, 1976

Category	New York Times		New York Daily News		Periodicals		CBS		All media	
	No.	%	No.	%	No.	%	No.	%	No.	%
Penal policy and prison conditions	220	45	52	15	28	61	30	24	330	32
Disturbances	90	18	38	11	3	6	17	14	148	14
Litigation	78	16	9	2	4	9	8	7	99	10
Human interest	33	7	18	5	9	20	22	17	82	8
Celebrities	11	2	211	58	2	4	39	29	263	26
Escapes	40	8	15	4	0		11	9	66	6
Editorials	12	2	10	3	0		0		22	2
Miscellaneous	11	2	8	2	0		0		19	2
All categories	495		361		46		127		1,029	

issues; there were only 13 segments on nursing homes, 41 on mental health, and 67 on welfare.

The Content of Prison News

We were able to code about 98 percent of prison-related news into seven categories: penal policy and conditions, disturbances, litigation, human interest, celebrities, escapes, and editorials (see Table 1). The fact that "penal policy" received the most attention (37 percent of total prison news coverage) should dispel the notion that the only prison news conveyed to the public concerns violence and scandal. The newspapers reported a wide range of policy issues, which can be more clearly analyzed in terms of four subcategories: statements on policy and conditions, reports and studies of policy, legislation, and new programs (see Table 2).

With respect to general information about prison conditions and policies, the newspapers reported such news as Mayor Abraham Beame's order to probe into recent increases of inmate suicides (*New York Times*, October 15, 1976:5). The newspapers reported the findings of various studies and investigations, particularly those announced by New York State's Correction Commission. The *Daily News* (November 21, 1976:21) reported the Correction Commission's findings on the use of tranquilizing drugs at Bedford Hills Correctional Facility. The *Times* (July 1, 1976:1) reported the same agency's conclusion that conditions at Attica are "just as bad, perhaps worse" than in September 1971, just before the inmate rebellion that resulted in the death of forty-three persons.

The newspapers covered the legislative fate of several bills concerning corrections in 1976. Both the *Times* (July 1:1) and the *Daily News* (July 1:75) covered the passage of a New York State bill that shortened misdemeanor sen-

Table 2. Number and percent of items in New York City newspapers devoted to penal policy and prison conditions, by category, 1976

Category	New York Times		New York Daily News		Both papers	
	Number	Percent	Number	Percent	Number	Percent
Statement on policy and conditions	117	53	24	46	141	52
Reports and studies of policy	39	18	8	15	47	17
Legislation	28	13	5	10	33	12
New programs	36	16	15	29	51	29
All categories	220		52		272	

tences so that 470 inmates would be released, the aim of the legislation being to ease overcrowding. Articles also appeared in 1976 on new prison programs such as conjugal visits (*New York Times*, February 14:25) and inmate grievance committees (*New York Times*, November 26:48).

Overcrowding appeared in all four subcategories of policy and conditions. The recurrent message disseminated to the public was that prisons are vastly overcrowded because of higher crime rates, higher conviction rates, longer sentences, and, of course, a shortage of correctional facilities. For example, the *New York Times* (January 5, 1976:1) reported:

> Arkansas is using mobile homes to house prisoners, and Florida is using tents. In Virginia a warehouse is being converted. South Carolina has advertised for abandoned schools and factories for use as prisons... Prisoners have had to sleep on mattresses on the floor in all these states ... [and] Georgia, Alabama, Florida, and Louisiana have had to stop accepting prisoners in their state facilities.

Magazines gave more coverage (61 percent) to penal conditions and policy than to any other category in 1976. For example, *Newsweek* (March 29:87) carried a story, entitled "Gospel behind Bars," devoted to religious freedom in prisons, and *Ebony* (November 26:83) published the article "How to End Sex Problems in Prisons." However, the emphasis of magazine coverage in this category differed from that of the newspapers: many articles presented a definite point of view rather than merely describing prison events. For example, *Intellect* (May:93; January:310) published two case studies, "Politics and Prison Reform: 3 Test Cases" and "Bleak House Lives: The Brooklyn House of Detention Case." Among popular topics for magazine coverage in 1976 were rehabilitation programs and employment opportunities for ex-prisoners. *Psychology Today* (October:129) published an article entitled "Prisoners Can Be Rehabilitated Now," and *Business Week* (November 8:106) carried "Matching Ex-Convicts to Jobs They Like." Most articles that we coded under penal conditions and policy covered specific issues. Titles include "1976: The Lesson Not Learned, the Results of Attica" (*Nation*, De-

[109]

cember:586) and "Rights of the Prisoners versus the State — Medical Experimentation" (*Current*, February:40). There were only two general surveys; *New Republic* (November 20:12) published "Imprisoned Americans," and *Commentary* (November:55) carried "Who is in Prison?" Very few articles dealt with overcrowding, the most popular policy topic for newspapers.[4]

CBS aired thirty stories (24 percent of its prison news coverage) on prison conditions and penal policy. Ten percent of CBS's coverage in this category was devoted to commentary, 33 percent to studies (for example, a survey of death row populations), 20 percent to new programs (such as alternatives to traditional incarceration), and 30 percent to the United States-Mexico negotiations for prisoner exchange. As in the newspapers, the topic of overcrowding was stressed in all subcategories (see Table 2) except the last.

These data refute the assertion that mass media prison coverage is dominated by accounts of violence. Only 11 percent of the total media coverage concerned prison disturbances. The *Times* devoted only 18 percent of its prison coverage to this topic; the *Daily News* devoted 11 percent. There were no front-page stories on prison violence in the *Times* during 1976; only two front-page stories appeared in the *Daily News* (both concerning an inmate strike at Attica).

Under "disturbances," we coded violations of penal rules and threats to order, including inmate violence,[5] guard brutality, illegal contraband, suicide, rape, riot, arson, stabbing, and inmate and guard strikes, slowdowns, and sickouts. The *Times* (December 3, 1976:10), for example, printed a story about an execution squad, operating at Massachusetts's Walpole Prison. The *Daily News* printed seven stories on inmate suicides.

The magazines and journals devoted almost no coverage to disturbances; the only three articles on the subject which appeared in 1976 were all printed in the *Nation*. One reported an inmate work stoppage at Attica (December 4:581), another a protest over food and living conditions at McNeil Island (December 11:627), and a third presented a general discussion of violence and tension in prisons (February 28:241).

CBS aired seventeen news segments on prison disturbances, for the most part riots and strikes. It devoted four segments to hunger strikes by Americans in Mexican prisons and four segments to an inmate strike at Attica. The transcription of its August 24 story on the Attica strike provides a good example of how CBS handles prison news.

---

[4] Two articles were specifically about overcrowding: *New Republic* (June 1976:5) published an article entitled "Population Explosion," and *U.S. News and World Report* (March 1, 1976:65) carried, "Yesterday's Baby Boom Is Overcrowding Today's Prisons."

[5] Riots were reported at Trenton State Prison, Rikers Island, and Great Meadow. Inmate strikes occurred at Attica, Great Meadow, and Green Haven.

HUGHES RUDD: Most of the two thousand *prisoners* at Attica — in New York State — went on *strike* yesterday, with a long list of grievances. Ordinarily prison strikes don't get too much attention, but this one did because of what's happened before.

SAM CHU LIN: When the smoke cleared away from four days of rioting in Attica Prison in 1971, officials counted forty-three people dead. They immediately ordered an investigation into the causes and, subsequently, instituted *reforms*. Nearly five years later, inmates claim — what they call — deplorable conditions still exist. Ninety percent of the prison population has called a general strike, refusing to leave cells for meals, work assignments or classes.

So far, the protest has been peaceful. The men have issued nine demands, including the limitation of all jail terms to five years, with the rest served on parole, relaxed conjugal visitation privileges and the confinement of inmates at facilities closer to their homes and families. Prison officials say they've been talking with a committee of fifteen inmates about the demands, but they emphasize that talks are not negotiations.

COMMISSIONER BENJAMIN WARD [Department of Correctional Services]: I'm not altogether certain myself, that it's something that has — that the legislature has to address. And these — these long-range requests are not — they're not even different. I mean, they've been around the prison reform request route for many years, and the legislature have — has to address itself to this and see whether or not they're going to make changes in these areas.

CHU LIN: Prison officials have not allowed the press to speak with inmates, saying such activity might interfere with their current talks. Continual dialogue, they say, means the situation is under control.

The "litigation" category includes prisoners' rights suits and court rulings on prisoner cases. The *New York Times* printed seventy-eight stories concerning prison litigation (16 percent of its total coverage), eight times that of the *Daily News*. Both papers carried front-page stories. The *Daily News's* headlines reported the dismissal of charges against Attica inmates and the indictment of two prison guards charged with abetting an escape from Rikers Island. The *Times* printed front-page stories on Attica and on the jury's verdict in the "San Quentin 6" trial.

The most heavily reported case was Judge Frank Johnson's landmark decision in *Pugh v. Locke*, declaring Alabama's prisons unconstitutional and establishing minimum standards for their future operation.[6] The *Times* devoted six

[6] *New York Times* articles on the Johnson ruling appeared in 1976 on January 14:69, col. 1; January 18:4, col. 2; January 19:17, col. 5; January 26:23, col. 2; February 1:32, col. 2; and December 5:43, col. 1. All of the media reported the decision. A *Daily News* headline on January 14:38, col. 1 stated "Prisons in Alabama Judged Unfit." CBS covered the ruling on its January 13 "Evening News" show. *Time* (January 26:65) carried the article "The Real Governor — The Rulings of Judge F. M. Johnson, Jr." A *Newsweek* story (January 26:43) was entitled "Snake Pits — Decision of Judge F. M. Johnson."

articles to this case and its impact. Judge Lasker's rulings on New York City's jails also attracted extensive media attention, as did such other matters as the verdict in the "San Quentin 6" case, the dropping of charges against Attica inmates, Attorney General Levy's suit against Illinois and Chicago prison officials for widespread deprivations of civil rights, and the Supreme Court's reinstatement of the death penalty. Acquittals and indictments pertaining to crimes committed inside the prison comprise the remainder of items in this category.

In 1976 four articles (9 percent) on prison litigation appeared in popular periodicals. Both *Time* and *Newsweek* devoted stories to Judge Johnson's ruling on Alabama prisons and to a New York court's dismissal of charges against 1971 Attica rioters. The only prison story to open a CBS news broadcast concerned the Supreme Court's ruling on the death penalty.

The mass media also carried human interest stories from prison. These generally depicted the lighter side of prison life: art exhibits, sporting events, concerts, educational programs, and even weddings. One story reported the reunion of a father and son in prison after a nineteen-year separation; both were serving minor sentences. Governor Carey granted amnesty to an ex-convict, Martin Sostre, who sought employment as a New York State assemblyman's aide. Both papers carried this story (*New York Times*, February 5, 1976:28; *Daily News*, February 11, 1976:43). There were also several articles on reformed ex-convicts currently employed in corrections.

The *New York Times* printed only thirty-three human interest stories — 6 percent of its prison coverage; the *News* was comparable at 5 percent. The magazines paid somewhat more attention to human interest (19 percent of their prison coverage). All but one article focused on particular prisoners; several dealt with inmates on death row. *Newsweek* (April 26, 1976:13) carried a piece about Carl Velleca, a Massachusetts prisoner who ran unsuccessfully for political office.

CBS presented twice the proportion of human interest stories (15 percent) as the *Times* or the *Daily News*. It covered Carl Velleca's political campaign, as well as the ordeal of Peter Reilly, who was mistakenly incarcerated for matricide. One "Morning News" broadcast closed with a segment on unusual criminals and their crimes. There were also several CBS stories in 1976 on pardons and clemencies. For example, on October 25, CBS reported the pardon of Willie Norris, the last known defendant from the Scottsboro Trial. One CBS segment spotlighted a ninety-one-year-old prisoner who, unable to cope with the outside world, declined parole and returned to prison. Two CBS segments were devoted to Johnson Van Dyke, who had spent sixty-six of his ninety-two years behind bars. His pardon when he was eighty-nine drew national attention; Johnny Cash wrote a song about his release. Another prisoner reported, on the air, that he was quite content with his life as a thief.

[112]

To our "celebrity" category we assigned all stories on famous or notorious inmates. In 1976 the *Times* reported 11 celebrity stories, concentrating on Watergate prisoners — for example, Gordon Liddy's campaign for prison reform, particularly liberalized mailing privileges (April 3:40; May 3:26; August 20:15). In contrast, the *Daily News* gave its most extensive coverage to celebrities; of its 211 stories, 144 were devoted to Patty Hearst. Readers were provided every detail of her prison experience, from her fears to her illnesses. The paper even reported when Patty won the right to have her hair cut. There were only two celebrity stories in the 1976 periodicals: one reported on Patty Hearst's prison experiences and the other on John Erlichman's. By contrast, CBS devoted 39 news segments, 29 percent of its prison coverage, to the activities of celebrity prisoners, perhaps reflecting TV's stronger orientation toward "stars."

The newspaper reports of escapes consisted of descriptions either of how the escapes occurred or of subsequent recaptures. The *Times* devoted only 8 percent of its total prison coverage to escapes, the *Daily News* only 4 percent. No escape stories were printed in magazines and journals. CBS carried twelve segments; half dealt with Americans escaping from Mexican jails.

Editorials concerning prisons appeared only in newspapers in 1976. There was a marked contrast between the *Times* and the *Daily News* editorials, reflecting their different political positions. The *Times* favored spending money to improve penal conditions (March 18:40), supported Herman Schwartz's nomination for chairman of New York State's Correction Commission (April 7:40), applauded Judge Lasker's rulings (January 22:30), criticized the City administration's failure to improve conditions in the Tombs (January 28:32), and urged Governor Hugh Carey to grant amnesty to the Attica inmates involved in the 1971 riot (October 11:37). The *Daily News*, on the other hand, called it "silly" to loosen mail censorship requirements and "assinine" to liberalize inmates' visitation privileges (January 15:31). It urged Judge Lasker "to come down from his ivory tower," (January 28:39) and stated that the United States should be skeptical about the prisoner exchange treaty talks with Mexico (September 28:33). In addition, the *Daily News* characterized the recent Attica inmate strike as a "con game" (August 25:39) and advocated a get-tough policy on parole (August 16:31).

Conclusion

Content analysis suggests several hypotheses and directions for future research. While it is hard to know what standard could be used to determine whether the media present an "appropriate" *amount* of prison news, comparisons of media coverage of a variety of "social problems" would be quite revealing. Our cursory comparison of prison news with coverage given to welfare, mental health, and nursing homes suggests that prisons are not being slighted.

Whether prison news is objective, accurate, and comprehensive or whether it is sensationalistic is another question. Once again it is a formidable problem to find appropriate tools for evaluation. Still, our analysis shows that there is more news on such topics as prison conditions and penal policy, legislative developments and prisoners' rights, than on brutality, violence, and escape. It seems clear to us that even a weakly motivated resident of the New York metropolitan area would learn a substantial amount about prisons by following either the print or electronic news media.

There are obvious and considerable differences among the media sources. The *New York Times* maintains a high standard of journalism and reflects as "intellectual" an orientation as can be found in a mass-circulation newspaper. It should not, however, be dismissed as a deviant case; it has enormous importance in shaping the attitudes of opinion leaders nationally. A regular reader of the *New York Times* would be well informed about prison matters.

It is more difficult to assess the level of information about prisons available to the public in other media. At least in 1976 no single news magazine paid significant attention to prisons or issues of penal policy. Articles on specific topics occurred infrequently. Such coverage is not distortive, but neither can it be relied upon for a clear picture of the prison landscape.

Surprisingly, even the *Daily News* presented a wide range of information about prisons and prisoners, despite its concentration on Patty Hearst. While the *Daily News* readers would not be nearly so well informed as readers of the *New York Times*, they would nevertheless be made aware of the problems of crowding, the search for new policies, and the judicial intervention into prison administration.

Television news is obviously less comprehensive than the news presented in the print media. Extraordinary events dominate TV coverage; the more mundane aspects of prison management, legislation, litigation, conflict, and philosophical debate are unlikely to appear on national televised news. The year 1976, in retrospect, was somewhat unusual from a prison-news standpoint because of the presence of the Watergate inmates in the federal prisons. In addition, the controversy over the treatment of Americans in Mexican prisons presented a prison issue with an international flavor — one appropriate for national news. Even including these stories, however, television coverage of American prisons in 1976 was "thin," primarily "snapshots" of disjointed events. It would be difficult for people for whom television is the sole source of news to develop an informed view of the current conditions and controversies in American prisons. In fact, their image of prisons in 1976 might have been distorted by pictures of the minimum security federal institutions housing the Watergate defendants.

There is a need for much research on how the American public forms its opinions about prisons as well as about other social issues. Our work could be usefully supplemented by content analyses of radio news presentations and of a large sample of metropolitan dailies and suburban chain newspapers. In the final analysis, what the public thinks about prison will play an important role in facilitating or impeding prison reforms. Therefore, the processes of opinion formation deserve the penologist's sustained attention.

REFLECTIONS ON THE DEFEAT
OF NEW YORK STATE'S PRISON BOND
COAUTHOR LAURA BERKOWITZ

Introduction: The Politics of Prison Construction

Massive growth of prisoner populations in most American states since the mid-1970s has touched off building and expansion controversies nearly everywhere (see Sherman and Hawkins 1981; Corrections Compendium 1982). While the merits of both the expansion and the anti-expansion positions are reasonably well known, surprisingly little attention has been paid to the politics of prison expansion. Which elites can be expected to favor expansion and which to oppose it? What is the position of the print and electronic media? When is mass opinion important and how is it shaped?

In 1981 New York State's political leaders narrowly failed in their efforts to convince the electorate to support a half-billion-dollar bond issue that would have financed the construction of three new state prisons and the substantial expansion of several older ones and expansion of local jails. New York's experience is not necessarily "typical," but neither is it unusual. The magnitude of New York's proposed expansion and the plebiscite that was convened to support or reject it make the New York case particularly noteworthy. Indeed, it is rare that a major criminal justice issue, especially a penological issue, is put directly to the voters for resolution. Analysis of the history of New York's prison bond, the election campaign, the role of the media, and the election results will, we hope, make a contribution to the study of penological politics and stimulate other related research elsewhere in the country.

Birth of a Bond

As did most other states, New York experienced an astronomical growth of its prisoner population during the last decade. In September 1972 there were

12,242 state prisoners; nine years later the count stood at 24,082, 10 percent above the system's total capacity. The Department of Correctional Services (DOCS) added approximately 5,500 beds between 1975 and 1980, but space lagged far behind admissions. When lengthy negotiations to lease New York City's jail complex at Rikers Island failed,[7] DOCS concluded that large-scale construction and renovation was the only alternative to an overcrowding disaster.

The idea of financing prison construction through a bond was first proposed in 1978. Proponents of prison expansion felt that spreading the cost of construction over thirty years would be politically easier than obtaining such a large amount of money in the annual legislative budget competition, particularly in light of the state's continuing fiscal problems. The bond was incorporated into the Senate's 1978 Omnibus Crime Bill but subsequently dropped, because the issue was thought too politically sensitive for a gubernatorial election year.

In June 1980, as prison crowding increasingly threatened prison operations, and following the mayor's scuttling of the Rikers option, DOCS Commissioner Thomas A. Coughlin and Howard F. Miller, state budget director, submitted to Governor Hugh Carey a plan calling for the creation of 4,078 state prison beds in three new maximum security prisons (housing 512 inmates each) and in renovated existing facilities. The governor in turn proposed a $375 million Public Safety Bond Issue, with by far the largest share to go to DOCS, but with $40 million earmarked for the state police, the mentally retarded, and the criminally insane and $100 million in loans to go to municipalities for expansion or renovation of jails, which were also extremely crowded. This last expenditure was included after the New York State Sheriff's Association threatened to oppose the bond unless it included money for local jail construction.

The bond attracted strong support in the legislature. The powerful chairman of the Senate Committee on Crime and Correction, Senator Ralph Marino (R-Nassau County), submitted a counter proposal that differed from the governor's plan in two ways: (1) the Marino bill provided money only for state and local corrections; "extras" such as the state police barracks and crime control centers were eliminated, (2) while the governor proposed *loans* to localities that undertook jail and penitentiary expansion, Marino provided

---

[7] DOCS began negotiations with New York City for the acquisition of Rikers Island in 1978. The legislature approved a $200 million appropriation to lease Rikers for 99 years. In 1980 New York City pulled out of negotiations because of pressing fiscal problems. If the State had been successful, Rikers would have added 5,000 beds to the system. The City subsequently obtained a court ruling requiring the State to take sentenced prisoners from Rikers within forty-eight hours (*Benjamin v. Malcolm et al.* 1981).

for fifty-fifty matching *grants*. The switch from loans to grants was an obvious attempt to enhance prison construction's grass roots appeal.

Negotiations among the two houses of the legislature, the governor's office, and the Division of Budget resulted in a compromise bill, the Security Through the Development of Correctional Facilities Bond Act of 1981. It passed the Assembly by a vote of 130 to 6, and the Senate 52 to 4. As the vote indicates, there was no serious legislative opposition. The absence of legislative opposition, however, did not indicate widespread consensus among the citizenry.

The final bill closely paralleled Marino's proposal. The state would sell $500 million in bonds that would mature serially over a thirty-year period, spreading the cost of repayment over three decades. Financial analysts calculated that if sold over four years at a 10 percent interest rate, the total cost to New York taxpayers would be $1,286,400,000. The revenue would be allocated in the following manner: (1) $350 million to DOCS for the construction of three maximum security prisons (512 beds each) in Ulster, Sullivan, and Greene counties and the expansion of existing facilities by 2542 beds, (2) $100 million in grants to the counties on a fifty-fifty matching basis for construction and renovation of local jails — the amount for which any municipality or county could apply being based on population, (3) $15 million on a matching basis ($490,196 per county) to all counties except New York City, Erie, Monroe, Nassau, Suffolk, Onondaga, and Westchester, (4) $10 million to New York City for jail expansion, (5) $25 million for the expansion and improvement of state penal facilities for juvenile offenders (Division for Youth) and for the criminally insane. The bill designated DOCS overseer of all funds distributed for state corrections and placed the Commission of Correction in charge of local disbursements. The Commission was granted discretion in disbursing bond funds to localities and was directed to consider, among other things, whether a locality complied with minimum health and safety standards and to what extent it made use of alternatives to incarceration, such as probation, fines, and community service.

The Campaign

Although the governor and virtually the entire legislature endorsed the prison construction bond, many citizens' groups opposed it as wasteful, ineffective, and immoral. Throughout the summer and fall of 1981, the contending camps attempted to sway the voters through publications, speeches, and advertisements. Both the print and electronic media gave a good deal of attention to the bond. Proponents and opponents frequently appeared on TV talk shows.

[117]

The Proponents

By far the most vigorous supporter of the bond was DOCS. Not surprisingly, it defined the creation of new prison space as essential to the effective and humane management of the prisons. DOCS officials, led by Commissioner Coughlin, campaigned vigorously. Coughlin argued that imprisonment deters crime and that prison expansion would make a significant contribution to public safety. He also warned that if more space were not made available immediately, "we had better be prepared for a major uprising in the institutions ... people have to have space." (*New York Times*, February 12, 1981:3). Finally, he presented prison expansion as a *fait accompli*; if the bond were not approved, more prison space would be built anyway — using hard tax dollars. It is interesting that neither DOCS nor the bond's other supporters emphasized the welfare of the prisoners: humanitarianism apparently had little political appeal.

Although DOCS paid lip service to the rule that as a state agency it could not campaign on political issues, as opposed to providing educational information, in reality it pressed its case with vigor. Wardens were called to Albany for instruction by a public relations expert on the best techniques for influencing employees and the public in favor of the bond. A DOCS task force operated as a full-time liaison between DOCS and voters. A half-dozen regular staff members worked full-time answering telephone inquiries, distributing leaflets, and providing detailed information packets to influential citizens' groups and newspapers. One task force member estimates that by late October the Department had sent out approximately one hundred thousand leaflets. A legal challenge to the Department's campaign activities revealed that it had spent $158,000 on the election.[8]

In addition to DOCS officials, numerous political leaders campaigned in behalf of the expansion program. Touting the bond as "a wise and necessary investment in our criminal justice and corrections system," Governor Carey appeared regularly on radio and television throughout the fall of 1981 (*New York Times* August 4, 1981:B-2). Carey warned that if the bond were defeated, the state might be forced to cut other programs in order to finance prison construction out of general revenues. The bond also enjoyed the support of New York's mayor, Ed Koch, who with characteristic bluntness argued that "for the public the issue is as simple as put up or shut up ... what good is everything else if you are not safe?" (*New York Times*, October 10, 1981:27).

[8] In late October, New York Public Interest Research Group (NYPIRG) sought a court order the restraining DOC's campaign activities. It charged DOCS with channeling public funds to an organization called the "Vote Yes on Proposition One Committee" and with stuffing state employees' pay envelopes with campaign literature. The state court refused to issue the restraining order. The suit did reveal, however, the amount that DOCS had spent on the campaign (*New York Times*, Oct. 24, 1981:A-27).

Senator Marino and his staff lent their efforts by circulating newsletters and pamphlets. Others, such as Senator Donald Halperin (D-Brooklyn) made frequent speeches and appeared on TV. Of course, the prison bond had the enthusiastic endorsement of law enforcement agencies. As Phil Caruso, president of New York's Patrolmen's Benevolent Association put it: "The P.B.A. favors the building of more prisons. In this way we can nullify the trite, longstanding excuse for leniency preferred by judges who blame their mercy-bent on a lack of jail space." (*New York Times,*, August 1, 1981:24).

To our knowledge, only one private citizen's group endorsed the bond — the Citizens' Crime Commission of New York City, comprised primarily of New York City businessmen. The Commission's arguments were similar to those of DOCS (in fact, many of their facts and figures came from the Department): prison space must be expanded if the state is to deal with crime effectively; incarceration is the safest and most effective method of crime control because it both incapacitates and deters; bonding is a fair and realistic method of financing prison construction. At the end of its October 1981 report, the Commission summed up its pro-construction arguments:

> If the public safety bond issue is not passed it will mean, at the least, that recent successful programs designed to incarcerate violent repeat offenders will fail. Worse, it may cause the unjustified release of dangerous criminals to prey on the public. Alternatively, it may create a nightmare of overcrowding and tension for prison inmates and staff. If approved, it will provide some breathing space for a criminal justice system which finds itself plagued by too few resources and too many predators.

The Opponents

Groups opposed to prison expansion began to mobilize against the bond as soon as it passed the legislature. The most important was a statewide coalition, Voters Against the Prison Construction Bond, sponsored by four liberal organizations traditionally active on criminal justice reform issues: the New York State Council of Churches, the New York State Coalition for Criminal Justice, the National Council on Crime and Delinquency, and the Fortune Society. Voters mounted a statewide campaign, distributing anti-bond literature, sponsoring public speeches and debates, and pressing its position on television and radio.

The anti-bond organizations can be grouped into three categories. The first is comprised of the criminal justice reform groups, for example, the Fortune Society, the Correctional Association of New York, and Prisoners' Legal Services. They consistently scrutinize and criticize prison conditions, and during the 1981 election they linked their anti-construction position to other "repressive" crime control strategies, such as mandatory sentencing. A second category is made up of public interest groups, including the New York Civil Liberties Union, the Citizens Union, and the NAACP. These groups linked their opposition to the bond to the broader concerns of underlying social injustices that imprisonment perpetuates and reinforces. Religious groups, such as the New York State Council of Churches, Genesee Ecumenical Ministries, the Mercy Prayer Center, the Unitarian Church, and the Quakers, comprise the third category. They especially stressed the failure of corrections to rehabilitate offenders and the moral and ethical problems posed by prison expansion.

The organizations that opposed the bond articulated a great many arguments; the main ones were these:

1. *Prison expansion is too expensive.* A $500 million bond issue would cost taxpayers nearly $1.5 billion. Four thousand cells would add as much as $80 million to the annual operating budget.

2. *Incarceration does not lower the crime rate.* Locking up criminals neither deters nor provides a significant incapacitation effect. Dan Pachoda, chairman of the Correctional Association of New York, argued that mandatory sentences have no deterrent effect on criminals. Many groups, including Coalition and the Correctional Association, cited the 1973 Rockefeller drug law as proof that mandatory sentences are an ineffective deterrent. The National Council on Crime and Delinquency estimated that the state would have to increase prison commitments by 264 percent in order to achieve a 10 percent reduction in crimes.

3. *Prison expansion cannot relieve overcrowding immediately.* Even if the bond issue were passed, it would take several years before the new cells would be completed, and by then they would not be needed; less costly alternatives could be used to reduce current overcrowding.

4. *There are less costly and more effective alternatives to incarceration.* Virtually all opponents of the prison bond acknowledged that the state faced a serious prison overcrowding problem, but they insisted that there existed non-incarcerative alternatives for bringing the prison population under control: increased use of probation, early release, fines, community service, diversion, and victim restitution. The Correctional Association of New York, the New York State Council of Churches, and Voters all claimed that a large percentage of prisoners could be placed in alternative programs with no danger to the public.

5. *Prison construction would deprive citizens of more pressing services.* Voters Against the Prison Construction Bond issued a position paper (August 1981) that explained: "We question the wisdom of allocating billions of dollars to build and maintain prisons while the state is confronted with cutbacks to government services of such magnitude. We also wonder how many teachers,

job developers, nurses, daycare workers, and librarians that $500 million bond issue can pay for."

6. *Prison expansion would perpetuate the racism, immorality, and injustice already perpetrated by imprisonment.* The anti-builders argued that incarceration should not be expanded because the effect would be to exacerbate discrimination against blacks and Hispanics. The New York Civil Liberties Union stressed that incarceration deprives individuals of important political freedoms. Many groups, including the New York State Coalition for Criminal Justice, emphasized the negative, nonrehabilitative impact that imprisonment has upon inmates: "Prisons are cost defective rather than cost effective. Rather than reducing crime, prisons in fact increase crime because they are so destructive of those persons sentenced to them. Removed from the communities to which they will ultimately return, prisoners are required to rehabilitate themselves in a near vacuum." The Coalition for Criminal Justice argued that greater crime reduction could be achieved by using the proposed prison construction money for education and job training.

Media Coverage

The prison bond campaign calls into question the often repeated view that prisons are brought to the public's attention only when there is a riot, scandal, or the equivalent. The campaign was very well covered in both the print and electronic media. This point is especially salient when one compares the attention given to the prison bond with that given to the Job Development Authority (JDA) bond, which appeared on the same ballot in the November election, and which proposed spending $150 million on loans for developing private sector jobs (see Table 3).

Table 3. Number of items in selected New York State newspapers devoted to state bond and JDA bond, by type of item, September 1 – Election Day, 1981

Type of item	New York Times	Syracuse Post-Standard	Ithaca Journal
Prison bond			
News features	9	10	3
Editorials	3	2	2
Letters to the editor	7	16	6
JDA bond			
News features	2	1	1
Editorials	1	2	1
Letters to the editor	1	0	2

The most important point to be made about the print media is that the newspapers, like the political leaders of both parties, were overwhelmingly in favor of the prison bond. Most editorials echoed the arguments of the pro-bond groups, rejecting alternatives to imprisonment as unsafe and impractical. For example, the *Syracuse Post-Standard* (October 12, 1981:A-8) stated that "the need for more prison space is desperate. Everyone is only too well aware of the great increase in crimes of violence and of the need for prisons in which to incarcerate criminals found guilty of such crimes."

Moreover, most editorials suggested that prison expansion was inevitable and that bonding was the best means of financing. The *New York Times* (November 3, 1981:A-18) noted that "the real issue is how to pay for cells that will have to be built one way or another. That's why voters should approve the prison bond." It rejected a moratorium on prison expansion as "holding prisoners hostage" (October 18, 1981:E-20), stressing that "sooner or later, the money will have to be spent. Better sooner, for it's not clear how the Prison System without even the prospect of relief, can long survive the current 10% overcrowding" (November 3, 1981:A-18). Similarly, the editor of the *Ithaca Journal* explained that "if there were an alternative to incarcerating felony offenders we'd support it . . . If there were a less expensive way to fix the problem we'd support it. But the fact is we're putting more criminals behind bars and we need room for them" (October 27, 1981:12).

Another concern that editorial writers expressed was that rioting might result from continued crowding. The *New York Times* (November 3, 1981:A-18) warned that overcrowded conditions "might well produce unrest, even riot." The *Syracuse Post-Standard* made the same prediction: "If we are to avoid a possible repetition of Attica riots, we must expand and rehabilitate our prisons" (October 12, 1981:A-8).

While the editorials were overwhelmingly pro-bond, the letters-to-the-editor columns ventilated both sides of the issue. Most proponents simply asserted the need for prison expansion in order to bolster public safety and alleviate prison overcrowding. A majority of writers opposing the bond stressed its expense. As one Syracuse resident put it: "Yes, we are concerned with crime but . . . who will protect us from the ever shrinking tax base that makes fewer and fewer of us pay more and more taxes" (*Syracuse Post-Standard*, October 22, 1981:A-10). An Albany writer made the same point: "A few million here. A few billion there. No wonder industry has fled south, taking our fine young people educated at our expense with them" (*Albany Times Union*, October 7, 1981:8).

The anti-expansion viewpoint was not limited to letters to the editor. Many newspapers carried stories about the bond's opponents. And some writers stressed the need for alternatives to incarceration. In late July, Tom Wicker of the *New York Times* advised that "New York, instead of building more cells at great cost, and putting more people in them at great cost, should try to keep more offenders out of prison, saving the taxpayers immense sums, possibly improving the crime rate, almost certainly not worsening it" (July 24, 1981:A-27). Furthermore, at least one article, perhaps anticipating upstate voter sentiment, openly denounced the bond as a tactic for shifting New York City's crime problem onto the entire state's shoulders. As one *Albany Times-Union* journalist complained: "Other than being a heavy drain on state finances, and thus a pain in the wallet to the rest of the state, the Big Apple contributes more prisoners to the state system than any other locality or area ... it's damned well time that New York City's control over much of the rest of the state and its desires should be terminated and the city itself a world of its own, should start bearing more of its own load" (October 29, 1981:7).

The Election

During the campaign there were no opinion polls with which to gauge public opinion on prison expansion. Given the support of politicians, media, and the general public for crime control, however, one would probably have wagered on passage.[9] But on November 3, 1981, New York's voters defeated the prison bond by 1,286,371 to 1,272,672 — a margin of 13,699 votes. How can we explain this vote?

Voter Participation

Given the intensity of the campaign and the political salience of issues of crime and punishment and new government indebtedness, the extent of voter apathy is notable. To begin with, only 58 percent of New York's eligible voters went to the polls at all, about average for an off-year election. (Voter turnout was 53 percent in 1979, 60 percent in 1977.)

Of those who did vote, 41.4 percent left the prison bond referendum blank. The JDA bond received almost the exact same percentage of blanks (43 percent), another indication that neither the salience of the issues nor the vigor of the campaign aroused the electorate. The sad fact is that a large percentage of voters have no opinion on clear-cut policy issues.

---

[9] As a leading writer on popular attitudes toward crime and victimization has noted: "there is immense public support for government activity against crime. Since 1971, the Gallup organization and the National Opinion Research Center have monitored people's opinions about government spending in ten major areas, including cities, education, health, defense, space, foreign aid, and crime. They have been asked if 'too much' or 'too little' has been spent on those, or if spending has been 'just about right.' Over that decade, crime has had the most support for more spending and it has also been the most unwavering on the list; while public enthusiasm for other issues has waxed and waned, the proportion thinking that government does not spend enough on crime has remained constant at about 70%" (Skogan 1981:22).

[123]

Analysis of the Vote

The prison bond was defeated in all but eleven of the state's sixty-two counties. As Table 4 and the map of New York State demonstrate, only in the five New York City boroughs did more than 60 percent of the voters support the bond. All three counties that passed the bond by a margin of 55-60 percent (Rockland, Nassau, Westchester) are in the New York metropolitan area. The remaining three pro-bond counties (Clinton, Oneida, and Broome), located upstate, passed the bond by narrow majorities. Thus, the vote on the prison bond exhibits the same upstate-downstate split that occurs in most statewide elections.

Table 4. Percentage of yes vote for New York State prison bond, by county.

County	Yes vote (percent)
Broome	50.4
Bronx	68.8
Clinton	53.5
Kings	67.3
Nassau	57.6
New York	62.4
Oneida	50.6
Queens	65.3
Richmond	64.7
Rockland	60.4
Westchester	57.1

These results carry a powerful irony. The prison bond's opponents were traditional liberal organizations, predominantly based in New York City. Their campaign against the bond reiterated familiar liberal arguments. However, New York City voters, traditionally the most liberal in the state, strongly *supported* prison expansion.

The bond's opponents campaigned upstate with some trepidation. Upstaters are more conservative, more Republican, and usually more responsive to law-and-order issues. Yet, the bond was handily defeated in all but three counties outside the New York City metropolitan area. Why?

New York City voters confirm what many analysts have been telling us (e.g., Bayer 1981): that urban dwellers have lost their patience with crime and violence in the streets.[10] Liberals no longer automatically oppose law-and-order issues. But what explains rejection of prison expansion in conservative upstate counties? Perhaps the cost of prison expansion was the decisive fac-

[10] Two Gannett News Service-Gordon Black polls, conducted in May and June 1982, confirm our observations. Residents of upstate New York (defined as all counties north and west of Rockland) indicated much less concern about crime than New York City residents. A majority of upstaters opposed almost every crime measure supported by those living in New York City and surrounding counties (*Ithaca Journal*, July 26, 1982).

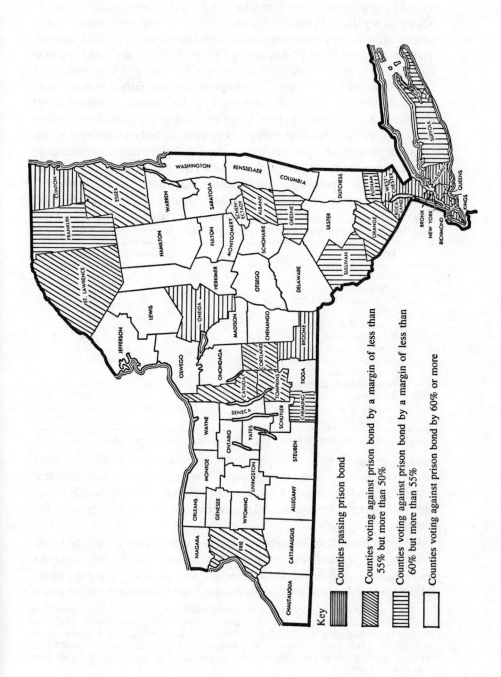

Key

▨ Counties passing prison bond

▨ Counties voting against prison bond by a margin of less than 55% but more than 50%

▨ Counties voting against prison bond by a margin of less than 60% but more than 55%

☐ Counties voting against prison bond by 60% or more

tor: why pay to lock up New York City's problems? This explanation does not wholly satisfy. It might make sense for many of the sparsely populated counties, but what about voters in the state's other large cities — Buffalo, Rochester, Syracuse, and Albany? Are they not affected by the same trends as New York City? It is very interesting that these upstate cities, with high crime rates and large minority populations, voted against the bond (albeit by lower margins than their contiguous rural counties), while Nassau, Westchester, and Rockland counties voted like New York City residents, despite all the obvious social and demographic differences between the city and its wealthy suburbs.

In order to draw sharper conclusions about the bond vote, we examined the correlations of county election results with five socioeconomic and demographic variables: population, percentage of nonwhites, per capita income, absence or presence of a state prison, and crime rate[11] (see Table 5). This

Table 5. Correlation of five independent variables with vote on New York State prison and JDA bonds for all counties and for all counties except downstate and metropolitan area, 1981

Variable	Prison bond	JDA bond
All counties		
Total population	.69	.73
Percentage of nonwhites	.72	.63
Crime rate	.66	.54
Presence of state prison	.20	.01
Per capita income	.46	.30
All counties except		
downstate metropolitan area[a]		
Total population	.26	.24
Percentage of nonwhites	.31	.21
Crime rate	.35	.24
Presence of state prison	.07	.17
Per capita income	.06	.04

[a]The five boroughs of New York City and Nassau, Westchester, and Rockland counties.

analysis reveals strong zero-order correlations between a county's vote on the prison bond and three of the factors: population; percentage of population that is nonwhite; and crime rate. A county's voting behavior is only weakly correlated with its per capita income and presence or absence of a state prison in the county.

We expected that more populated counties would favor the prison bond, since they would tend to be more urban, have greater fear of crime, and have fewer informal sanctions to deal with serious nonconformity. Our expectation is borne out by the data; there is a strong positive correlation (.686) between

[11] These independent variables were derived from the following sources: (1) population: 1980 census; (2) percentage of nonwhites: 1980 census; (3) per capita income: *Survey of Current Business* 61, no. 4 (April 1981), U.S. Dept of Commerce Bureau of Economic Analysis (figures are from 1979); (4) presence of a prison: *New York State Legislative Manual* 1974-79:673-675; (5) crime rate: New York State Division of Criminal Justice Services, *Annual Report* 1980 (figures are for 1980).

population and the percentage of yes votes. When New York City and the three downstate counties that voted for the bond are omitted, however, the relationship is substantially reduced (.263).[12] Outside the New York City metropolitan area a county's population is not a powerful determinant of its prison bond vote. This fact supports our observation that the prison bond vote did not reveal any sharp divergence between New York's urban centers and nonurban counties.

The larger a county's nonwhite population, the more likely it was to vote for the prison bond (.720), although once again the relationship decreases markedly (.311) when New York City and the three surrounding counties are omitted from the analysis. This trend suggests one of three hypotheses: (1) minorities are most in favor of prison expansion because they suffer most as crime victims and believe that they will be better off with more offenders incarcerated; (2) minorities are most sympathetic with prisoners and support prison expansion as a way of alleviating human suffering; (3) white voters in counties with large minority populations disproportionately favor prison construction because they fear crime, minorities, or both. It is unfortunate that neither we nor other researchers had the opportunity to carry out individual polling on the bond, for to have done so would have enabled us to determine which, if any, of these hypotheses is valid.

We hypothesized that the greater a county's crime rate, the more support it would give to the bond, because of greater fear and concern about crime. This hypothesis was born out by the data: the correlation is .661 for all counties and .350 outside the New York City metropolitan area. With the New York City metropolitan area omitted, the relationship between crime rate and the bond vote is higher than any of the other pairings, making crime rate the best single determinant of how upstate counties voted on the prison bond.

There are several reasons why counties with state prisons might have supported prison expansion: the desire to improve working conditions at the local facility; general support for law enforcement and particular support for corrections; self-interest, that is, the desire for more jobs and job security. We hypothesized that counties slated for new prison construction would be especially likely to support the bond since it meant construction jobs, long-term employment, and other economic benefits. The results show only a weak positive relationship between the presence of a state prison and support for the bond (.196). The only upstate county with a state prison to approve the bond was Clinton, and it provided only a narrow margin of victory (53.5 percent).

[12] In the text and in the tables, we present the results of our analyses for all New York counties and for all counties excluding New York City, Westchester, Nassau, and Rockland. We do this because the data suggest that something is going on in the pro-bond counties. If the data were analyzed only in aggregate form, results might be shown which only hold true in the pro-bond counties but which, because of the pro-bond counties' enormous population, are strong enough to distort the statewide reality.

Many counties with large state prisons, such as Chemung County (Elmira) and Wyoming County (Attica), voted against prison expansion. Even the counties proposed as sites for the three new prisons (Ulster, Sullivan, and Greene) voted no on the bond; in Ulster County the bond picked up less than 30 percent yes votes, one of the lowest percentages in the state.

The same ballot that contained the prison bond issue also carried a referendum for a Job Development Agency bond; the latter, however, passed by a vote of 60 percent. The success of the JDA bond referendum may be attributed to lower cost ($150 million), the lack of any organized opposition, and/or voter support for creating new jobs in the private sector. Whatever the reasons, and despite the differences in outcome, there was a high correlation (.73) between the votes on both bond issues. Indeed, a county's support for the JDA bond is a better predictor of its vote on the prison bond than any of our socioeconomic variables. Moreover, the pattern of correlations between votes on the two bonds and the independent variables are similar, albeit of slightly different magnitudes, except for the presence of the state prison, which is more highly correlated with the prison bond than with the JDA bond (see Table 5).

Does the vote on the prison bond simply represent a reaction to bond referenda generally rather than a specific response to prison construction? There is undoubtedly much to substantiate this hypothesis. There are, after all, consistent voting patterns in any jurisdiction. A large segment of the electorate is apparently likely to hold a general and diffuse view toward "bonds," without giving the specifics much attention. But for some portion of the voters, the bond issue was particularly salient — notably for the New York metropolitan area and counties with a state prison facility; in these counties there was a greater tendency for voters not to leave the prison bond blank.[13]

Multiple regression analysis confirms the correlation analysis. The stepwise regression technique is a type of multi-variate analysis that, beginning with the strongest independent variable, proceeds by adding the variable that explains most of the remaining variance, until there are no variables left that can make a statistically significant contribution. Table 6 shows that with all New York counties included only two variables explain a significant amount of variation in the prison bond vote: percentage of nonwhite population and the crime rate ($R^2 = 55.68$). When the metropolitan (pro-bond) area was excluded, crime rate explained only a small amount of the variance in the percentage of yes vote on the prison bond, but the R^2 fell to 12.28. If all counties are included in a multiple regression of percentage of nonwhite population, crime rate, population, presence of a prison, and per capita income on the percentage of yes vote on both referenda, the independent variables

[13] Voters in counties with prisons were much more likely to express an opinion on the prison bond. The percentage of blank vote on the prison bond correlates highly with the percentage of blank vote on the JDA bond, but where a prison exists, the prison bond was significantly less likely to have been left blank.

explain 57.77 percent of variance of the prison bond vote and only 43.1 percent of the JDA bond vote (see Table 7). If the vote on the JDA bond is added to the independent variables, it becomes the sole significant predictor and the R^2 increases to 69.33.

Table 6. Stepwise regression of six independent variables with percentage of vote on New York State prison bond in all counties and in all except downstate metropolitan areas, 1981.

Step	Constant	Percentage of nonwhites	Crime rate	R^2
All counties				
1	36.17	.758 (8.05)		51.91
2	24.25	.537 (4.00)	.00199 (2.24)	55.68
All counties except downstate metropolitan areas				
1	29.48		.00216 (2.70)	12.18

NOTE: The *t* statistic in parentheses represents the value of the data after they have been transformed to fit a normal distribution. It is a useful statistic with which to calculate statistical significance.

Table 7. Multiple regression of percentage of yes vote on New York State prison and JDA bonds, all counties, 1981

Variable	Model 1 Coefficient	Model 2 Coefficient	Model 3 Coefficient	Model 4 Coefficient
Prison bond				
Percentage of nonwhites	.46 (3.3)	.39 (2.25)	.20 (1.5)	.17 (1.0)
Crime rate	.002 (2.2)	.002 (1.7)	.001 (1.9)	.001 (1.7)
Per capita income	.001 (1.6)	.001 (1.1)	.001 (1.8)	.001 (1.4)
Presence of state prison	0.8 (0.4)	1.1 (0.6)	2.2 (1.3)	2.3 (1.34)
Total population		.000 (0.7)		.000 (.32)
Vote on JDA bond			62.0 (4.6)	61.0 (4.5)
R^2	57.77	58.14	69.48	69.53
JDA bond				
Percentage of nonwhites	.004 (3.6)	.004 (2.4)		
Crime rate	.000 (.98)	.000 (0.6)		
Per capita income	.000 (0.2)	-.000 (-.2)		
Presence of state prison	-.022 (-.4)	-.019 (-1.1)		
Total population		.000 (.8)		
R^2	43.10	43.75		

NOTE: *t* statistic in parentheses, see note to Table 6.

The results for the JDA bond are rather different (see Table 7). The best predictor of a county's vote on the JDA bond, when all New York State counties are included, is the percentage of nonwhite population, although less

Table 8. Stepwise regression of six independent variables with percentage of yes vote on New York State JDA bond, all counties, 1981

Step	Constant	Percentage of nonwhites		R^2
1	.5197	.00490	6.34	40.14

NOTE: No significant predictors for all counties exclusive of downstate metropolitan areas.

variance is explained than for the prison bond (40 v. 51.9 percent), and no other variable contributes significantly to the equation. Without the New York City metropolitan area, all of the independent variables together fail to explain a significant amount of variance (see Table 8).

We are left with the conclusion that the different outcomes on the two bonds are best explained by the crime rate and percentage of nonwhites in a county. The more crime and the more nonwhites, the more likely a county will support prison expansion. Taking the state as a whole, the percentage of nonwhites is the best predictor of the prison bond vote, but upstate, crime rate is the best predictor.

The Failure to Halt Prison Construction

The most startling aspect of the prison bond referendum is that its defeat has had no impact on the construction plans and timetable of the Department of Correctional Services. The Department's building program, which began before the bond, is still on track. If anything, it has been expanded by new initiatives to purchase several abandoned air force bases and other properties and to convert mental hygiene facilities to correctional institutions.[14]

It is now clear that prison expansion had actually begun as early as fiscal year 1980, when the legislature increased the capital construction budget from $106,926,659 to $309,637,850; not all of these monies were spent, however. If the bond had passed, some of the funds it produced clearly would have been used to pay back general revenue although this stipulation appeared nowhere in the bond bill or referendum. In the wake of the bond's defeat, the fiscal year 1983 capital construction budget appropriated 62.8 million new dollars and reappropriated $178.6 million for prison expansion. One third of the DOCS budget is for continued expansion of the prisons. The determination of the state's political leadership of both parties to build more prisons is unshaken.

Commissioner Coughlin, and no doubt other proponents of the prison

[14] In retrospect, the result should not be surprising. New York State political leaders have always showed imagination in circumventing the referendum requirement. Perhaps the best example is the moral obligation bond invented by Governor Rockefeller; it allowed the state to raise money without putting the issue to the voters at all (see McClelland and Magdovitz 1981).

bond as well, find no contradiction between defeat of the bond and continued construction.

> I don't believe the voters of New York turned down the bond issue because they don't want more prisons. Nor do I believe that the bond issue was defeated because our policies are ineffective, which they are not.
>
> The people of this state don't want to throw in the towel in a fight against crime just when we are beginning to score significant gains.
>
> I feel that the bond issue was defeated on the question of financing — that the bond issue was not palatable because of its long term cost.
>
> It is extremely important that you [DOCS employees] support the continued expansion of our state prisons with the appropriations in this budget. [*Correctional Services News*, March-April 1982:1,4]

Conclusion: The Many Dimensions of Correctional Politics

Correctional politics, the contest for influence and power over prison policies and practices, occurs on many levels. On most of these levels, research has hardly begun. Thus, it is worth briefly reviewing the prison bond controversy for the clues it provides for future studies.

First, there is the state legislature. Many commentators seem to think of the legislature as a monolith, a single "mind set." Legislators obviously differ substantially on criminal justice matters, and it is important to identify the different coalitions and the constituencies they represent.

Typically, criminal justice and penal legislation must emanate from specialized committees, such as New York's Senate Committee on Crime and Correction. The chairmen of such committees frequently wield enormous influence, and their approval may be essential if a particular bill is ever to become law. Who tends to control such committees, how they operate, and how partisans can win approval are vital issues for those of us interested in correctional policy.

The executive branch is obviously just as important as the legislature in formulating correctional policy, perhaps more so. The governor's position on penal issues is, of course, essential, but he is likely to defer to special criminal justice aides in his "kitchen cabinet" or to the director of the department of corrections. The governor's relationship to the director will, of course, be important in determining the degree to which corrections has an inside track to the executive centers of power and influence. The director himself is increasingly likely to be a corrections specialist whose own career is more closely tied to his performance as a correctional administrator than to his connections with a particular political incumbent. It is a likely hypothesis that the director and the departmental elite are the most powerful interest group effecting correctional legislation.

The director must compete in the executive budget competition with other departmental heads and must obtain funds for a "service" that has little, if any, political constituency. One might therefore be led to the conclusion that corrections will always be short-changed. We believe this is not the case for several reasons: the most important is that while expenditures on corrections may not help the governor, policy failures may hurt him. An administration can be rocked by riots, scandals, legislative or media exposés, or court suits declaring the prisons violative of basic human rights. A second reason why prisons do not fare poorly in comparison with other state services is the gubernatorial and legislative desire to demonstrate that something is being done about crime and violence. A governor may believe that there is political capital to be made from increasing the correctional budget.

There is also, of course, a complicated political relationship between the executive and legislative branches. Even if the director of corrections is successful in the executive budget competition, he must also be able to defend his budget and territories before the legislature, particularly the powerful appropriations committees. In addition to purely political considerations, success may depend upon the professional competency of departmental personnel in providing convincing projections, trend data, and diverse technical information.[15]

In our view, the scant writing that does exist on correctional politics exaggerates the importance of public opinion. Typical citizens spend little or no time thinking about correctional policy, just as they are unlikely to give much thought to other state functions — such as those dealing with the mentally ill and retarded, highway maintenance, supervision of the state police, or setting of policy for the state university system. This does not mean that the citizen is not exposed to information about prisons. Justice Byron White once said that "there is no iron curtain drawn between the Constitution and the prisons of this country" (*Wolff v. McDonnell* 1974). Neither is there an iron curtain drawn between the public and the prisons. Information is available and plentiful, but politics is the occupation of politicians and interest groups, not of some amorphous entity called "society" or "the public." Of course, obeisance to our political traditions requires that competing groups constantly invoke "society" or "the public" for their respective causes.

The citizenry rarely gets to express its opinion on correctional policy. And when it does have such an opportunity, as in the case of the New York State prison bond referendum, it reveals itself to be confused and apathetic. This is not, to re-emphasize, a feature peculiar to the public's attitude toward crime and punishment, but a general characteristic of a mass democracy in which citizens and voters are overwhelmed with scores, even hundreds, of highly significant issues competing for their limited time and attention.

[15] In this regard, the department's relationship to the legislative fiscal office may be as crucial as its relationship to particular legislators.

[6]

The Guard's World

COAUTHOR NORMA CROTTY

For generations, criminologists have entered the prison world to study the backgrounds, personalities, attitudes, values, and criminal careers of the inmates. Consequently, there exists a rich sociological literature describing the norms and roles of the inmate social system. The prison guard, however, has rarely been the subject of scholarly research. The student interested in the social origins of the guards, their work, and their ideology is hard pressed to find even cursory data.

The lack of academic interest in prison guards underscores the public's disdain for them. In their famous 1943 criminology text, Harry Elmer Barnes and Negley Teeters criticized the guards' "lock psychosis" resulting from a routine of "numbering, counting, checking and locking." Donald Clemmer, in his 1940 seminal study of the social organization of the prison community, observed that "a considerable portion of the employees have a spirit of retaliation toward inmates." Nevertheless, he urged that guards not be judged too harshly.

The[ir] occasional atavism is matched, no doubt, in other prisons and in the free world as well. Guards do not possess the reformer's zeal. They have their own lives to live; they have their own little frustrations, sorrows, and tragedies, and few people, guards included, have a "sense of state." The personality problems of employees in prison may be quite as serious as those of the inmates with whose care they are charged. The student of social science does not hate a stupid, brutal guard, just as he does not hate the feebleminded rapist.[1958:158]

The assumption that prison guards are incompetent and psychologically, morally, and socially inferior has been reinforced by subsequent commentators.

Reprinted in slightly different form from *Guard Unions and the Future of the Prisons* (Ithaca, N.Y.: New York State School of Industrial & Labor Relations, 1978).

Richard McCleery's (1960) well-known study of a Hawaii prison portrayed the guards as reactionaries who were subverting the goals of the reform regime. The same charge is often repeated by prison administrators frustrated in their attempts to implement vaguely defined prison reforms. The commission that investigated the 1971 Attica rebellion labeled the guards as racists. (New York State Special Commission on Attica 1972). Prison reform activist Herman Schwartz (1972a) has referred to guards as "frightened, hostile people." The public also tends to stereotype the prison guard as brutal, racist, and dim-witted. A Louis Harris survey in the late 1960s found that only 1 percent of high school seniors had ever even considered jobs as prison guards. (Joint Commission on Correctional Manpower and Training 1969).

Few studies are available to confirm or deny the public's negative stereotype. Some data indicate that, contrary to popular opinion, guards adhere to the basic tenets of liberal criminology. A 1968 survey conducted for the Joint Commission on Correctional Manpower and Training by Louis Harris found that 98 percent of a sample of line personnel believed that correctional agencies should give primary or secondary emphasis to rehabilitation. A survey of all certified corrections officers in Illinois found that six out of ten officers disagreed with the assertion that "rehabilitation programs are a waste of time and money." This study concluded:

> The Illinois prison guard survey data do not support the stereotype of the guard as a stern — even brutal — disciplinarian. No extreme desire to punish prisoners is evident. Indeed, the guards' opinion as to the causes of crime and the purposes of imprisonment parallels the liberal sociopolitical position. The recent trend toward punitive justifications for imprisonment may leave the guards in the anomalous position of having greater commitment to rehabilitation than the academic penologists and prison administrators.[Jacobs 1978:193]

Because most prisons are located in remote rural areas, the guards tend to be drawn from the ranks of the unemployed and marginally employed in small towns and farm areas. A study in Illinois found that 41 percent of the respondents were unemployed at the time they became guards (Jacobs 1978). The great majority of all prison guards are white males; in 1968 only 10 percent of line corrections officers were nonwhite. In that year the average age of a corrections officer was about forty, and only 10 percent of the guards had educational credits beyond high school (Joint Commission 1968). Only 54 percent of the guards in Illinois had a high school diploma; eleven guards in the entire state had four-year-college degrees. Training for the position is the exception rather than the rule.

As a result of the occupation's negative stereotype and the marginal education of the work force, guards are typically the lowest-paid security personnel in public service. The 1967 President's Commission on Law Enforcement and the Administration of Justice reported that in 1965 corrections officers' entering salaries were under $4,000 a year in twenty-four states. Corrections officers often take second jobs to support their families.

A career officer in effect commits himself to a life sentence in prison. The gruesome conditions in most American prisons do not need to be documented here. The reader need only turn to the report of the Special Commission on Attica to find a chilling description of a "typical" American maximum security prison. In addition to being dirty, malodorous, and confining, prisons are dangerous. The guard faces the constant possibility of being attacked or taken hostage. Few people realize that guards in maximum security prisons are unarmed, except for those in the wall towers. Ironically, the prisoners frequently carry or have access to knives, pipes, or bits of glass or metal. In addition, the guards are vastly outnumbered, sometimes by as much as a hundred to one. It is therefore not at all surprising that the guards and their unions have strongly emphasized security and safety in their demands for better conditions.

A Guard's Role

The most obvious characteristic of prison work is its routine (*see* Jacobs and Retsky 1975). The prison is to a great degree a closed and timeless society where days, weeks, and months pass monotonously. With the exception of infrequent riots, hardly anything exceptional occurs. One day's regimen is like the next's. As Donald Cressey (1965:1024) has pointed out, "Most guards have nothing to do but stand guard; they do not use inmates productively any more than they themselves are used productively by prison managers. Guards manage and are managed in organizations where management is an end, not a means."

Still, guarding is not a monolithic occupation. A new recruit finds a variety of assignments paralleling the different facets of a prisoner's existence. Guards supervise the cell houses, dining areas, and shops; transport prisoners to hospitals and courts; take turns serving on the disciplinary board; sit perched with rifles in the towers on top of the walls; and protect the gates leading into and out of the interior. Unscheduled activities range from informal counseling to breaking up fights to escorting prisoners on family visits in the community.

The cell house is the basic living unit of the traditional maximum security prison and the guards who work there are the busiest in the prison. At Stateville Penitentiary in Illinois, for example, each circular cell house holds approximately 250 inmates, supervised by no more than five guards and frequently as few as two, depending on the shift and who shows up for work. (Absenteeism is

[135]

high.)[1] In the course of a day's work, the guard stationed at the cell house gate is required to open and close the steel-barred door for inmates whose work or visits require movement in and out of the cell house. Another guard may distribute medicine, mail, and laundry; answer telephones; and supervise maintenance activities. A third guard is positioned in an enclosed observation post in the middle of the cell house where he can see into every cell. The most important responsibility of the cell house guard is conducting the "count" — determining several times a day if all inmates are accounted for. If there is a miscount, all operations and movement cease. A guard who is responsible for causing a miscount may be liable to discipline.

The cell house is also the most dangerous place for the guard; there he is clearly at the mercy of the inmates. In case of emergency there is no safe exit. The guard knows that he could be overwhelmed or taken hostage at any time. An unpopular cell house guard fears more than rough treatment during a riot; at any time he might be assaulted, thrown off a gallery, or pelted with objects thrown from the upper tiers.

The majority of guards during the day shift are assigned to work areas such as the mechanical store, the metal factory, or the yard. Some are assigned to maintenance crews in the cell house or to recreation areas. Some of these guards are analogous to factory supervisors, although, as Cressey (1965) points out, the guard really has no counterpart in the business or industrial world. One may enter a prison workshop and see no activity whatsoever; the guards may be sitting in an office or standing in a corner talking. The guard in the work area requires only minimal compliance from the men assigned to him; yet, like his counterpart in the cell house, he is likely to have his authority "corrupted by reciprocity" (Sykes 1956:157–62). That is, in order to meet minimum requirements, such as the repair of furniture or storage of boxes, the guard may have to overlook certain breaches of the rules. This accommodation may ultimately prove unstable if inmates escalate demands for favors in exchange for cooperation. The newly recruited guard invariably receives the warning to remain aloof from inmates lest the cycle of corruption and blackmail destroy his authority.[2]

[1] John M. Wynne, Jr. (1978:12) reports that "in 1975, in New York, correctional employees' time off for disability was 300 percent higher than the state average. Sixty percent of the disability leave in this period resulted from heart, emotional or drinking problems, all of which are frequently associated with severe emotional stress."

[2] The following warning is presented for use in guard training by the American Correctional Association, "Corrections Officers Training Guide" (unpublished booklet, n.d.):23. "Bribery usually begins as a result of being too intimate with inmates. They offer a cigar, cigarettes, or some trivial article. Each time this is done a closer contact is made and finally they come through with what they really want the officer to do. They may work the officer into a compromising position by securing information from him which may make it appear to his superiors that he has been passing on confidential or department information. Or it may be that an inmate is a witness to some incident involving the officer, which, if known, would not add to his reputation for

The work area guard also seems to establish the closest relations with inmates. Working together engenders camaraderie. Work assignments usually consist of a small number of inmates, and conversation between inmates and guards develops spontaneously. Guards assigned to workshops often have skills they can pass along to inmates who may be grateful to their "teacher." Sometimes work assignment guards and their subordinates even become friendly. One guard at Stateville noted that it is not rare for a guard "to unburden things to an inmate that he would not tell his wife." In such circumstances, if he is not careful, the guard's authority may be "eroded through friendship" (Sykes 1956).

The work unit guard often becomes dependent on his men for the skill and expertise that they have developed over the years. Chronic understaffing encourages delegation of small tasks to inmates eager to ingratiate themselves with the guard or to relieve their boredom. A locksmith, machine operator, or agricultural worker may become indispensable to the prison regime, especially where the turnover rate is so great that an inexperienced guard finds himself supervising a task about which he knows nothing. This situation also tends to undermine the effective exercise of the guard's authority.

There are two security jobs in the maximum security prison, the towers and the gates. Except for telephone or walkie-talkie communication with security headquarters, the tower guard has no contact with other individuals during the eight-hour shift. He cannot bring a radio or reading matter into the tower. If caught reading or dozing, the guard is liable to be severely disciplined. In many prisons the loneliness, uncomfortable temperatures, and boredom make this task more like punishment than a viable job assignment. Traditionally, assignment to the towers on top of the prison wall was reserved for recruits, partially incapacitated old-timers, and those unable to manage inmates. In recent years, however, increased violence in some prisons has led veteran guards to request transfer to the towers. Sometimes seniority rights have made it possible for the most experienced guards to bid for these positions. That such posts are now sought after is a telling commentary on the deterioration of internal order.

Tower work places the guard in a position of open confrontation with inmates. All that is needed to remind an inmate of the nature of the institution or the purpose of the custodial staff is a glance at the walls. The tower guard symbolizes the stern hand of the community that has exiled the inmate. This hostile interaction between the tower guard and the inmate is continuous and uncomplicated.

---

efficiency and reliability. Self-protection, being a powerful instinct, the officer might ask the inmate to keep quiet or to falsify his testimony when questioned. This is the beginning of bribery, and it may get the officer on the inmate's payroll from that time on."

Despite the vital importance of tower duty, the guard is often ill equipped to handle emergencies. His position, uncomfortable both physically and existentially, impairs his ability to act decisively in critical moments. In addition, the rules relating to the use of deadly force are difficult to interpret. Guards frequently lack training in both the regulations and mechanics for using firearms. It is therefore understandable that training has become a salient union issue.

An outsider entering the maximum security prison is frisked, stamped, and checked by guards positioned at a series of gates, each successively closer to the heart of the prison. The guard may not open the gate unless the visitor has been approved. The gate is an attractive job for an ambitious individual, since the guard is in constant contact with high-ranking security personnel and civilian administrators. Assignment to the gate is one route to promotion to sergeant. The guards at the gates and those stationed in the visiting room represent the institution to the streams of outsiders — students, relatives, lawyers, legislators — who enter the prison each day. Their brief but superficial contacts with staff, inmates, and outsiders require a vareity of social skills. Top administrators realize that the entire staff is often judged by the behavior and appearance of those guards in front-line positions. Conscious efforts are made to choose those who will make the best impression. Despite these efforts, tension frequently develops between guards and visitors who resent questioning, searches, and other security measures.

The division of labor sketched above is applicable only to the lowest-ranking guard — the line officer. There are usually three ranks above the line officer — sergeant, lieutenant, and captain. The work of a guard sergeant is similar to that of a sergeant in the army. Directly familiar with the line officer's work, he manages his unit, fills jobs requiring special responsibility (such as gatekeeper at various key points in the institution), and often substitutes for absent line officers. In addition, a sergeant is usually in charge of cell houses, work units, and the hospital. But whether or not sergeants exercise real supervisory authority is a lively issue in defining appropriate bargaining units in corrections.

Lieutenants serve as the prison's police force. When there is a disturbance in a cell house or on a work assignment, the lieutenants are called upon to stop a fight or to "walk" an inmate to isolation or forcibly remove him from his cell. When they are not responding to trouble, the lieutenants roam about the institution checking and "shaking down" (searching) inmate and lower-ranking guards.

There are only a handful of captains. They rarely have time to exercise personal supervision over a specific prison area. Instead, they are assigned to shift commands or to full-time administrative duties, which may include chairing the assignment or disciplinary committees. They have been saddled with increasing amounts of paper work, including personnel evaluations and budgets. The power of the captains has dwindled in recent years because college-educated professionals have come to dominate prison management. Some captains also claim that the emergence of public employee unionism undermines their authority and the paramilitary chain of command.

The social distance between lower- and higher-level guards is reinforced by the paramilitary organization, whereby information originates below, but initiative and decisions come from above. Discipline parallels that of the military: the line officer is often scrutinized as closely as the inmate under his surveillance. Alleged trafficking in contraband is said to justify periodic shakedowns of the line officers. Lieutenants inspect both guards and inmates to see that they are working properly at an assignment. Just as guards are required to write tickets (disciplinary reports) on inmates' rule violations, so too do superiors, and sometimes inmates, compile reports on guards' infractions of the rules. Guards are also encouraged to write tickets on each other. The disciplinary board for guards is similar to the tribunal that hears inmate cases. Like the prisoners, rank-and-file officers and their unions have pressed, often successfully, for greater procedural and substantive rights in recent years.

The Emergence of Unionization

Low prestige, poor pay, unpleasant working conditions, and strict discipline make prisons ripe for unionization. Nevertheless, there have been obstacles, the most important of which is the rank-and-file's strong sense of identification with the warden and top members of the custody force. In such a hierarchical and authoritarian institution as the prison there is a tendency to respect and emulate those at the top of the pyramid. In addition, before the advent of public employee legislation, wardens wielded sanctions sufficient to defeat most organizing efforts among the rank and file.

While the public employee union movement of the 1960s was probably powerful enough to bring many guards into the union's ranks, there were other earlier forces, internal to corrections, that transformed the prison and made unionization attractive to line personnel. The end of World War II released major reform energies in American society. Despite a great deal of talk about reform and rehabilitation, however, concrete improvements in prison conditions were modest. The unfulfilled aspirations and expectations of the prisoners probably engendered the wave of prison riots that swept the United States in the early fifties. These riots in turn stimulated further demands for reform.

By the late 1950s and early 1960s the ideology of rehabilitation had gained ascendency among the public and among many influential administrators within state prison systems. This ideology was marked by commitment to attitudinal change, best accomplished, it was thought, by therapy and training programs. Many prison systems were renamed "departments of correction" and the guards were rechristened "corrections officers." The prison guards were now expected to become agents of change. The 1967 President's Commission on Law Enforcement and Administration of Justice called for the prison to be transformed into a "collaborative regime" where the corrections officers would function as front-line treatment staff.

The guards no longer knew what was expected of them. There were no firm directives on how to function as counselors, and they were still required to carry out their traditional disciplinary role. This attempt to combine treatment and disciplinary tasks in the same role put the guards in a difficult position. They felt betrayed by the public and by college-educated administrators who seemed to favor the inmates. More and more educational and vocational programs were introduced. Some prisoners earned college credits and degrees. Even worse, from the guards' perspective, was the increasing intervention of the federal courts on behalf of prisoners' rights. All the while, the guards' pay remained abysmally low, and their conditions of employment declined in the face of increasing hostility and violence brought about by racial conflict and the organization of prisoners into gangs and other types of solidary groups (*see* Jacobs 1976:476–82).

In addition to the emphasis on rehabilitation, a trend toward professionalization produced a new breed of college-educated administrators to dominate the top prison positions. Many of these administrators were trained in sociology and psychology and brought with them a personal commitment to serve the prisoners. Some did not disguise their contempt for the guards and often blamed them for the failure of rehabilitation programs to reduce recidivism as liberal penology had promised they would. Thus, the guards were alienated from this new breed of administrators who, they felt, no longer represented their interests. It was a short step to defining the administrators as "management" and "bosses."

During this period more and more jobs traditionally handled by guards were turned over to civilians. Heretofore anyone who worked in the prison had been a member of the guard force; now many of the "cleaner" jobs were turned over to civilian counselors, teachers, work supervisors, nurses, and secretaries. The guards were left with their traditional security functions and little else, while prestige passed to the civilians. Under such conditions it is understandable that the union's emphasis on respect and dignity had strong appeal.

The prison population of the mid- and late sixties also changed. After World War II there had been a massive movement of poor southern blacks to northern cities. By the late fifties, and certainly by the mid-sixties, the prison populations of the big industrial states had black majorities. The young blacks flooding the prison systems were politicized, or at least shared a widely disseminated vocabulary of social protest (*see* Miller 1974:210-37). They were more prone to violence than their predecessor generations, as indicated by the steady rise in the nation's violent crime rate. A new wave of prison violence, individual and collective, in the late 1960s and early 1970s left the guards tense and apprehensive. In contrast to the administration's apparent kowtowing to liberal prison reform groups, the union represented the guards' interest in security, authority, and discipline.

Unionism did not spring up suddenly in state prisons. Low pay, poor working conditions, and the disintegration of the prison's traditional system of authority and organization sowed the seeds of discontent. These factors made unionization possible but not inevitable. Long years of organizing were required, and even then, success could not have been fully achieved without change in the law governing labor relations in the public sector.

[7]

Collective Bargaining
and Labor Unrest

COAUTHOR LYNN ZIMMER

On April 18, 1979, nearly all of New York State's prison guards (approximately seven thousand employees)[1] walked off the job at the state's thirty-three penal facilities. It was by far the largest strike by prison employees in American history. It also represented a major challenge to New York's Taylor Law because the strike involved, for the first time, a large number of highly visible state employees capable of capturing public attention throughout New York State. In addition, of course, the prison strike posed an enormous administrative and logistical problem since the prisons could not be shut down; services had to be continued and life and property had to be protected.

To keep the prisons operating, Governor Hugh Carey called up over 12,000 National Guardsmen, one of the largest activations under state authority in the nation's history and by far the largest for any public sector strike. The guardsmen initially encountered sharp resistance from picketing prison guards: during the first days of what proved to be a seventeen-day strike, the prison guards threatened and perpetrated a good deal of violence and property damage.

Ultimately, with the use of the National Guard and with crucial assistance from the courts, state officials were able to impose their contract terms on the

Reprinted with permission, in slightly different form from *Industrial & Labor Relations Review* 34, no. 4 (July 1981):531-44.©1981 by Cornell University. All rights reserved.
[1] The total number of state employees on strike was approximately 8,200 because the guards are part of New York's Security Services bargaining unit, which includes a wide variety of security personnel, such as museum caretakers, state university police, and park rangers. Most of these noncorrectional members of the unit honored the strike, as did many "civilian" prison employees represented by other unions.

union. One needs to speak carefully about the state having "won the strike," however, because the resentments that caused the strike have not been ameliorated and, in fact, may even have been intensified by the state's use of the anti-strike penalties.

The sheer magnitude and disputive nature of this strike, both for the New York State Department of Correctional Services (DOCS) and the Office of Employee Relations (OER),[2] make this strike worthy of an extended "institutional analysis," in the tradition of Clark Kerr and Abraham Siegel (1954), William Gould (1972), and Bernard Karsh (1958). Analysis of this strike reveals, in addition, the importance of enriching labor relations studies with the insights provided by the sociology of occupations. It would be a gross oversimplification to explain the 1979 guard strike only in terms of collective bargaining strategies. Indeed, we believe that such strategies were neither the most important cause of the strike nor the most important factor in bringing the sides back together. We therefore emphasize how an understanding of the guards' occupational role and of the social organization of the work environment explains the occurrence of the strike and the way it was conducted.

Causes of the Strike

Like coal miners, loggers, and longshoremen, prison guards tend to live in relative isolation from the larger society and to work under conditions of constant danger. Even in the best of times, the level of tension and stress is high (*see* Brodsky 1977); in bad times, the guards and inmates may be locked in mortal combat. The nature of prisons and of prison guards' work, however, establishes merely the structural preconditions for frustration, discontent, and collective protest. To understand how those preconditions were translated into the emotion-ridden strike that erupted in 1979, against even the advice of the union negotiating team,[3] one must understand the growing discontent that has engulfed the guard force over the past decade.[4]

Large-scale sociopolitical and legal forces have dramatically changed the guards' job, leaving them concerned about the erosion of their authority, resent-

---

[2] OER is the agency responsible for negotiating contracts on behalf of the state government, initiating legal actions against striking unions, and imposing certain penalties against strikers.

[3] The negotiating team originally voted to accept the state's offer but changed its decision when the overwhelming rank-and-file opposition became evident. Thus, the strike should be viewed as a "protest from below." It is reminiscent of many early private sector labor strikes and perhaps indicates something basic about the "natural history" of public sector unionism too.

[4] Before the 1979 strike, New York correction officers had threatened to strike on several occasions and had engaged in at least five limited job actions (*see* Jacobs and Crotty 1978: 30-31).

ful, and angry. After the Attica riot in September 1971, New York prison guards felt that the slew of reforms that were instituted undermined their role. The New York State Special Commission report on Attica (1972) branded the guards as racist and poorly trained and called for wholesale reform of New York State's prisons.

In addition, court decisions have weakened the guards' disciplinary prerogatives. Judicial involvement in the prisons these days severely restricts the guards' use of physical sanctions, requiring that any use of force be accurately documented. Line officers' decisions are subject to repeated review and are frequently reversed or modified. The extension of due process to inmates charged with disciplinary infractions means that prisoners can challenge a guard's version of the "facts." A 1970 New York State law requires each prison to have an Adjustment Committee made up of three prison employees (at least one nonuniformed and one above the rank of sergeant) to review all inmate infractions. The committee must give inmates an opportunity to explain their behavior and can choose not to impose punishment if the inmate shows a "genuine intention to cooperate." The New York State Commission of Correction, reorganized and revitalized because of the Attica riot, keeps a close watch on New York prisons and investigates charges of abuse. The very existence of the commission reinforces the guards' perception that the inmates "have taken over the prisons."

The result of these legal and organizational changes is that guards feel they do not have the ability to apply effective discipline. They can no longer "prevent trouble" by throwing suspected troublemakers into isolation; instead, more stringent due process requires "a case" built on solid evidence. A guard from Coxsackie explained, "it used to be if an inmate gave you trouble, you had the authority to lock him up. Now, a guard can't do . . . anything on his own . . . . We're nothing but figureheads anymore.[5]

Throughout the 1970s, in spite of the rhetoric of reform, the guards were defined even more than before as disciplinarians and had lower prestige within the prison organization. In fact, treatment staff often identified with the inmates, blaming the guards for institutional problems and for the failure of rehabilitative programs — a practice that served only to reinforce and legitimate the prisoners' traditional disdain for and hatred of the guards.

The guards perceived a loss of moral status as well. To them the increase in prisoners' prerogatives and material goods indicated enhanced respect for inmates. Reformers, including members of the department's central office, seemed committed to ameliorating the pains of imprisonment whenever pos-

[5] Quoted in *Schenectady Gazette*, April 30, 1979:4. Interestingly enough, this feeling of loss of authority is shared by young guards who entered the system after Attica. Indeed, new officers may be more inclined than older ones to exaggerate the advantages of the "good old days."

sible. Inmates are now allowed, for example, to wear street clothes rather than uniforms. They receive earphones for the prison radio station as standard issue and are allowed to possess their own radios and tape players. If they have funds, they can make unlimited purchase of cigarettes and toiletries from the commissary and keep nonperishable food in their cells. They can receive uncensored mail and they have access to religious and political materials many guards believe to be racist and revolutionary.

In addition to providing generous visitation privileges, the DOCS has initiated a Family Events Program to help inmates retain family ties. Each inmate is given at least two opportunities a year to invite family members to ethnic club picnics, prison organization picnics, or "conjugal visits," which take place in trailers on the prison grounds. Vocational and educational programs, including access to a free college education, have increased dramatically over the last decade; at Auburn, for example, over 15 percent of the inmates are enrolled in college courses. Inmates close to release can apply for the work release or early release programs.

Some of the guards' resentment over the inmates' increased rights and benefits is due to the fact that they complicate the guards' job by increasing inmate movement around the prison, thereby multiplying opportunities for assaults, drug taking, and other violation of the rules. More important, however, is the guards' belief that these reforms signify public sympathy for prisoners and corresponding ingratitude, even antipathy, for the job being done by the guards. One Elmira officer sarcastically predicts that the prison will some day be renamed "Elmira Recreational Facility." "You've got to make everybody in prison comfortable, like they were in camp" *New York Times*, April 1979:B1.) One simply cannot understand today's prison guards, or prison labor relations, without appreciating the extent to which the guards feel rejected, shunned, and even despised by "society."

Another factor that contributes to job strain and discontent is racial integration. While the inmate population shifted from a white to a black majority in the 1960s, the guard force remained nearly all white. Under political and legal pressures during the 1970s, especially after Attica, more black guards were brought into the system (in 1971 only 6.1 percent of the guards were black or hispanic; by 1979 their percentage had increased to 20.1). Although the largest increase in black guards has been at the downstate facilities, the impact of the increase has been felt statewide.

One frequently hears complaints from white guards that the DOCS sacrificed "recruitment standards" in order to increase the number of minority employees. For many white upstate guards who have never known any blacks except inmates, black means inmate; they fear that black officers will feel loyalty to black inmates rather than to fellow officers.

The best documented example of racial tension in the guard force can be found in the eight-year struggle over promotions. When only two blacks made the eligibility list for sergeant in 1972, a group of minority officers challenged the civil service examination. After two years of litigation, a court ordered the DOCS to adopt a nondiscriminatory promotional system and racial quotas for future promotions. When the DOCS complied, white guards sued, claiming reverse discrimination; the Second Circuit Court of Appeals struck down the quota system but sustained the invalidity of the original exam. The minority officers' request for a Supreme Court review of this decision was denied in 1975. During the period of litigation, all permanent appointments were held in abeyance, creating instability at the first level of prison management and, of course, tense intrastaff race relations. Although permanent appointments are now being made, litigation on the issue continues (*see Kirkland v. DOCS* 1974; 1975; 1980).

Racial tensions reverberate through the collective bargaining system, too. Minority officers represent 20 percent of the guard force but hold no leadership positions within the union. Feeling that the union does not represent them fairly or respond to their special needs, minority officers have formed the Minority Correctional Officer Association (MCOA) to fight discrimination within the union and the DOCS.

Collective Bargaining and the 1979 Strike

We have identified three underlying causes of the worker discontent that culminated in the 1979 strike: loss of control, loss of status, and intrastaff racial tension. Now we must ask why the collective bargaining system, set up explicitly to resolve conflicts between employers and employees over wages and conditions of employment, was unable to ameliorate this widespread malaise. Our thesis is that collective bargaining could not prevent the guard strike because the issues that caused the strike are not easily addressed within the collective bargaining framework.

The state and the guards' union have three basic avenues of communication: labor-management committees, the grievance procedure, and contract negotiation. Negotiation is the appropriate avenue for pursuing monetary and fringe benefit gains; it is not well suited, however, to handle the kinds of discontent that caused this strike. Guards did not negotiate for greater control over inmates, higher status, or a segregated work force. Perhaps, in theory, they could have advanced the first two of these concerns through innovative negotiation, but in practice neither side showed anything like the skill or creativity that would have been required.

The grievance system, while a valuable tool, is limited, because it is designed to resolve specific disputes over administration of the contract, not matters of policy and social organization. Labor-management committees,[6] while potentially the broadest avenue, have usually discussed mundane matters like the need for new lighting, mess hall schedules, parking problems, and forced overtime. It is conceivable that the issues that caused the 1979 strike could have been discussed at these meetings; but they are extremely difficult to articulate and, in any case, they would have been beyond the power of local administrators to solve.

It is also possible to contend that the operation of collective bargaining in the New York correctional system aggravated the underlying organizational strains and thereby contributed to the 1979 strike. First, the collective bargaining system itself established the potential for organized collective action by seven thousand prison guards. No matter how deep the guards' discontent, organized, statewide, collective protest involving thousands of people would not have been likely without a union structure. To put it differently, unionization, collective bargaining, and exclusive representation all increased the capacity of prison guards to pull off a statewide strike.

Second, the status of labor-management relations at the state and local levels also contributed to the 1979 strike. Contract administration places additional strains on the skills, abilities, and cooperative capacities of management and workers; in the New York State DOCS there is evidence that neither side has been successful in coping with its labor relations role. One superintendent (warden) complained to us that he has little time to devote to running the prison because of the necessity of administering the contract and responding to union grievances. Another complained that his union president is "dumb and incompetent" and that the central office gives in to union grievances merely to pacify "the crazies." Although some administrators have come to terms with the reality of collective bargaining and the sharing of power it entails, others continue to resist any suggestion that they must share authority with the union. For them, the union, like the inmates and outside prison reformers, is just another usurper of their legitimate authority. One

---

[6] The contract states that labor-management committees will be established at the executive, departmental, and local levels to discuss implementation of the contract and "other matters of mutual interest." (Executive meetings are those that take place between union officials and high administrators at the DOCS.) Because the contract does not mandate the frequency of these committee meetings or the manner in which they should be conducted, their success, especially at the local level, depends mostly on the quality of the labor-management relationship. At some facilities, formal meetings are rarely scheduled because there is ongoing communication between union leaders and administrators. At others, meetings are rarely scheduled because they result in shouting matches. It is therefore difficult to generalize about the usefulness of these committees for solving problems.

simply has to understand that in prisons, authority is the coin of the realm. How to gain authority and how to hold on to it are the constant preoccupations of inmates, guards, and administrators. In this struggle for power, some administrators see the union as a mortal enemy; consequently, they view all union activities with suspicion and apprehension.

The style and aptitudes of union leaders also vary from facility to facility. At some prisons, local leaders remain active for many years and maintain good working relationships with administrators. At others, however, there is a constant flow of new union officials, many of whom lack the experience and skill for successfully processing grievances or conducting labor-management meetings. At still others union leaders are simply too combative to engage in the constructive give-and-take that could lead to stable labor relations.

Third, to some extent local union leaders have been pushed into a militant stance by the rank and file, who watch them closely for signs of weakness and cooptation. The rank and file seem to have an exaggerated view of their union's power. This places the union leaders in a precarious position: effective labor relations requires compromise, but maintaining credibility with the rank and file requires unceasing opposition to the department. This pressure on union leaders to "get tough" has increased with the growing dissatisfaction of the rank and file, putting further strains on relations at the negotiating table.

With expertise, respect, and a genuine interest in cooperation generally missing in the ranks of both management and union, labor relations have been marked by a decade of tension and stress. They worsened in the period immediately before the strike, as suggested by the doubling from 1976 to 1978 of fourth-step grievances filed by the union.[7] This tension was reflected in the 1979 contract negotiations.

Rank-and-File Rejection of the Contract

Negotiators from OER and the guards' union, the American Federation of State, County and Municipal Employees (AFSCME) Council 82, met in December 1978 to begin talks to replace the guards' contract, which was scheduled to expire in March. While the contract negotiations proceeded in a rather conventional manner, both sides were aware of a growing discontent within the guard force and of the possibility of a strike. Indeed, from the outset union

---

[7] This increase in grievances cannot be explained by the increase of less than 10 percent in the number of correction officers over this period. Although there may have been several immediate causes of the increase, such as a union effort to "flood the system" or the unwillingness of superintendents to settle matters at the facility level, the increase in grievances nevertheless signifies increased tension and strain.

leaders claimed that their members would not agree to many of the terms offered by the state. The issues that had the most important consequences for the strike and its resolution were wages, seniority, and workers' compensation leave.

President Carter's voluntary wage guidelines complicated the bargaining over wages, as the parties disagreed over whether the suggested maximum increase of 7 percent included only wages or both wages and fringe benefits. State negotiators first offered a wage increase of 5.3 percent, which was raised to 7 percent later, when the union dropped its request for an increased clothing allowance. Still, breaking the 7 percent barrier was very important to the guards because they wanted to be recognized as more important and more "worthy" than other state employees. State negotiators were adamant, however, about not exceeding the 7 percent figure, which recently had been agreed to in negotiations with the Civil Service Employees Association (CSEA), representing the vast majority (108,000) of state employees. The CSEA contract had not yet been ratified and state officials feared than a higher raise for the guards would jeopardize its acceptance.

A second area of major disagreement was seniority rights covering post and shift assignments. The guards felt that those who have served their time in high-contact positions have earned the right to transfer to less demanding and less dangerous assignments. Correction administrators stressed their need for more discretion in making assignments, however, in order to prevent inexperienced officers from being concentrated in posts that have the most inmate contact and, consequently, the most significance for security and control.[8] Administrators also wanted more discretion in assigning the large number of female officers working in the facilities for males. OER responded to these complaints by seeking some changes in the decade-old seniority provision. Union negotiators were loath to make concessions on the highly symbolic seniority issue because the rank and file perceived it as the heart of their collective bargaining agreement.

A final issue causing major disagreement was a state-suggested change in workers' compensation leave. The guards' contract provided six months' full pay for absences caused by job-related injuries or diseases. The state pointed out that correction officers use far more workers' compensation than other state employees (5.6 as opposed to 1.7 days per person per year) and that fewer than one-third of the guards' absences were due to inmate-related injuries. OER negotiators hoped to ease the state's financial burden by charging

---

[8] Prison administrators have consistently blamed the guards' seniority clause as the cause of many major problems with the prisons. The Attica Commission even cited seniority as one of the underlying causes of the Attica uprising (*see* New York State Special Commission on Attica, 1972:126).

the first ten days of such absences to sick-leave accruals, the standard procedure for many other state employees. The union reacted emotionally to this
proposal, seeing in it a lack of appreciation for the special occupational haz-
ards of prison work.

By late March, with these issues still unsettled, the two sides announced an
impasse and called upon mediators from the Public Employee Relations
Board (PERB). After lengthy negotiations the state put forward a new pack-
age — a first-year across-the-board increase of 7 percent and a second-year
reopener on wages, seniority, and workers' compensation. A fourteen-to-
eight majority of the union negotiating team accepted this new offer on April
5, but the dissenters warned that the tentative agreement would not be ratified
by the members.

Perhaps to prevent a revolution from below, Council 82's Policy Committee, made up entirely of correction personnel, called an emergency meeting
and voted unanimously to reject the contract without sending it to the membership. The committee claimed that the rank and file's vehement reaction to
the news of the tentative settlement indicated that neither the 7 percent increase nor the reopeners were acceptable. Without sending the contract out
for membership acceptance or rejection, the committee requested the state to
return to the bargaining table.

State negotiators did not want to reopen negotiations on the issue of wages,
feeling that there was little room to move in view of the pending ratification
vote on the CSEA agreement. Thus, OER took the position that without a
negative vote on its last offer by the rank and file, the tentative agreement was
binding and the state was legally constrained from returning to the table.[9] In
addition, OER director Meyer Frucher insisted that the president's wage
guidelines and the state's fiscal problems made 7 percent the best offer that the
state could make.

Although, under these circumstances, it hardly seemed an opportune time
to strike for higher wages, the pressure on union leaders to stand up to the state
was insurmountable. Guards voiced their dissatisfaction with the wage pack-
age and the reopeners, but more important, as one union official later said, "It
was as if the members wanted to strike to show the department something; the
details of the contract didn't matter a bit. The contract provided the time to
strike, but underlying problems provided the enthusiasm." On April 19,
1979, 8,200 state employees walked off the job.

---

[9] OER officials maintained that an earlier PERB decision, *Union Springs Central School
Teachers Assoc.* (1973), prohibited further bargaining until the original contract had been sent
out for ratification by the rank and file. This position was rejected by the State Supreme Court
(*see, New York State Inspection, Security, and Law Enforcement Employees v. Hugh Carey et al.*
1979).

Conducting a Strike

The early hours of the strike presented a severe challenge to DOCS officials and to local prison administrators around the state; neither had expected that any walkout would be statewide or so widely honored. The percentage of the guard force honoring the strike varied from a low of 27 percent at Bayview to a high of 100 percent at Elmira, Hudson, and Parkside.[10] At some institutions sergeants and lieutenants left with the rank-and-file guards, but at others, such as Elmira and Auburn, supervisors either left a few days later or stayed inside for the duration of the strike. Some officers walked off the job without securing their posts or waiting for replacements. Some superintendents ordered the last shifts to remain on duty, but such efforts were futile.

Many civilian prison employees, represented by CSEA or the Professional Employees Federation (PEF), stayed home from work, some in sympathy for the guards' cause, many in fear of crossing the picket lines. In virtually all the state's thirty-three prisons, only skeleton crews were left to maintain security and vital services. This small number of personnel could simply not guarantee the health and safety of the inmates. Therefore, Governor Carey quickly declared a state of emergency and ordered New York's National Guard into twenty-nine of the state's thirty-three penal institutions.[11]

Although the National Guard had been notified in February 1979 of the possibility of a guards' strike, prestrike plans did not contemplate such a large mobilization and deployment. It took almost two full days for the twelve thousand National Guardsmen to reach all of the upstate prisons. During that time, there was considerable fear and apprehension expressed by both the highest state officials and the inmates. The Commission of Correction dispatched twenty observers to the facilities to monitor the situation.

It was during the first few days that the picket lines were the most volatile and the greatest number of threats and acts of violence occurred. Indeed, it would not be inaccurate to speak of the guards during this period as engaging in a controlled riot. They vented their anger against anyone who remained on the job and against the National Guard as well. Picketers at some prisons refused to allow National Guard trucks containing troops and supplies to enter, thereby necessitating a helicopter airlift. Harassment of National Guardsmen and destruction of National Guard property were regular occurrences. Prison administrators and inmates were also targets of the guards' anger.

[10] These percentages were calculated on the basis of DOCS figures of available personnel at each facility on Friday, April 27, 1979.

[11] Three minimum security facilities (Rochester, Hudson, and Camp Summit) did not need National Guard assistance since all inmates were either relocated or furloughed during the period of the strike.

Throughout the state, families of nonstriking prison personnel received threatening phone calls.[12]

The highly explosive nature of the picket lines was exacerbated by the inability or unwillingness of many local law enforcement agencies to control the picketers. In many small towns, local police and prison guards are members of a single subculture; the police did not want to take action against law enforcement colleagues, who were their friends and neighbors. In addition, police officers, now unionized themselves, undoubtedly sympathized with the wage demands of fellow law enforcement personnel.

Governor Carey ordered the state police into many prison communities in order to stabilize picket line conditions. They investigated 452 incidents and made 170 arrests for such acts as trespassing, criminal mischief, burglary, arson, assault, supplying prison contraband, and possession of stolen property.[13] Most of these charges were subsequently dropped "for lack of proof." We have in fact been unable to substantiate a single felony or misdemeanor conviction arising out of the strike.

Resolving the Strike

In order to deter public employees from striking, the Taylor Law prescribes sanctions against individual strikers (the two-for-one salary penalty) and the union (a loss of dues check-off), if it has authorized or condoned a walkout. In addition, the state is authorized to seek an injunction that can be enforced by the court's contempt power, if it is not obeyed. It was these coercive powers, rather than some negotiating breakthrough, that finally brought an end to the strike.

On the first day of the strike, alleging irreparable damage to the people of New York, the state obtained a temporary restraining order. Immediately, OER served the order and soon thereafter moved to have the union leaders held in contempt for refusing to abide by it. After several days of hearings, the court fined the union $450,000 plus $100,000 per shift as long as the strike continued and sent the union's executive director to jail for thirty days.[14]

---

[12] For an extreme example of the tension between strikers and National Guardsmen, see *New York Times*, April 23, 1979:2.

[13] See *The Trooper: New York State Police Magazine* 17, no. 5 (July 1979):4.

[14] The court provided that the entire fine would be reduced to $100,000 if Council 82 members returned to work by 8:00 the following morning. They did not and the contempt fine grew to the staggering sum of $2,550,000. After the strike had been settled, the union successfully moved for a reduction to $1,220,000 (*see State of New York v. Security Unit Employees* 1979). Still later, the union succeeded in having the fine reduced to $150,000 by claiming that payment of the larger amount would limit the union's capacity to fulfill its statutory duty of representing employees in the bargaining unit. The state entered no objection (*see State of New York v. Security Unit Employees*, 1980).

As noted, the striking guards faced an automatic forfeiture of two days' pay for every day on strike. The amount of the penalty depended on an employee's salary, but the average for a line officer was approximately $126 per day. This meant that by the tenth day of the strike each striker had lost over $1,200. Council 82 leaders began to worry that the strike might collapse. Toward the end of the second week strikers began to trickle back to work at some of the prisons.

In the face of these penalties, the union's only hope of victory was a deterioration of conditions within the prisons. This deterioration never occurred, primarily because the National Guard was able to serve successfully as a replacement force. The Guard took no chances; it deployed massive manpower, filling every guard post with two National Guardsmen. And since each Guardsman worked twelve hours per day, instead of eight, the amount of coverage was even further increased. It also approached this extraordinary assignment quite cautiously. The Guard was initially limited to providing "humanitarian services" (primarily food and medical care) rather than the full range of correctional duties. Only as administrators and Guardsmen became more confident did the facilities move from total lockup (in which all inmates were confined to their cells around the clock) to a more normal routine. Each facility progressed at its own pace, but by the end of the first week all mess halls were opened and prisoners were receiving recreation, showers, visits, and commissary privileges on a regular basis. Only educational and industrial programs were not resumed.

The relationship between inmates and Guardsmen blossomed into a "honeymoon period" similar to that which had occurred during other guard strikes around the country (*e.g.*, Ross 1978). Inmates claimed that by being treated humanely, their dignity had been restored: "the National Guard . . . they treat us like human beings. They give us respect and we give it back. The regular guards don't" (quoted in *Western Reporter* [Warsaw, N.Y.], May 1, 1979:3). A National Guardsman who served on an Auburn cell block voiced a similar sentiment: "They respected us and we respected them; after that, everything else was easy." Newspaper and television reports of the National Guard were extremely favorable and even the most apprehensive superintendent rated the Guardsmen as entirely capable. In fact, a kind of euphoria took over, some wardens jokingly suggesting that OER stop negotiating and fire all the guards; they claimed that the prisons had never run so smoothly.

The strategic use of New York's state police also contributed to the state's ability to withstand the strike. Over eight hundred troopers worked twelve-hour shifts monitoring the picket lines, investigating crimes by striking guards, manning prison guard towers, and patrolling prison perimeters. These tasks were assigned to the state police rather than the National Guard because they required the use of weapons, which the Guard refused to issue to its members.

Because OER could rely on the National Guard, state police, and the Taylor Law sanctions, it had little incentive to compromise. In addition, the state was determined not to offer higher wages to the guards because of the pending CSEA agreement. Productive negotiations were further hampered by the preoccupation of OER and Council 82 officials with the contempt litigation, which took eight days to complete. Perhaps the most formidable constraint on negotiations, however, was a scarcity of negotiable issues. Because the basic causes of the strike could not easily be formulated into contract clauses, union negotiators continued to focus exclusively on wages, seniority, and workers' compensation.

As the penalties against Council 82 and the strikers mounted, the state was in a position to wait for the guards to capitulate. There was pressure on the state to reach a face-saving compromise if it could be achieved without endangering the CSEA agreement, however. The single most important factor pushing state negotiators toward a compromise was the fear that some serious problems might emerge within the prisons. In spite of favorable reports about the performance of the National Guard, there was no precedent for such an extended deployment and it could not be assumed that the Guardsmen could serve indefinitely. Indeed, some superintendents noticed strain in the ranks of the National Guard as their prison duty dragged on. State negotiators could not discount the possibility of violence. The injury or death of Guardsmen, administrators, or inmates would have adversely affected public opinion and hurt the governor politically. The constant possibility of lethal violence adds a dimension to labor relations in corrections that is not present in most other public agencies.

Perhaps most important, state negotiators had to consider making at least minor concessions in order not to demoralize totally and further embitter the guards. If the state had simply broken the strike without making any concessions, the guards might have returned to the prisons in a mood to subvert the system. It was the guards, after all, who would ultimately have the responsibility of managing the facilities; the state had to be concerned about preventing "mutiny" after the strike.

By the tenth day of the strike, state negotiators offered the union a new three-year contract similar to that which had been tentatively accepted by the CSEA. It called for a maximum 7 percent pay increase each year (depending on the Cost of Living Index); the reopeners on workers' compensation and seniority were dropped. The only "extras" for the guards were a fifty-cent-per-week increase in preshift lineup pay and "training bonuses" of three hundred and two hundred dollars for the next two years.[15] While none of these benefits came close to compensating for fines, they may have helped the guards save face.

Although the union team quickly agreed to the new terms, the final settlement was delayed almost a week over the issue of amnesty. The union requested OER to seek a gubernatorial pardon for their jailed executive director, to pressure local law enforcement agencies to drop all criminal charges against strikers, to intercede at PERB to retain Council 82's dues check-off privileges, and to drop all DOCS disciplinary charges. The state refused most of the union's amnesty formulations but finally agreed to refrain from taking disciplinary action merely for striking. The state retained the right to charge employees for illegal actions while on strike. A special tripartite reconciliation panel was to be set up to arbitrate all grievances arising out of such charges.[16] On May 3, the union negotiating team voted to accept the new contract and the prison locals agreed to return to work. On May 5, National Guard units returned home. New York's prison guards returned to their posts with little to show for seventeen days on strike except that they had demonstrated to the state that "they weren't going to take it any more." The most serious prison employee strike in American history was over.

Strike Aftermath

Shock waves continued to reverberate through the prisons in the weeks and months after the strike had officially ended. At the outset, DOCS and the Commission of Correction worried about possible reprisals by guards against inmates who had supported the National Guard publicly or had worked to help maintain prison operations. Therefore, the commission sent observers to monitor five maximum security facilities, potential trouble spots because of traditionally bad labor relations or considerable hostility during the strike. Although

[15] After the strike, the state decided to give these training bonuses to all prison workers, whether or not they were AFSCME members and whether or not they honored the strike. Thus, the guards could not claim only they "benefited" from the strike. Indeed, the fact that nonguards and nonstrikers received the same bonus helped to fan the flames of the guards' poststrike discontent. The first year bonus was actually paid in September 1979, several months before the start of the skills communication training. The second bonus was received a year later, again before the "stress training" program began. Money for the training was obtained from a grant from the Law Enforcement Assistance Administration.

[16] The tripartite reconciliation panel was never set up because the department never followed through on its disciplinary charges.

inmates at several institutions did allege brutalities and reprisals,[17] we cannot conclude that the number of such incidents was unusual or strike-related. Still, the presence of the observers, reminiscent of the post-Attica period, undermined the lack of normality during these months.

While there was relative calm between guards and inmates, serious tension existed between the guards and local administrators. A cloud hung over the prison as administrators pondered disciplinary charges and investigated officers who were thought to have engaged in illegal activities during the strike. Superintendents originally filed about 250 charges, but half of these were dropped by the central office, to the great disgust of some local officials. In the cases that remained, DOCS sought the dismissal of sixty guards, fanning the flames of rank-and-file discontent. (More than three years after the strike, these cases were still "pending"; it is clear that no action will ever be taken.)

The returning strikers also directed hostility toward guards and civilian employees who had remained on the job. The strikers' anger was undoubtedly intensified by the fact that those who crossed picket lines earned generous overtime pay while the strikers suffered substantial deductions; guards normally earning three hundred dollars a week took home almost two thousand dollars in overtime pay.

At Attica, loyalty has been symbolized by jackets and tee shirts proclaiming "we walked the line in '79." The striking and nonstriking workers have had difficulty working together, and administrators at Attica forecast a permanent division between them. One local union leader, interviewed a year after the strike, said that he still would not talk to any of the "scabs" or give union cards to any of the trainees who worked during the strike.

The Future of Prison Labor Relations

While the case study of a single strike does not allow us to claim success or failure for collective bargaining in New York's prisons, we can identify the strengths and weaknesses of the system and the need for further research and institution building. What is clear from our study is that while collective bargaining may create opportunities for increased labor-management communication, it also has limits. It almost certainly cannot shoulder the full burden of personnel problems within the prison system. Collective bargaining seems best suited for negotiation over wages and benefits and for solving sharply defined

---

[17] Thomas LeClair (1980), the monitor assigned to Elmira, cited five major incidents between inmates and officers in the immediate poststrike period.

grievances over contract administration. It is not well suited for solving the emotional and deep-seated discontents that caused the 1979 guard strike. Furthermore, attempts to rely solely on collective bargaining to solve all personnel problems may so strain the process as to undermine its potential to do what it can do best. Collective bargaining is simply no substitute for effective personnel management.

Neither, as we have emphasized, does analysis of the structure and operation of collective bargaining provide a satisfactory framework for understanding this strike or the current state of labor-management relations. This case study strongly suggests the importance of linking research on particular occupations and worker subcultures with industrial relations research. Furthermore, we believe there is a strong need to carry out research on the role of the National Guard and the courts in deterring and resolving public sector strikes. The existence of a replacement force such as the National Guard greatly strengthens the state's bargaining position and must be accounted for in any analysis of critical strikes in the public sector (*see* Jacobs 1982). Likewise, the capacity and willingness of courts to enjoin strikers and enforce legislative penalties can be decisive in producing a particular strike outcome and must be a factor in future negotiation strategies.

While the Taylor Law sanctions were effective in breaking the strike and perhaps in suppressing the willingness of many public employees to strike in the future, it may be hypothesized that these sanctions further alienate dissatisfied workers like New York's prison guards. In the months following the strike, guards complained bitterly about the two-for-one penalties.[18] The commissioner of correction's poststrike observer at Elmira reported that the implementation of these penalties, as well as the pending dismissal actions, created intense anti-state sentiment and constant threats of a wildcat strike (LeClair 1980).

It might be useful to compare the highly unstable poststrike period in New York with a poststrike situation in Montana, where a guard strike occurred at approximately the same time (Jacobs and Zimmer 1980). Like their New York counterparts, the Montana guards ultimately settled for little more than the state originally offered. While Montana guards face many of the same problems, particularly loss of status and authority, their strike and its aftermath were never marked by the extreme tension, hostility, and violence that

---

[18] One complaint continually voiced was that the state was willing to absorb the cost of the strike but not to give a more substantial raise. The guards probably overestimate the cost of the strike when compared with a higher wage increase. The cost of the strike was estimated to be about $41 million, which includes approximately $1 million per day for the National Guard. OER claims that the long-term costs of even a 1 percent larger pay increase would have been much greater.

appeared in New York. There are many differences between these two correctional systems, of course, but one salient difference is that public employee strikes are legal in Montana.

In New York's poststrike period, the guards and their union continued to press their battle against "the system." Nearly every guard, at the union's encouragement, filed a petition with OER to challenge the two-for-one penalty. Within twenty days of the strike, OER had received nearly seven thousand affidavits, which had to be processed individually. OER granted more than 2,600 hearings, which took more than three years to complete.[19] Union leaders encouraged officers to manipulate absences to create overtime to compensate for the fines levied against strikers. Council 82 lawyers managed to have the contempt fine reduced to $150,000, with the stipulation that the guards not engage in another strike for a three-year period. The PERB hearings covering the union's possible loss of its check-off rights dragged on for almost two years. The hearing officer found Council 82 in violation of the Taylor Law for violating "the rules of good faith bargaining," and PERB ordered an eighteen months' suspension of the dues check-off.

If this case study shows anything, it is the need for prison officials to create new mechanisms for addressing the guards' discontents. Perhaps DOCS should embark on an educational program to help guards see their changing role in the context of broader sociopolitical change. Both guards and administrators must begin to understand that their loss of authority is the product of a wholesale redefinition of the status of marginal groups in American society. That explanation does not make the loss any less real. The great challenge for corrections is to develop an administrative system that can maintain control in the context of the legal and humane reforms of the last fifteen years. This is no small undertaking. Such a system could be realized only if there is commitment by all segments of the prison staff.

DOCS might address the guards' perceived loss of status by stressing "professionalism" and a more realistic assessment of public opinion. Somehow, administrators must broaden the guards' world view so that they cease to see themselves as locked into a zero-sum competition with prisoners for status. Obviously, this is easier said than done, but only solutions that take into consideration the nature of the occupation and of the worker subculture can be successful. Perhaps DOCS could develop career ladders that provide more opportunities for guards to move into treatment or administrative positions, or establish work teams that treat security and treatment personnel as equal team members rather than as competitors. Another alternative is to rebuild the guard force along more paramilitary lines, such as those govern-

---

[19] Penalties were excused in 43.5 percent of the cases, partially excused in 13.5 percent, and denied in 43 percent.

ing state police, in which esprit de corps and professionalism are high. Such a force would ideally take pride in its contribution to professional law enforcement. Further, to increase career opportunities for guards, police agencies might someday be willing to make a few years of service in corrections a prerequisite to appointment.

Racial tensions within the prison work force must also be addressed. While deep-seated racial prejudices are difficult to eradicate, the DOCS might do well to embark upon a constructive race relations program, perhaps borrowing from the armed forces, where such programs have been used extensively for many years.

Much must also be done to make labor-management relations more constructive. The question whether collective bargaining is appropriate for a uniformed service such as corrections was resolved in the affirmative more than a decade ago. The typical private-sector adversary relationship, however, is not appropriate for a department with the responsibility of securing, programming, and, it is hoped, reforming violent men. High-level administrators must finally come to terms with collective bargaining, putting aside their concerns about their diminished authority and their charges that unionization is the major cause of all that is wrong in prisons. Local administrators must accept unionization as a permanent feature of the corrections environment and thereby accept the reality of more participatory decision making. Once superintendents accept the responsibility for good labor relations at their own facility, fewer grievances will need to be handled at the central office or by OER. Training may help administrators make these attitudinal changes and develop more effective labor relations skills. In addition, DOCS and the guards' union might mandate more frequent meetings between superintendents and local union leaders. At some facilities, representatives from labor and management meet only when there are problems and, thus, only in adversary roles. To be effective, communication must exist before problems emerge.

For its part, the union must identify the issues that can be brought into the collective bargaining system and articulate them coherently. If stress is a real concern, for example, then the union should develop proposals for reducing it and for treating those who are suffering. If discipline is ineffective, realistic proposals that recognize prisoners' rights must be put forward.

Somehow the union must reduce worker expectations about what collective bargaining can accomplish. The prison guard rank and file tend to feel that there is no limit to what can be gained by being "militant." This lack of realism must be corrected if union leaders are to represent their members' interests effectively. Until these changes occur, there is danger that job dissatisfaction will be expressed as collective protest, including strikes and job actions, rather than by constructive proposals for more effective administration.

[8]

Race Relations and
the Guards' Subculture

COAUTHOR LAWRENCE J. KRAFT

A consistent demand of prison reformers, national commissions, and rioting prisoners has been the recruitment of minority personnel to replace veteran rural white prison guards, who are charged with being unsympathetic, brutal, and racist. Consider the following statement by prison reform activist Herman Schwartz (1972:50):

> The guard population is drawn from the extremely conservative residents of these rural areas, who become guards for the pension, and often as a second job to a farm or other occupation. These people usually have no sympathy or understanding for the strange urban groups, with their often unfamiliar and often immoral life styles, with their demands and their resentments. Racial prejudice is often present for the white backlash is particularly powerful among such rural types, even apart from the prison.

The prestigious National Advisory Commission on Criminal Justice Standards and Goals (1973) observed:

> There are other problems regarding recruitment of minority staff. In the past, those few who were brought into the system felt pressure to become like their white counterparts. By doing so, they suffered an identity crisis with minority offenders. As black, Chicano and Indian offenders have become politicized, they increasingly have rejected traditional minority staff. Extreme conflict has resulted in some institutions. Black inmates want black staff with whom they can identify....

Reprinted in slightly different form from *Social Problems* 25, no.3 (February 1978): 304–18.

Correctional agencies must become sensitive to this issue. They should abandon policies and practices that weaken identification between members of these groups and launch programs that capitalize on cultural differences as opportunities to improve their programs rather than as problems to contend with.

The need for a role model to admire and emulate is undeniable. All youth need heroes. So do adults. Corrections should provide them among its staff, rather than weed them out. Both white and minority staff must be trained to accept this program goal.

The twentieth demand of the rioting Attica prisoners in September 1971 was to "institute a program for the employment of significant numbers of black and Spanish-speaking officers." The New York State Special Commission on Attica (1972:xviii) stated:

> Racism among Attica officers may be no greater than what is present in society at large, but its effect is more intense at Attica. The prisoner can find no escape from it — there is no way to avoid confrontations and unpleasant experiences when the interaction is so ever-present and the quarters so close.... [But] the relationship between most officers and the inmates was characterized by fear, hostility, mistrust, nurtured by racism....
> Training for correction officers must sensitize them to understand and deal with the new breed of young inmates from the urban ghettos and to understand and control the racism within themselves.

In describing the deplorable overcrowding and other abuses of the Alabama prison systems, federal district court judge, Frank Johnson, wrote in *Pugh v. Locke* (1976):

> The problems posed by understaffing are aggravated by the fact that most of the large institutions are located in rural areas of the state. The guards, drawn largely from the local population, are practically all white and rural in contrast to the predominately black and urban inmate population they supervise. A number of witnesses testified that staff members address black inmates with racial slurs, further straining already tense relations....
> Defendants shall immediately institute an affirmative hiring program designed to reduce and having the effect of reducing the racial and cultural disparity between the staff and the inmate population.

The assumption is that because minority prison guards share the same socio-economic and cultural background as the minority prisoners, they will treat them more humanely and relate to them more effectively. It is also assumed that minority prisoners will view the authority of minority guards as more legitimate.

A contrary hypothesis, drawn from the sociology of occupations, suggests

[161]

that the role demands on the prison guard are both so encompassing and restrictive that all guards, regardless of social background and prior beliefs, will inevitably develop hostile attitudes toward the prisoners. Sociological studies of the police (Niederhoffer 1967; Skolnick 1966) have repeatedly confirmed the segmentation of that work force from the wider society and its hostility toward those minority groups with which it most frequently comes in contact. Nicholas Alex's (1969) study of the New York City Police Department found that those who have the most contact with the police make no distinction between black and white officers. Indeed, the black officer is more likely to react forcefully against minority citizens because of his role strain, despite his awareness of the white officers' racism and his own marginality on the force. In a subsequent book, however, Alex (1976) points to the politicization of minority police officers in cities like New York and Chicago, perhaps undercutting the continued validity of his earlier observations.

Like the policeman, the prison guard is physically and existentially segmented from the mainstream of society (Jacobs and Retsky 1975; Jacobs 1977). Uniforms (Roucek 1935), and the system of paramilitary rank and discipline reinforce in-group solidarity and distance from the prisoners. There is every reason to expect that prison guards constitute at least as tight knit an occupational group as the police and that their occupational role is equally restrictive.

The situation of constant oppositional interaction makes it difficult for the guard to establish affective relations with the prisoners. Not only is it difficult to transcend the role of disciplinarian, but as Sykes (1956) points out, the guard is constantly preoccupied with maintaining authority. The guard who attempts to be a "good Joe" may lose the capacity to maintain order and discipline. The formal orientation of the new officer as well as the lore of the occupation warn against allowing oneself to be corrupted through "reciprocity." It is said that once an officer accepts a favor from a prisoner or breaks a rule on the prisoner's behalf, the officer will be blackmailed into further improper acts.

That the relationship between guard and inmate is one of structured conflict, which cannot be surmounted even by racial and ethnic ties, is the dramatic conclusion of a well-known Stanford experiment (Haney, Banks, and Zimbardo 1973). The experimenters randomly assigned white Anglo-Saxon male college student volunteers to roles of guard and prisoner in a "mock prison" constructed in the basement of a university building. Both groups were dressed appropriately. The guards were given simple rules to enforce and were told to maintain order. Conflict between the two groups grew so intense that the experiment had to be stopped. The "prisoners" showed signs of psychopathology, especially depression. Many "guards" acted in an authoritarian manner, even sadistically. This experiment is often cited to support the proposition that the behavior of guards and inmates is a product of their organizational roles, and is independent of such extrainstitutional variables as education, age, political orientation, and race.

At issue sociologically is whether the otherwise decisive background variable of race will modify the guard's behavior or whether guarding is such a tightly structured and organized occupation that all guards, regardless of race, will feel and act the same way toward prisoners. As a matter of public policy, it is important to know whether the infusion of young black guards into the prisons will ameliorate the atmosphere of tension, fear, and hostility. If not, an important plank in the reform platform will give way, again raising the larger question of the capacity of this society to find humane, practical, and principled solutions to the problems of imprisonment.

The Sample

Our sample consisted of 231 in-service guards from the Stateville and Joliet maximum security prisons in Illinois. The questionnaire was administered to 252 of the approximately 600 Stateville and Joliet guards. We excluded 9 officers who did not identify both race and rank, 7 who were of some other racial group, and 5 who were lieutenants or captains. The sample includes 5 guards (3 whites, 2 blacks) who had not yet achieved civil service certification and 20 sergeants (11 whites, 9 blacks).

The Stateville and Joliet prisons are located approximately thirty-five miles southwest of Chicago. They stand about seven miles apart and are administered separately. Approximately 75 percent of their combined prison population is black; another 10 percent is Latino. The great majority of prisoners are drawn from the core areas of Chicago. While blacks make up only 12 percent of all guards in the state, 63 percent of all black Illinois guards are at Stateville and Joliet. Nineteen percent of Joliet's and 32 percent of Stateville's guards are black.

One of us administered a questionnaire to the guards as they rotated through the Correctional Academy between summer 1974 and fall 1975. In the later months of the project the academy staff administered the questionnaire as a regular part of the training week. Periodic on-site visits and informal conversation with guards who had completed the questionnaire revealed no special problems. Anonymity was assured and preserved. A comparison of responses given in the early months with those of guards who filled out the questionnaire several months later shows no systematic variations.

Demographic Composition

Seventy-two percent of the respondents were white ($n = 165$) and 28 percent were black ($n = 66$).

[163]

The black guards have less seniority. Seventy-two percent of the black guards, but only 26 percent of the white guards, have less than four years' seniority. This difference is not surprising since the overwhelming majority of black guards entered the system as a consequence of affirmative action pressures in the early 1970s. Up until 1963, only 30 black guards had ever been appointed to positions at the two prisons, but in 1972 alone there were 142 black appointees. This number grew by 1974 to 184, constituting 42 percent of all appointees for that year.

The black guards are younger. Their mean age is thirty-seven years (median=32) compared to a mean age of forty-three years for the whites (median=45). Sixty-two percent of the blacks, as compared to 30 percent of the whites are thirty-five years of age or under. They are also better educated. Thirty-nine percent of them have had some college compared to 21 percent of the whites; 28 percent of the blacks and 38 percent of the whites have not completed high school; only 5 percent of the blacks, but 15 percent of the whites have no high school at all.

The black guards are more likely to come from an urban background. Thirty-six percent of the blacks and only 11 percent of the whites grew up in a metropolitan area. Twenty-three percent of the blacks grew up in the country or on a farm in comparison to 36 percent of the whites; only 14 percent of the blacks but 34 percent of the whites, have a small-town (population less than 25,000) background. The black guards are also more likely to identify with the working class and to consider themselves politically liberal. Sixty-seven percent of this group said they identified with the working class and 33 percent with the middle class. This compares with 60 percent of the white guards who identified with the working class, and 40 percent with the middle class. Asked their political and social views, 57 percent of the blacks and 25 percent of the whites said either "very" or "somewhat" liberal; on the other hand, 16 percent of the blacks and 31 percent of the whites described themselves as either "very" or "somewhat" conservative.

If reformers, commissioners, and the prisoners are correct, then these black guards should have a much more sympathetic attitude toward the prison population made up substantially (approximately 75 percent) of black inmates from the core areas of Chicago. In addition, we would expect to find that the black guards give greater support to rehabilitation as the primary rationale for imprisonment, that they express less support for their superiors, most of whom are white, and that they are less committed to the goals of the institution and to their occupation in general. Moreover, we would expect these differences to emerge more sharply for the less experienced and younger guards.

The Findings

In the discussion that follows we compare the responses of black and white guards on a series of questionnaire items about their attitudes toward the inmates, their job, the staff, and the system, and on their commitment as a prison guard. (See tables). We also examine racial differences within two guard subgroups: those guards with less than four years' experience and those under forty years of age. The first subgroup, the newer guards, corresponds to those guards hired after affirmative action was mandated. The second subgroup, the younger guards, corresponds to those guards below the mean age of all guards in our sample. (See tables.)

Inmate Orientation

If those who have demanded greater minority representation in correctional institutions to cure the organizational conflict between prisoners and guards are right, black guards, especially those who are younger and less "institutionalized," will feel less social distance from the prisoners and be more likely to accept the prisoners' moral worth and humanity. Our data fail to support this hypothesis. In fact, on several questionnaire items the black officers show less empathy for the prisoners than do their white colleagues.

On the questionnaire item most relevant for assessing social distance — "How similar are correctional officers and inmates?" — responses show virtually no racial differences (see Table 9). The vast majority of all guards (n=231), especially the younger blacks (n=38), think that inmates "try to take advantage of officers whenever they can." Blacks give less support to the statement that most inmates are "decent people," although they are more likely to agree that a smaller percentage of inmates "belong in prison." Almost the same percentage in both races think that "most inmates lack morals."

Contrary to our expectation, the less experienced black guards are not consistently more "inmate-oriented." Eleven percent of this subgroup (n=47), for example, strongly disagree with the statement that "most inmates are decent people." A greater proportion of less experienced blacks than of any other subgroup are in strong agreement with the assertion that "inmates take advantage of officers whenever they can." They also tend to think, however, that "fewer prisoners belong in prison," and that prisoners do not "have too many rights." They are generally less morally indignant about inmate behavior and slightly more tolerant of homosexuality. The less experienced white guards, on the other hand, express the most consistently negative attitudes toward the inmates of any guard subgroup.[1]

When asked whether black guards "get along better with inmates," the majority of all guards answer negatively (see Table 9). The black guards themselves are more likely to think that being black matters; the majority of less experienced black guards ($n=47$) agree that black guards relate to prisoners more effectively. But on an open-ended question that asked guards to list three problems of their job, only five whites and none of the blacks mention race; this despite the obvious racial separation in the officers' dining

Table 9. Responses of guards to questions and statements regarding attitudes toward inmates, by experience, age, and race (percent).

	All guards ($n=231$)		New guards[a] ($n=90$)		Young guards[b] ($n=94$)	
	White ($n=165$)	Black ($n=66$)	White ($n=43$)	Black ($n=47$)	White ($n=56$)	Black ($n=38$)
"In your opinion, when just considered as people, how similar are guards and prisoners?"						
Very similar	21.7	27.7	16.3	29.8	26.8	26.3
Somewhat similar	35.5	26.2	34.9	25.5	33.9	21.1
Somewhat different	25.9	26.2	30.2	23.4	30.4	28.9
Very different	16.9	20.0	18.6	21.3	8.9	23.7
"Only a few inmates are troublemakers; most of them are decent people."						
Strongly agree	8.5	9.5	4.7	8.9	7.3	8.1
Agree	66.1	58.7	53.5	60.0	65.5	67.6
Disagree	22.4	23.8	34.9	20.0	23.6	18.9
Strongly disagree	3.0	7.9	7.0	11.1	3.6	5.4
"The courts have given inmates so many rights that it is practically impossible to maintain satisfactory discipline."						
Strongly agree	39.1	23.1	54.8	23.4	43.3	21.1
Agree	48.4	43.1	42.9	40.4	47.2	44.7
Disagree	10.6	27.7	2.4	29.8	9.4	28.9
Strongly disagree	1.9	6.2[c]	0.0	6.4[d]	0.0	5.3[e]
"Inmates try to take advantage of officers whenever they can."						
Strongly agree	33.3	39.1	38.1	41.3	30.4	45.9
Agree	55.8	51.6	54.8	45.7	57.1	51.4
Disagree	10.9	9.4	7.1	13.0	12.5	2.7
Strongly disagree	0.0	0.0	0.0	0.0	0.0	0.0

Continued on next page

[1] The responses to a series of open-ended questions that allowed respondents to acknowledge how inmates influenced their job, assignment, and shift also resulted in very little racial difference. Whites more often mention working with inmates as a disadvantage, while blacks are more likely to perceive it as an advantage. The differences, however, are small and inconsistent. Among guards with less than four years' experience, for example, blacks more often consider working with inmates to be a disadvantage of the job.

Table 9 continued

	All guards (n=231)		New guards[a] (n=90)		Young guards[b] (n=94)	
	White (n=165)	Black (n=66)	White (n=43)	Black (n=47)	White (n=56)	Black (n=38)
"Of the inmates you know, how many of them do you think belong in prison?"						
Less than 10%	1.9	9.7	4.8	13.6	1.8	13.5
About 25%	3.7	8.1	0.0	6.8	1.8	5.4
About 50%	14.8	19.4	9.5	22.7	10.7	24.3
About 75%	33.3	35.5	35.7	27.3	55.4	32.4
More than 90%	46.3	27.4[c]	50.0	29.5 (6.0)	30.4	24.3
"How many inmates practice homosexuality?"						
10% or less	50.3	37.5	40.5	32.6	37.0	27.0
About 25%	36.5	40.6	42.9	43.5	47.3	48.6
About 50%	11.3	15.6	19.0	15.2	10.9	18.9
75% or more	1.9	4.7	4.8	8.7	3.6	5.4
"What is your opinion of inmates who practice homosexuality?"[f]						
No different	6.8	12.5	5.0	15.2	7.6	18.9
Normal	11.8	14.1	10.0	17.4	17.0	16.2
Lack morals	39.1	35.9	42.5	41.3	50.9	32.4
Sick	46.9	43.8	52.5	34.8	33.3	40.5
"Most inmates lack morals."						
Strongly agree	6.7	6.3	4.8	6.5	5.5	5.3
Agree	43.9	40.6	52.4	34.8	34.5	36.8
Disagree	46.3	50.0	42.9	54.3	58.2	55.3
Strongly disagree	3.0	3.1	0.0	4.3	1.8	2.6
"In the past few years the respect shown officers by inmates has . . ."						
Increased	17.6	26.6	11.6	28.3	8.9	27.0
Stayed the same	10.3	14.1	9.3	15.2	12.5	16.2
Decreased	72.1	59.4	79.1	56.5	78.6	56.8[c]
"Black guards get along better with inmates than whites do."						
Strongly agree	5.5	18.5	7.0	19.1	5.6	15.8
Agree	25.0	29.2	32.6	36.2	33.3	42.1
Disagree	59.8	40.0	51.2	27.7	57.4	34.2
Strongly disagree	9.8	12.3[g]	9.3	17.0	3.7	7.9

NOTE: All percentages and statistics are based on the responses of those guards who answered specific questions. Nonresponse rates of over 5% of a given sample for a given question are reported in parentheses.

[a] All guards with less than four years' experience.

[b] All guards under forty years of age (56% of young guards are also new; 63% of new guards are also young).

[c] $x^2 p$ .005.

[d] $x^2 p$ .001.

[e] $x^2 p$ .05.

[f] Open-ended question; all responses coded.

[g] $x^2 p$ .01.

room and the racial hostility of blacks separated from the force (Jacobs and Grear 1977). This finding contrasts with studies of police (Stark 1972), of prison guards (Wright 1973), and with actual prison experience. In April 1976, for example, a letter was sent to the governor of Illinois by an organization calling itself the Afro-American Correctional Officers Movement, which complained of the racist oppression of minority employees and inmates at Stateville and other Illinois prisons. Their seventeen demands included the removal of "Ku Klux Klan organizers" from Stateville.

Job Orientation

While black officers may feel no closer, socially, to the prisoners, do they support a more relaxed correctional process that, according to the reformers' position, would create an atmosphere more conducive to self change? We found no such support on the part of the black guards. The majority of officers of both races disagree with the statement that "correctional officers should be rough with inmates occasionally to let them know who is boss," but blacks, especially those with less seniority, more often give approval to the statement (see Table 10).

The number of disciplinary reports of rule violations by prisoners also shows blacks to be more active disciplinarians. Three-fourths of the whites ($n=165$) but just over one-half of the blacks ($n=66$) manage their jobs while writing two or fewer disciplinary tickets per week. This is not an artifact of different job assignments, for within a subsample of those twenty-six whites and seventeen blacks who work in the cell houses, 73 percent of the whites and 29 percent of the blacks write two or fewer tickets per week.

On the other hand, the strongest questionnaire support for the proposition that black guards are more favorably oriented to the prisoners is their attraction to those assignments requiring intensive inmate contact. While the majority of whites prefer the towers, blacks prefer the cell houses. A fair number of blacks even chose isolation, detention, and segregation as the best duty assignment.

Preference by blacks for high-contact assignments might suggest that they are less fearful. It is true that fewer of the less experienced blacks voluntarily mention "danger" as a problem of the job, but when forced to respond to a question asking how dangerous being a prison guard is, blacks are more likely to answer "extremely dangerous." On the open-ended questions only small percentages of guards mention danger as a disadvantage or problem of their assignment or shift. Here, too, proportionately more younger black guards mention danger than any other subgroup.

Table 10. Responses of guards to questions and statements regarding attitudes toward their jobs, by experience, age, and race (percent)

	All guards (n = 231)		New guards[a] (n = 90)		Young guards[b] (n = 94)	
	White (n=165)	Black (n=66)	White (n=43)	Black (n=47)	White (n=56)	Black (n=38)
"Correctional officers should be rough with inmates occasionally to let them know who is boss."						
Strongly agree	3.1	4.6	4.8	6.4	3.6	5.3
Agree	19.6	32.3	28.6	36.2	25.5	31.6
Disagree	65.0	53.8	52.4	46.8	56.4	55.3
Strongly disagree	12.3	9.2	14.3	10.6	14.5	7.9
"Although understanding may be important in helping inmates, what is really needed is strictness."						
Strongly agree	26.3	18.5	40.5	17.0	21.8	21.1
Agree	60.0	56.9	50.0	57.4	63.6	55.3
Disagree	10.0	20.0	7.1	21.3	9.1	21.1
Strongly disagree	3.8	4.6	2.4	4.3[c]	5.5	2.6
"What are the three most serious problems that a correctional officer must face while he is on the job?"[d]						
Responsibility	23.4	35.8	16.2	33.3	19.6	34.4
Order and security	40.9	49.1	43.2	47.6	41.2	43.8
Conflict with inmates	21.2	15.1	21.6	14.3	19.6	21.9
Physical danger	51.8	49.1	59.5	45.2	56.9	40.6
Superior officers	19.0	7.5	24.3	9.5	21.6	9.4
Other guards	12.4	7.5	13.5	4.8	15.7	9.4
Race	3.6	0.0	8.1	0.0	5.9	0.0
	(18.0)	(19.0)	(14.0)	(11.0)	(9.0)	(16.0)
"About how many tickets do you write each week?"						
0	35.4	28.6	21.4	24.4	29.6	25.0
1–2	42.2	28.6	42.9	26.7	31.5	25.0
3 or more	22.4	42.9[c]	35.7	48.9	38.9	50.0
"What is the *best* job assignment?"						
Towers	36.3	17.5	33.3	12.2	25.5	8.6
Cellhouses	7.0	22.8	4.8	24.4	5.9	25.7
Services	14.6	10.5	11.9	14.6	15.7	11.4
Wards	5.1	14.0	2.4	14.6	5.9	17.1

Continued on next page

NOTE: All percentages and statistics are based on the responses of those guards who answered specific questions. Nonresponse rates of over 5% of a given sample for a given question are reported in parentheses.

[a] All guards with less than four years' experience.
[b] All guards under forty years of age (56% of young guards are also new; 63% of new guards are also young).
[c] $x^2 p$ .05.
[d] Open-ended question; all responses coded.
[e] $x^2 p$ .01.

Table 10 continued

	All guards (n = 231)		New guards[a] (n = 90)		Young guards[b] (n = 94)	
	White (n=165)	Black (n=66)	White (n=43)	Black (n=47)	White (n=56)	Black (n=38)
Armory, guard hall, telephone center, warden house	17.2	15.8	28.6	9.8	27.5	22.9
Any other	19.7	19.3	19.1	24.4	19.6	14.4
		(12.0)		(13.0)	(9.0)	(8.0)
"What is the *worst* job assignment?"						
Towers	28.0	43.6	28.2	53.8	42.9	60.6
Cellhouses	22.7	20.0	25.6	17.9	16.3	15.2
Wards	32.0	20.0	30.8	15.4	26.5	15.2
Any other	17.3	16.3	15.4	12.9	14.2	9.1
	(10.0)	(15.0)	(9.0)	(17.0)	(13.0)	(13.0)
"How dangerous is working as a correctional officer?"						
Extremely 1	35.1	47.5	42.1	52.3	35.2	44.4
2	7.1	3.3	15.8	4.5	13.0	5.6
3	16.2	16.4	10.5	18.2	16.7	16.7
4	20.8	21.3	13.2	15.9	20.4	25.0
5	12.3	3.3	10.5	0.0	11.1	2.8
6	3.2	4.9	2.6	6.8	1.9	2.8
Not at all 7	5.2	3.3	5.3	2.3	1.9	2.8
		(6.0)	(12.0)	(6.0)		

Staff Orientation

The higher ranks of the custody force at the Stateville and Joliet prisons are dominated by white southern Illinoisians. Almost all of the top administrators are white, although they have diverse backgrounds and typically have at least an undergraduate college education. Until the early 1970s, blacks were unrepresented among both the administrators and top guards. A comparison study of guard "dropouts and rejects" (Jacobs and Grear 1977) found that among those officers leaving the force, whites were consistently more favorably disposed to their superiors. Seventy-three percent of the nonwhites who left the prisons by resignation or discharge within six months attributed their greatest difficulties to their relationships with superior officers.

Among in-service officers, however, blacks give more positive responses to questions concerning administrators and superior officers (see Table 11). Fifty-four percent of the blacks (n=66) and 46 percent of the whites (n=165) disagree with the statement that "lieutenants are more sympathetic to the problems of inmates than of guards." There is identical support for the statement that "when a problem arises between an officer and an inmate the warden and other administrators usually support the officer." Since younger blacks show stronger support for the prison administration than any other subgroup,[2] at least a substantial segment of black officers who make it past the six-month civil service probationary period are quite a different breed from those whose employment at the prison ends within the first six months.

These findings may indicate that there is a highly effective process of (de)selection operating within the guard force. Those black officers most attracted to the prisoners and most antagonistic toward the prison regime either resign, are fired, or change their attitudes. Jacobs and Grear (1977) found that, compared to the nonwhite officers who left the force within six months, nonwhites who served longer had more positive attitudes toward superiors. The same situation of structured conflict which forces black police officers to rely on their white colleagues, even though they do not socialize with them or even respect them, may exist in maximum security prisons. The black officer is in a particularly difficult position of role strain because he cannot satisfy the demands for solidarity and support pressed upon him by both the prisoners and the prison administrators. A guard either identifies with the prisoners and risks being fired, resigns, or comes to accept the ruling authority as necessary and legitimate.

System Orientation

Both black and white guards support "rehabilitation" as the primary justification for imprisonment (see Table 11). The younger whites are the exception, stressing the importance of the prison for protecting society. A significantly higher percentage of blacks than whites mentions punishment as the primary purpose of imprisonment; whites mention deterrence and protection of society much more frequently. If any sharp difference emerges, it is that relatively more black guards express a punitive orientation.

Ambiguity on whether guards responded with what "is" or what "should be" the justification for imprisonment is avoided by looking at responses to the statement "The primary purpose of a correctional institution *should be* to punish convicted criminals" (see Table 11). Blacks again answer affirmatively more often than whites. On the other hand, significantly fewer blacks (23 per-

---

[2] The feeling is apparently not reciprocated. The top custodial officers, most of whom are white southern Illinoisians, are very suspicious of the recent wave of black recruits. An outside departmental evaluation of Stateville (Irwin 1974) found: "The new breed who make up the second strata [of guards] are younger, more often black, and come from Chicago. These younger guards have been pouring into the system because it is one job that has opened up to blacks and other minorities... The old guards mistrust and resent the new breed intensely. They feel that the new guards lack discipline, a respect for authority, a sense of the importance of maintaining vigilance against the violent and escape prone convict population. Moreover, and this may be more serious, the old guard feels that the new breed, since they are urban and perhaps from the same neighborhood as many of the convicts, may even identify more, in fact, secretly cooperate with the convicts."

Table 11. Responses of guards to questions and statements regarding attitudes toward prison staff and correctional system, by experience, age, and race (percent).

	All guards (n = 165)		New guards[a] (n = 90)		Young guards[b] (n = 94)	
	White (n=165)	Black (n=66)	White (n=43)	Black (n=47)	White (n=56)	Black (n=38)
Staff orientation						
"When I began, the veterans were friendly and helped me learn."						
Strongly agree	12.2	21.5	9.3	19.1	9.1	21.1
Agree	47.6	40.0	55.8	38.3	41.8	47.4
Disagree	30.5	27.7	27.9	29.8	38.2	21.1
Strongly disagree	9.8	10.8	7.0	12.8	10.9	10.5
"In general, lieutenants are more sympathetic to problems of inmates than to problems of correctional officers."						
Strongly agree	22.5	14.3	38.1	17.4	20.4	5.3
Agree	31.9	31.7	16.7	30.4	27.8	34.2
Disagree	38.1	39.7	35.7	41.3	42.6	52.6
Strongly disagree	7.5	14.3	9.5	10.9	9.3	7.9
"When a problem arises between an officer and inmate, the warden and other administrators usually support the officer."						
Strongly agree	4.8	4.7	4.7	4.3	8.9	2.6
Agree	54.8	56.3	51.2	56.5	48.2	60.5
Disagree	34.3	29.7	34.9	30.4	35.7	26.3
Strongly disagree	6.0	9.4	9.3	8.7	7.1	10.5
System orientation						
"What, in your opinion, is the main reason for putting an offender in prison?"[c]						
To deter	13.9	7.8	23.3	10.9	16.1	8.1
To punish	22.3	40.6[d]	20.6	34.8	19.6	37.8
To rehabilitate	39.2	48.4	37.2	52.2	35.7	45.9
To protect society	33.1	18.8[e]	37.2	21.7	46.4	18.9[e]
"The primary purpose of a correctional institution should be to punish convicted criminals."						
Strongly agree	9.4	6.3	9.5	6.5	11.1	2.7
Agree	31.3	45.0	31.0	43.5	29.6	54.1
Disagree	45.0	27.0	40.5	26.1	46.3	27.0
Strongly disagree	14.4	20.6[e]	19.0	23.9	13.0	16.2
"Rehabilitation programs are a waste of time and money."						
Strongly agree	10.6	6.3	14.6	6.5	3.7	5.4
Agree	29.2	17.2	24.4	13.0	33.3	18.9
Disagree	47.8	43.0	46.3	41.3	46.3	45.9
Strongly disagree	12.4	32.8[f]	14.6	39.1	16.7	29.7
"Why do inmates commit crimes?"[g]						
Sick	51.8	50.8	60.5	46.8	53.6	57.9
Born criminals	13.9	10.8	11.6	12.8	14.5	13.2
Free choice	57.6	53.8	53.5	53.2	65.5	55.3
Broken homes	49.4	58.5	60.5	55.3	46.4	68.4
Poverty	52.4	61.5	62.8	61.7	62.5	65.8

Continued on next page

Table 11 continued

	All guards (n = 165)		New guards[a] (n = 90)		Young guards[b] (n = 94)	
	White (n=165)	Black (n=66)	White (n=43)	Black (n=47)	White (n=56)	Black (n=38)
"Why are there so many members of minority groups in prison?"[g]						
Sick	2.2	1.9	2.9	2.6	0.0	0.0
Inferior	19.4	13.0	25.7	10.5	20.8	6.1
Inability to conform	5.2	0.0	0.0	0.0	8.3	0.0
Violent subculture	31.3	24.1	25.7	28.9	43.8	27.3
Lack of opportunity	41.0	63.0[e]	34.3	60.5[e]	37.5	63.6[e]
Lack of education	23.1	18.5	17.1	18.4	18.8	18.2
Broken homes	10.4	5.6	5.7	5.3	6.3	9.1
Lack of religion	9.7	3.7	8.6	5.3	6.3	3.0
Racism	6.0	13.0	11.4	10.5	10.4	12.1
	(19.0)	(17.0)	(19.0)	(19.0)	(14.0)	(13.0)

NOTE: All percentages and statistics are based on the responses of those guards who answered specific questions. Nonresponse rates of over 5% of a given sample for a given question are reported in parentheses.

[a] All guards with less than four years' experience.

[b] All guards under forty years of age (56% of young guards are also new; 63% of new guards are also young).

[c] Open-ended questions; all responses coded.

[d] $x^2 p$ .01.

[e] $x^2 p$ .05.

[f] $x^2 p$ .005.

[g] Multiple choice question; respondents able to select more than one answer.

cent) than whites (40 percent) agree with the assertion that "rehabilitation programs are a waste of time and money."

Except that blacks are more likely to mention "lack of opportunity," there are no substantial racial differences in perceptions of or reasons given for the high proportion of minority prisoners, or for causes of crime in general. Lack of opportunity is a preferred explanation for all subgroups, except the younger whites who subscribe to the view that the minority subculture is more violent. About one in ten guards of both races think "racism" is a reason.

Job Commitment

The prison guards at Stateville and Joliet do not plan to change jobs; two-thirds of them expect to be on the force five years from now. When presented with the choice of six alternative occupations, one-half to three-fourths of our respondents would prefer the job they now hold; there are no significant differences between blacks and whites (see Table 12). The most attractive alternative for all officers is private security guard, followed by policeman. Garbage collector is the least attractive.

Table 12. Responses of guards to questions and statements regarding job commitment, by experience, age, and race (percent)

	All guards (n = 231)		New guards[a] (n = 90)		Young guards[b] (n = 94)	
	White (n=165)	Black (n=66)	White (n=43)	Black (n=47)	White (n=56)	Black (n=38)
"Suppose that you were offered a job as a . . . at the same salary you are now making as a correctional officer. Would you take the job?"						
". . .construction worker. . ."						
Sure would	7.3	7.7	16.3	6.4	7.3	7.9
Probably would	7.3	1.5	9.3	2.1	5.5	2.6
Don't know	6.7	16.9	16.3	19.1	7.3	21.1
Probably not	21.2	20.0	9.3	12.8	23.4	21.1
Definitely not	57.6	53.8	48.8	59.6	56.4	47.4
". . .policeman. . ."						
Sure would	15.1	21.5	30.2	25.5	30.4	18.4
Probably would	13.9	12.3	16.3	14.9	14.3	21.1
Don't know	7.8	15.4	18.6	19.1	14.3	18.4
Probably not	16.9	16.9	18.6	8.5	14.3	13.2
Definitely not	46.4	33.8	16.3	31.9	26.8	28.9
". . .garbage collector. . ."						
Sure would	3.6	3.1	4.7	4.3	3.6	0.0
Probably would	5.4	4.6	4.7	4.3	5.4	7.9
Don't know	4.8	9.2	4.7	8.5	3.6	10.5
Probably not	18.1	18.5	16.3	12.8	16.1	15.8
Definitely not	68.1	64.6	69.8	70.2	71.4	65.8
". . .factory worker (assembly line). . ."						
Sure would	3.6	7.7	4.7	6.4	1.8	2.6
Probably would	6.6	4.6	9.3	4.3	3.6	5.3
Don't know	1.8	9.2	2.3	8.5	1.8	10.5
Probably not	22.9	15.4	14.0	6.4	17.9	13.2
Definitely not	65.1	63.1[c]	69.8	74.5	75.0	68.4
". . .auto mechanic. . ."						
Sure would	4.2	7.7	7.0	6.4	3.6	10.5
Probably would	6.6	12.3	4.7	17.0	0.0	15.8
Don't know	5.4	6.2	9.3	6.4	10.7	5.3
Probably not	21.7	18.5	20.9	12.8	26.8	15.8
Definitely not	62.0	55.4	58.1	57.4	58.9	52.6[c]
". . .security guard in bank or store. . ."						
Sure would	15.7	20.0	20.9	17.0	16.1	21.1
Probably would	21.1	20.0	25.6	19.1	21.4	21.1
Don't know	7.8	10.0	7.0	10.6	7.1	10.5
Probably not	21.1	15.4	16.3	12.8	25.0	10.5
Definitely not	34.3	33.8	30.2	40.4	30.4	36.8
"Thinking ahead five years from now, do you think you will still be a correctional officer?"						
Yes	70.7	67.2	73.2	67.4	72.7	57.1
No	29.3	32.8	26.8	32.6	27.3	42.9
		(11.0)				(8.0)

Continued on next page

Table 12 continued

	All guards (n = 231)		New guards[a] (n = 90)		Young guards[b] (n = 94)	
	White (n=165)	Black (n=66)	White (n=43)	Black (n=47)	White (n=56)	Black (n=38)
"Would you like to see your son become a correctional officer?"						
Yes	20.6	36.5	25.6	40.0	24.0	31.6
No	74.2	60.3	69.2	57.8	70.0	68.4
Up to him	5.2	3.2	5.1	2.2	6.0	0.0
	(6.0)				(9.0)	
"Suppose that you were at a party and someone you didn't know very well asked you what you do for a living. How would you feel telling him that you are a correctional officer?"						
Very proud	34.9	42.2	44.2	46.8	37.5	43.2
Somewhat proud	12.0	9.4	18.6	8.5	17.9	13.5
Just like any job	47.0	34.4	30.2	29.8	37.5	27.0
Somewhat embarrassed	5.4	7.8	4.7	6.4	5.4	10.8
Very embarrassed	0.6	6.3[c]	2.3	8.5	1.8	5.4

NOTE: All percentages and statistics are based on the responses of those guards who answered specific questions. Non-response rates of over 5% of a given sample for a given question are reported in parentheses.

[a] All guards with less than four years' experience.

[b] All guards under forty years of age (56% of young guards are also new; 63% of new guards are also young).

[c] $n^2 p$ .05.

For less experienced and younger blacks, police work is more desirable, but it still ranks second to private security. Among the less experienced and younger whites, there is an indication of a "frustrated policeman syndrome." For this group, guard work may reflect a strong desire to work in law enforcement.

Although a majority of guards of both races would not like to see their sons follow their occupation, blacks more often would approve such a choice. Their response may reflect the fact that job opportunities for blacks continue to lag far behind those available to whites. State employment offers a salary, security, and promotional opportunities better than what many individuals from a minority background can find in the private sector. But it may well be that being a prison guard or a police officer is more stigmatizing for black officers than for whites. Members of the minority community more frequently come into direct contact with society's agencies of social control and are more likely to hold a police officer or prison guard in contempt (Alex 1968). While black officers in our sample are slightly more proud of their occupation than whites, young blacks are twice as likely to find themselves "embarrassed" to tell people what they do for a living.

Conclusions

Although the black correction officers are younger, more urban, better educated, and more liberal than their white colleagues, there were no consistent differences in their attitudes toward prisoners, staff, correctional goals, or their occupation. Why?

It is possible, as with all survey research, that the guards' responses were self-serving. Respondents may have provided the "socially desirable" answers. Historically, officials have been secretive about prison procedures, and guards may be particularly wary of stating their true feelings.

Another explanation of our failure to find significant differences in the attitudes of black and white guards on a variety of measures is that the prison organization may succeed in screening out black guards who are sympathetic to the prisoners before the officers complete their six- to nine-month probationary service. Support for this hypothesis is found in a study by Jacobs and Grear (1977) which reveals "a picture of guard recruits, particularly blacks, failing to meet the expectations of old time and top echelon guards and refusing to accept the definition of the situation prescribed by the elite." Those who do not go along with the system either resign or are fired.

Finally, prison guard may be a "master status" (Hughes 1958) that washes out extraorganizational allegiances. Since there are no consistent attitudinal differences between guards with less than four years' seniority and other guards, complete socialization into a guard subculture and adoption of an occupational ideology must be established before the fourth year and perhaps as early as the six-month point when an officer is either certified or dismissed. Conflict between prisoners and guards may be so structured into organizational roles that only a certain kind of "working personality" enables the officer to survive.

We emphasize that recruitment of minority guards is itself an important societal goal, because it expands job opportunities in an area where minorities have been traditionally excluded. For this reason alone, increasing the proportion of black guards is socially justifiable as well as legally compelled. We should not unquestioningly accept, however, the belief that this change in the demographic composition of the work force will automatically have a salutary effect on the atmosphere of the prison. It is important to recall that prison conflict has not been limited to situations in which rural white guards confront urban, black prisoners. Extreme violence has occurred in such institutions as the Tombs, Rikers Island, and the Cook County Jail, where the majority of both guards and inmates are black. Historically, of course, violent riots have broken out in state prisons where a majority of both guards and prisoners have been white.

Perhaps Sykes (1958) was closer to the truth two decades ago when he dismissed changing patterns of guard recruitment as a means for reforming the prison. He, like some other recent observers, stressed how attitudes and behavior are built into the organization of the maximum security prison. Our data support this hypothesis. While answers to a questionnaire may not be perfect indicators of behavior on the job, there is nothing in these responses to suggest that black guards treat inmates with greater respect or sensitivity. They do not hold more rehabilitative views. Neither have they aligned themselves with the inmates against the administration.

[9]

Female Guards in
Men's Prisons

Some county jails, state correctional systems, as well as the Federal Bureau of Prisons, have begun hiring women to fill guard positions in men's prisons. This departure from previous policy descends from the social and political power of the women's movement, federal equal employment opportunity law, the public employee union movement, and the penological theory that women guards will contribute to prisoner rehabilitation by "normalizing" the penal environment. Opponents of this change, including rank-and-file male guards, dispute the capacity of women to maintain order and discipline. They also argue that stationing women guards in cell houses invades male inmates' right of privacy. Furthermore, some critics resist the idea of women guards in men's prisons because they fear it will require broadening the role of male guards in women's prisons.

Like many other contemporary issues of penal policy, the opposite-sex guard question is now being thrashed out in the courts. Women have attacked explicit employment restrictions in all-male prisons as well as apparently neutral height and weight requirements that disproportionately disqualify them. In a few cases, prisoners themselves have sought to reverse on privacy grounds a state correctional department's decision to hire opposite-sex guards.

The issue facing corrections is whether prisons will continue as single-sex institutions or whether women employees will have a major role in penal administration. My view is that concerns for a stable penal environment and prisoners' privacy complaints are not insurmountable obstacles to equal employ-

Reprinted, by permission, in slightly different form from the University of Toledo *Law Review*, 10 (Winter 1979).

ment opportunities. In those jurisdictions that employ women guards in men's facilities, the experience so far indicates no breakdown of order.[1] Structural changes in the cell houses and selectivity in assignments can greatly mitigate, and possibly resolve, the more thorny privacy problem.

The time is now ripe to cast off traditional stereotypes about both women and prisons.[2] The notion that men's prisons must inevitably be powder kegs of violence may prove to be more a consequence of societal expectations than an immutable feature of penal institutions.[3] It may be that institutions perpetually braced for violence do indeed experience it, or at least perceive that they are experiencing it. Perhaps if women were more fully integrated into the prison staff, expectations of conduct would change and violence would decrease. In any case, despite the dangerousness of prisons, Title VII (42 U.S.C. §2000e − 2) requires that women be allowed to compete individually for all positions in corrections.

Dothard v. Rawlinson

Dothard v. Rawlinson (1977) provides a starting point for analyzing the policy issues and legal problems associated with the sexual integration of the prison guard force. Prior to graduating from the University of Alabama with a degree in correctional psychology, Dianne Rawlinson applied to the Alabama Board of Corrections for a job as a correctional counselor, commonly known as a prison guard. Despite her superior educational qualifications, she was rejected because she failed by five pounds to meet the minimum statutory weight requirement for the position. Rawlinson filed a sex discrimination charge with the Equal Employment Opportunity Commission. After receiving a right-to-sue letter, she brought a federal class action charging that Alabama's height and

[1] There are no published studies on the performance of women guards. I draw this conclusion from informal interviews with prison officials in New York, Illinois, Minnesota, California, and the Federal Bureau of Prisons.

[2] Those who "instinctively" feel that women cannot function in the front lines of law enforcement should recall the fate of a similar stereotype about the capacity of blacks to serve in military combat. The myth that black soldiers could not fight was not dispelled until the Korean War (*see* Moskos 1973).

[3] I know of no sound research that documents crime rates in prisons. In a previous publication I pointed out that the number of very serious crimes at Stateville Penitentiary, Illinois' largest maximum security prison, was quite small. This conclusion was surprising in light of guards' and inmates' claims to the contrary (Jacobs 1976a). None of the other articles in the volume in which my article appeared shows that prisons are any more dangerous than core areas in our big cities. I believe that the data would show most prisons to be less dangerous. No one has yet proposed banning women from dangerous inner city areas. It seems strange to assume that many women who have grown up in high crime rate areas have not developed the savvy and street sense to deal effectively with male prisoners.

weight qualifications for law enforcement positions violated Title VII. She also challenged an administrative regulation, adopted during the pendency of the lawsuit, barring women from "contact positions" (posts requiring "continual close proximity to inmates" in men's maximum security prisons).[4]

The three-judge district court held that height and weight qualifications that disproportionately disqualify women constitute prima facie violations of Title VII (*Meith v. Dothard* 1976). Since the Alabama Board of Corrections failed to show how height and weight requirements are job related, the court enjoined their use. The court also struck down the state's "no contact" rule because the state failed to produce evidence showing that women could not serve successfully in men's prisons. Indeed, plaintiff's witnesses testified that females were successfully serving in several Alabama male youth facilities and that women guards in other correctional systems had contributed to the "normalization" of the penal environment. The court rejected arguments that maximum security prisons are too dangerous for women and that the presence of women guards would infringe upon the privacy of male prisoners.

The Supreme Court (*Dothard v. Rawlinson* 1977), in an opinion by Justice Potter Stewart, affirmed the elimination of the height and weight requirements, but reversed the invalidation of the no contact rule, holding that the guard position falls within the bona fide occupational qualification (bfoq) exception (§703(e)) to Title VII. Justice William Rehnquist, in a concurring opinion joined by Chief Justice Warren Burger and Justice Harry Blackmun, suggested that height and weight requirements might well be upheld in other contexts. Justice Thurgood Marshall, joined by Justice William Brennan, agreed that the height and weight requirements could not pass Title VII muster, but disagreed about the legality of the no contact rule. Justice Byron White dissented because he did not think there had been a prima facie showing of sex discrimination.

Rawlinson is the first decision by the Supreme Court, or any federal appellate court, upholding an employer's claim that a job should be limited to members of one sex. The case is all the more remarkable because the Supreme

---

[4] Administrative Regulation 204 provides that positions with the Alabama Board of Corrections will be open to members of both sexes, except where a process of "selective certification" designates a position as only appropriate for members of one sex. The grounds for obtaining a selective certification are the following:

A. That the presence of the opposite sex would cause disruption of the orderly running and security of the institution.

B. That the position would require contact with the inmates of the opposite sex without the presence of others.

C. That the position would require patrolling dormitories, restrooms, or showers while in use, frequently, during the day or night.

D. That the position would require search of inmates of the opposite sex on a regular basis.

E. That the position would require that the Correctional Counselor Trainee not be armed with a firearm.

Court chose to broaden the reach of Title VII's bfoq exception in spite of a three-judge lower court finding that there was no evidence to support the employer's claim. In effect, the Supreme Court held that the lower court was clearly erroneous, without being able to point to any evidence on the record showing that women could not serve successfully in Alabama's men's prisons. Unfortunately, the opinion reflects a "gut reaction" rather than a careful consideration of women's statutory rights to equal employment opportunity and the realities of prison life.

Since *Rawlinson* is the Supreme Court's first pronouncement on the scope of Title VII's bfoq exception, the full implications of the decision for women's employment opportunities are not yet clear. It was in the context of Alabama's very dangerous and poorly managed maximum security prisons held unconstitutional in *Pugh v. Locke* (1976) that Justice Stewart's opinion upheld the exclusion of women from the guard force on the ground that they would be vulnerable to assault by "predatory sex offenders." Perhaps the opinion will not warrant finding a bfoq exception in less deplorable prisons in other states.[5]

The deference paid to the claims of prison officials by the Supreme Court's *Rawlinson* majority strongly suggests that women could be legally excluded from all maximum security prisons, and perhaps from medium and minimum security institutions as well. Prisons, by definition, are populated by individuals who pose serious threats to the community, and all maximum security prisons hold at least some "predatory sex offenders." Unless prospective women guards are able to prove the negative — that they will not be more vulnerable to attack and will not destabilize the prison regime — the momentum of the *Rawlinson* decision will probably lead other courts to conclude that the role of women in men's penal facilities should be limited. The effects of the decision may also radiate to juvenile institutions, other male-dominated law enforcement agencies, such as the police, and even to the armed forces, where women have made important strides in the last few years.[6]

Height and Weight Standards

Despite the *Rawlinson* holding that neutral height and weight standards cannot be used to bar applicants from guard positions, this ruling may actually open

[5] In *Gunther v. Iowa State Men's Reformatory* (1979), an Iowa case that followed closely on the heels of *Rawlinson*, a district court judge held that security concerns did not justify limiting women's employment opportunities in the Iowa Reformatory. The judge explained that "[T]he Supreme Court painstakingly limited its decision upholding a male bfoq in the Alabama penitentiaries to that peculiarly inhospitable environment. Anamosa [the Iowa Reformatory] is no rose garden; neither is it the stygian spectre which faced the Supreme Court in *Dothard v. Rawlinson*." The decision was upheld by the Circuit Court; the Supreme Court denied *certiori*.

[6] For an overview of litigation on the military, see Beans (1975); for sex discrimination suits against police, see *Smith v. Trovan* (1975); *Officers for Justice v. Civil Serv. Comm'n of San Francisco* (1975); *Peltier v. City of Fargo* (1975); *Hardy v. Stumpf* (1974).

the way for law enforcement departments to limit job opportunities for women. We will consider this issue — as did the *Rawlinson* Court — before examining Title VII's bfoq exception.

The *Rawlinson* majority held that national statistics on the sex distribution of height and weight showed that the minima imposed by Alabama disproportionately disqualified women from law enforcement positions and thus constituted a prima facie violation of Title VII. According to Justice Stewart, the Board of Corrections had not carried its burden of proving how height and weight minima are job related. This much of the opinion would be a victory for women's efforts to achieve equality of employment opportunity were it not for the Court's suggestion that strength might be upheld as job related. Law enforcement agencies might now be tempted to establish strength tests, or to justify height and weight requirements on the ground that they are correlated with strength.

Justice Rehnquist's opinion, in which Chief Justice Burger and Justice Blackmun joined, supports this reading of *Rawlinson* as a retreat from Title VII's mandate for equal employment opportunity. Justice Rehnquist concurred in that part of Justice Stewart's opinion which invalidated the height and weight requirements because he did not think that the district court's conclusion — that there was no evidence in the record to demonstrate a relationship between height and weight and strength — was clearly erroneous. Justice Rehnquist emphasized, however, that the district court's conclusion was "by no means *required* by the proffered evidence." If the lower court had decided that there was sufficient evidence to demonstrate such a relationship, Justice Rehnquist certainly would have permitted the height and weight criteria to stand. Thus, he stated, "In other cases there could be different evidence which could lead a District Court to conclude that height and weight *are* in fact an accurate enough predictor of strength to justify, under all the circumstances, such minima." Justice Rehnquist's warning that the Court's decision should not be taken as a repudiation of height and weight qualifications for law enforcement jobs opened a door that most lower courts had assumed was closed.[7] He also pointed

---

[7] In *Officers for Justice v. Civil Serv. Comm'n of San Francisco* (1975), the San Francisco Police Department attempted to justify its 5'6" height requirement for Q-2 patrol positions on the basis of a relationship between a police officer's height and the frequency of assaults against him. Despite a weak positive correlation, the court refused to permit the department to maintain the test. On the other hand, in *Smith v. Troyan* (1975), the Sixth Circuit accepted the 5'8" height requirement for East Cleveland police officers on the grounds that (1) taller officers have a psychological advantage and (2) there is an advantage of height in effecting arrests and emergency aid. The court rejected the 150-pound weight requirement as having no correlation to physical strength or to psychological advantage.

In response to the many questions raised by these suits, a study was undertaken to consider whether height is related to police performance (White and Bloch 1975). Police departments from Dallas; Oakland; Nassau County, New York; and Dade County, Florida, submitted data. Since the participating departments used different formats for recording personnel information the authors could not make performance comparisons among the various groups. Nonetheless,

out that a corrections department could justify height and weight qualifications because of their relation to the appearance of strength, which contributes to the effective exercise of authority. The validity of this hypothesis is not supported by evidence in the *Rawlinson* case or by research data. Social psychological data suggest that the impact of size on the successful exercise of authority is probably not great. Research on the relationship between height and status or authority tends to show the reverse of the relationship suggested by advocates of height standards. Several recent studies show that perception of height is affected by the status attributed to the one perceived. The results were the same when status was conferred either by social standing, academic achievement, or employment position (*see* Koulack and Tuthill 1972; Wilson 1968; Dannenmaier and Thumin 1964).

Police departments and other agencies, which have revised their height and weight requirements in response to a slew of recent federal court decisions, may interpret *Rawlinson* as a signal to resurrect old standards or to construct new ones. Future litigation may focus on whether women, who tend to be smaller and lighter than men, fail to project the appearance of strength.

The Importance of Strength

In *Rawlinson*, the Alabama Board of Corrections did not introduce evidence on the relation between height and weight and strength. It is possible that in future litigation law enforcement agencies will be able to prove that these variables are correlated, especially if strength is defined in terms of capacity to lift heavy weights. Mere correlation, however, does not contradict the fact that height and weight criteria would bar from employment many small and light individuals of both sexes who could lift as much weight, or more, than taller, heavier persons. Therefore, if the ability to lift weight is job related, a department of corrections should still be required to test applicants individually rather than relying on height and weight as a crude surrogate for strength. This is especially true because height and weight criteria discriminate against women and hispanics — two groups protected by Title VII (*see, e.g., Castro v. Beecher* 1971).

We know, of course, that law enforcement agencies, particularly departments of correction, are not really trying to screen out poor weight lifters. These agencies are looking for employees who can handle physical confrontations competently. While research has disclosed no data on the relation between height and weight and the ability and willingness to use physical force, these

---

within several of the groups studied, seniority and duty assignment significantly affected officer performance, while height did not. Furthermore, in two departments (Nassau County and Dallas) where the experience variable was controlled, height differences had negligible effect on performance. Unfortunately, the study is almost exclusively confined to data on officers 5'7" and taller. It is possible that under that threshold, performance would be affected.

variables do not intuitively seem to be strongly correlated. Common experience reinforces the notion that self-defense skills are easily learned and displayed by individuals of all sizes and shapes. Aggressiveness and courage may be even less dependent on size. Prisoners themselves, a group disproportionately representative of highly combative persons, do not appear to vary from the rest of the population (of similar-aged persons) in height and weight. And even if smaller persons generally test lower on physical combat skills, those who apply for law enforcement positions are a self-selected sample. Short, light individuals who seek careers in law enforcement may be unusual in the degree to which they have developed highly effective combat skills.

Studies in various police departments lend no support to the contention that the appearance of strength is an important qualification for law enforcement work. A Portland study found no significant relation between a police officer's height and the probability of being assaulted (McNamara 1973). Cheryl Swanson and Charles Hale (1975) found little difference between the heights of assaulted and nonassaulted police officers in thirteen southwestern ciities. Peter Bloch and Deborah Anderson's (1974) careful analysis of the District of Columbia Police Department concluded that taller officers perform more poorly than smaller ones. Taller officers were given lower overall performance ratings by the department and lower ratings on the Chief's Survey on their general ability to patrol. They were less likely than shorter officers to have received favorable comments from the public, and they were observed to evoke comparatively poor reactions from victims. The only favorable relation found between height and performance was that tall men were observed to receive more favorable reactions when they handled arguments inside residences.

Most important, the final report of a year-long study on patrolwomen in Washington exploded many of the myths about women's reactions to violence. Observers noted that neither sex had a general advantage during threatening situations encountered on patrol. Additionally, the majority of citizens rated men and women about the same in handling aggressive behavior. A similar study done in New York City concluded that women had greater success than men in cooling violent situations (Sichel 1978).

There is simply no compelling, or even strong, evidence to justify excluding smaller and lighter individuals from law enforcement jobs. At the very least, Title VII should put the burden on employers to demonstrate that height and weight are strongly correlated with a specific operational definition of strength which can be shown to be job related. Even when this burden is met, law enforcement agencies should be compelled to test applicants individually rather than exclude them categorically. This is especially true where, as here, such characteristics as height and weight disproportionately exclude members of groups explicitly protected by Title VII.

Qualifications for Prison Guards

Unfortunately the prison guard has not been the subject of much scholarly study; little is known about the extent to which guards must rely on force and coercion. There is a body of research, however, that does suggest that skillful interpersonal relations are more important than physical force (Sykes 1956:257–62; Glaser 1964). Of course, guards must effectively exercise authority. An officer must be able to tell prisoners what to do and what not to do and must stop a fight if one breaks out. But on a day-to-day basis, a guard's authority and effectiveness depend more upon negotiation and accommodation than coercion.

The prison guard is expected to carry out a wide range of activities, from reporting prison rule violations to counseling prisoners about personal problems.[8] Duties such as supervising and keeping order among prisoners, taking required action in emergencies to prevent escapes or suppress disorders, and enforcing rules require the ability to exercise authority confidently. But each guard is far outnumbered by prisoners, and the need to coexist for months and years with prisoners places a premium on maturity, leadership, self-confidence, judgment, and effective interpersonal relations. It is simply not necessary (and probably not possible) for a guard to rely on force or threat of force to carry out job responsibilities. Numerous women employees who successfully function in tough juvenile institutions, as well as physically unfit and aging male guards who work in maximum security prisons, attest to this fact as does the absence of any requirements for guards to remain physically fit after they join the force. It should also be recalled that women teachers, secretaries, nurses, and administrators have been regularly functioning members of the prison staff, for at least the last decade. While their duties differ from those of prison guards, they still experience much sustained contact with prisoners, and the degree to which they are now accepted is instructive — earlier in the century it would not have been thought possible to employ women in these roles either.

Corrections departments might do well to require good health and physical fitness and then evaluate candidates on a variety of measures. Some candidates, deficient in combat skills, may compensate by their experience, moti-

[8] The Alabama Board of Corrections provides the following job description: "Patrols prisons and prison yards; stands watch in halls, at gates, or in wall towers; makes regular reports to supervisors. Supervises and keeps order among prisoners assigned to work in prison kitchens, shops, mills, laundries, or on farms. Enforces regulations covering sanitation and personal care. Inspects all traffic into and out of prison proper. Maintains constant watch for and reports unusual conditions or disturbances; keeps firearms in readiness for use if necessary; takes required action in emergencies to prevent escapes or suppress disorder; assists in recapture of escaped prisoners. Explains to inmates rules, procedures and services available at correctional institutions; counsels individual inmates regarding personal problems, educational and vocational opportunities and work assignments. Evaluates inmate behavior and adjustment to a correctional environment; submits evaluation reports. Instructs inmates in personal hygiene, discipline and proper etiquette. Performs related work as required."

[185]

vation, and skill in interpersonal relations. A well-balanced guard force might be composed of several different types of guards who might even be following divergent career paths. Some athletic types might seek to move up the custody ranks to lieutenant and captain, while other guards, oriented toward interpersonal relations, might aspire to become counselors, trainers, and the like. Whatever the job qualifications, the important point is to break away from stereotyped thinking about both prisons and sex roles.

The No Contact Rule

The second and more far-reaching issue in *Rawlinson* was whether Alabama could justify its refusal to hire women for contact positions in men's maximum security prisons under the bona fide occupational qualification (bfoq) exception to Title VII.

> "Notwithstanding any other provision of this subchapter [42 USC §§2000e − 1 to 2000e − 17], (1) it shall not be unlawful employment practice for an employer to hire and employ employees, for an employment agency to classify, or refer for employment any individual, for a labor organization to classify its membership or to classify or refer for employment any individual, or for an employer, labor organization, or joint labor-management committee controlling apprenticeship or other training or retraining programs to admit or employ any individual in any such program, on the basis of his religion, sex, or national origin in those certain instances where religion, sex or national origin *is a bona fide occupational qualification reasonably necessary to the normal operation of that particular business or enterprise* . . . . [emphasis added.]

Prior to *Rawlinson*, courts had construed the bfoq exception very narrowly. In *Weeks v. Southern Bell Telephone Co.* (1969) the employer sought to exclude women from jobs that required lifting more than thirty pounds. The Fifth Circuit found that Congress intended to allow women to decide for themselves what jobs are too physically demanding or dangerous.[9] The court held that to establish a bfoq, "the employer has the burden of proving that he had reasonable cause to believe . . . that all, or substantially all women would be unable to perform safely and efficiently the duties of the job involved." The Court of Appeals for the Fifth Circuit reaffirmed this holding in *Diaz v. Pan American World Airlines* (1971), where it rejected the district court's finding

[9] In part, the Court said: "Moreover, Title VII rejects just this type of romantic paternalism as unduly Victorian and instead vests individual women with the power to decide whether or not to take on unromantic tasks. Men have always had the right to determine whether the incremental increase in remuneration for strenuous, dangerous, obnoxious, boring or unromantic tasks is worth the candle. The promise of Title VII is that women are now to be on equal footing. We cannot conclude that by including the bona fide occupational qualification exception Congress intended to renege on that promise" (*Weeks v. Southern Bell Tel. Co.* 1969:236).

that customer preference for female stewardesses justified the exclusion of males from the occupation. The Ninth Circuit in *Rosenfeld v. Southern Pacific Co.* (1971) rejected a railroad's argument that certain jobs should be certified as "male only" with an even narrower interpretation of the bfoq exception: "Equality of footing is established only if employees otherwise entitled to the position, whether male or female, are excluded *only on a showing of individual incapacity.*"

With this background of judicial disinclination to accept the bfoq defense, it is not surprising that the three-judge district court in *Rawlinson* rejected the (state) employer's contention that being male should constitute a bfoq for the position of prison guard. It concluded that "labelling a job as 'strenuous' and then relying on stereotyped characterization of women will not meet the burden of demonstrating a bfoq. There must be some objective, demonstrable evidence that women cannot perform the duties associated with the job."

Although Justice Stewart acknowledged that Congress intended the bfoq exception to be very narrow, he found that the deplorable conditions of the Alabama prisons, fueled by the presence of "predatory male sex offenders," justified the exclusion of women. He reasoned that a woman could not successfully serve as a prison guard in the Alabama prisons because womanhood itself made female officers uniquely vulnerable to sexual assault, thereby increasing the instability of the total prison environment.

The validity of Justice Stewart's opinion is questionable in light of the facts. The only evidence on the record of a woman's special vulnerability was testimony of one attack on a female clerical worker in an Alabama prison and "an incident" involving a woman student who was taken hostage during a visit to one of the maximum security prisons. The record did not provide comparative data on the percentage of male guards involved in similar conflicts with prisoners during the same time period. Thus, there was no basis for concluding that women are more susceptible to assault than men.[10] The Su-

---

[10] There are no empirical studies on this subject to date. Personal inquiry indicates that no major problems have appeared in the states that have moved to expand job opportunities for women in corrections. Illinois officials report that there have been no attacks on female officers by male prisoners since they have been introduced into male facilities. As of November 1977, 39 women officers and 28 trainees are serving in medium or maximum male facilities. Despite a knife attack on one woman officer at Attica, New York's corrections officials feel that the sexual integration of the guards has been a success. Approximately 157 women are serving in male facilities throughout the state. (Subsequent to the attack at Attica a prisoner committee presented a formal apology.)

The California Attorney General filed an amicus brief that informed the Court that "[T]he integration of women into the staffs of previously all male facilities has been going on for more than ten years" (Motion of State of California for Leave to File Brief as Amicus Curiae and Amicus Curiae Brief, *Dothard v. Rawlinson* 1977:3).

In a personal interview conducted with Warden Nelson, he reported that during the first two years of operation there were no sexual assaults to his knowledge on female staff at the Metropolitan Correctional Center despite the fact that they made up approximately one-fourth of the force

preme Court's handling of the issue is even less satisfactory because it treated the lower court's findings as clearly erroneous.

Even if evidence had been offered to show that women were more frequently assaulted than men, it would still have been arguable that Title VII prohibits excluding all women from the job. Guidelines published by the EEOC specifically state that such wholesale exclusion undermines the basic thrust of Title VII: "The principle of nondiscrimination requires that individuals be considered on the basis of individual capacities and not on the basis of any characteristics generally attributed to the group" (EEOC Guidelines on Sex Discrimination, 29 C.F.R. §1604.2(a)(ii)(1976). Proof that more women than men are assaulted is not incompatible with the possibility that some (and possibly many) women either are not victimized or are victimized less frequently than most men. To justify a blanket exclusion of all women, a state should be required to prove that the cause of assaults on women officers is necessarily connected with "womanhood" and does not vary among individual women. Justice Stewart made exactly this point by asserting that by being a woman, a female guard was more likely to be assaulted by "predatory sex offenders." This "conclusion," however, was not based on the record. One could not determine from the record whether predatory sex offenders are more likely to assault female guards than male guards. It is hardly farfetched to suggest that prisoners with poor self-images and sexual maladjustment might be prone to strike out against male authority figures. On occasion male guards have been homosexually raped, especially during riots (Jacobs 1977; State of New Mexico 1980). Moreover, the record did not indicate whether the two "incidents" involving women were perpetrated by "sex offenders." This unsupported premise in the majority opinion seems to reflect nothing more than a "gut reaction" that it is not appropriate for women to serve in male maximum security prisons.

Assuming that the unproven assertion that female guards are more likely to be assaulted is true, it is still insufficient justification for denying women the opportunity to choose a dangerous occupation. Title VII promises to end employment discrimination based upon notions of "romantic paternalism,"

---

and were assigned duties without regard to sex. While the MCC is a federal jail, not a state prison, it handles a wide range of state and federal prisoners, the former residing at the jail when they are in town on writs.

The situation in Illinois's state prisons is similar. According to the chief of program services, "The reaction of the line staff is mixed with some being totally supportive, some being amused, and some being outright hostile [sic]" (letter from Philip G. Shayne, Chief of Program Services, State of Illinois Department of Corrections to James B. Jacobs, November 10, 1977).

Commenting on his experience with female guards in Illinois's Joliet Correctional Center (an all-male maximum security prison), Warden Dennis J. Wolff said, "The presence of women is long overdue. We're glad to see women in our facility. It adds a new dimension to corrections. It's a little too soon to say, but I tend to think that women are more respected than male guards" (Kleinman, *As Guards Women Help Bring Down Prison Walls, Chicago Tribune*, February 5, 1978).

and allow women to work in dangerous occupations if they so desire. Many courts have stated that employers must have reasons, other than the protection of women workers, to justify discriminating on the basis of sex. In this regard, Justice Stewart stated, again without explanation, that the extra vulnerability of women to attack (by "predatory sex offenders") would have a ripple effect on the whole prison environment, endangering the lives and safety of other guards and employees. At best, this is an unproven hypothesis; there simply are no data to support it. Even if valid, it should not have ended the analysis. One still needs to consider whether any increase in overall dangerousness would suffice to exclude all women or whether increased instability in the penal environment, unless substantial, is a cost which must be borne in order to vindicate other societal goals and individual rights. After all, the extension of all constitutional rights to prisoners arguably increases danger to some degree — at least this could be said of decisions limiting censorship and arbitrary discipline. A few attacks, more or less, in the "jungle atmosphere" of the Alabama prison should not justify a categorical denial of employment opportunities for women. To hold the contrary would mean that women could legally be barred from all administrative, medical, educational, and clerical positions on the ground that their presence marginally increases overall instability.

Justice Marshall's dissent observed that running a state penal system in violation of the Eighth Amendment should not justify employment discrimination against women.

> The statute requires that a bfoq be "reasonably necessary to the normal operation of that particular business or enterprise." But no governmental "business" may operate "normally" in violation of the Constitution... A prison system operating in blatant violation of the Eighth Amendment is an exception that should be remedied with all possible speed, as Judge Johnson's comprehensive order in *Pugh v. Locke*, is designed to do. In the meantime, the existence of such violations should not be legitimated by calling them "normal." Nor should the court accept them as justifying conduct that would otherwise violate a statute intended to remedy age-old discrimination. [*Dothard v. Rawlinson* (1977):345].

Justice Marshall also warned that the notion that women are "seductive sex objects" is a traditional basis for treating them as second-class citizens:

> with all respect, this rationale regrettably perpetuates one of the most insidious of the old myths about women — that women, wittingly or not, are seductive sexual objects. The effect of the decision, made I am sure with the best of intentions, is to punish women because their very presence might provoke sexual assaults. It is women who are to pay the price in lost job opportunities for the threat of depraved conduct by prison inmates. Once again, "[t]he pedestal upon which women have been placed has . . . upon closer inspection been revealed as a cage" (citing *Sail'er Inn, Inc. v. Kirby* (1971).

Finally, if a woman's vulnerability to sexual assault does significantly increase the instability of the penal environment, the special advantages that women staff members could bring to the job might outweigh the disadvantages associated with increased dangerousness. Justice Stewart did not discuss the advantages women guards might bring to the prison. This point, however, should not be overlooked. As Justice Marshall said in his dissent:

> Presumably, one of the goals of the Alabama prison system is the eradication of inmates' antisocial behavior patterns so that prisoners will be able to live one day in free society. Sex offenders can begin this process by learning to relate to women guards in a socially acceptable manner.

The same point was made at the trial in *Dothard* by Ray Nelson, an expert witness for the plaintiffs and at the time warden of the Federal Bureau of Prisons' Metropolitan Correctional Center in Chicago. He stated that it was the policy of the Federal Bureau of Prisons to move toward "normalization" of the prison environment by integrating women into the guard force at men's institutions.[11] Theoretically, a prisoner will be better prepared to adjust to society by learning how to function in a realistic custodial environment. Since prisoners, (especially) including "predatory sex offenders," will have to learn how to live in a world populated by both sexes, it is important to allow them to interact "normally" with women while in prison. Norval Morris and Gordon Hawkins (1969:133), two prominent penologists, strenuously advocate the sexual integration of the guard force for this reason. Additionally, they argue that "women bring a softening influence to the prison society, assisting men to strengthen their inner controls through a variety of deeply entrenched processes of psychological growth."

Prisoner's Privacy

The Supreme Court in *Rawlinson* did not address the issue of prisoners' privacy rights as an independent justification, under either Title VII's bfoq exception or the Constitution, for limiting women's employment opportunities in corrections. In light of recent decisions against prisoners, one suspects that the Court was not anxious to resolve *Rawlinson* by recognizing a privacy right or interest, despite the fact that such a position might have been more defensible

---

[11] Compare the normalization theory articulated in the Amicus Brief of the State of California submitted in behalf of the plaintiff in *Rawlinson*, at 3: "The Department of Corrections and the Youth Authority have adopted as one of their primary responsibilities a policy of "normalization" within their respective institutions. Officials of these departments believe that rehabilitation will be enhanced by providing an environment which includes trained and competent professional staff of both sexes because that environment more closely approximates society than does a unisexual institution."

[190]

than the one the Court actually took. The courts will be required to deal with the privacy issue if prisoners attempt to use the Civil Rights Act (42 U.S.C. §1983) to challenge the presence of opposite sex guards, or if correctional departments claim that prisoners' privacy justifies a bfoq even when prison conditions do not justify a bfoq on *Rawlinson* grounds.

Privacy, Nudity, and Bodily Integrity

Constitutional Rights

The constitutional right of privacy propounded by the Supreme Court in *Griswold v. Connecticut* (1965), and relied upon by the Court in such cases as *Eisenstadt v. Baird* (1972) and *Roe v. Wade* (1973) continues to defy definitive explication. The very concept of privacy has so many meanings and connotations that one searching for either a philosophical or a legal point of departure is inevitably left disappointed and frustrated.[12] Any attempt to develop a unified theory of privacy, constitutional or otherwise, is clearly beyond the scope of this chapter. We can be certain, however, that no Supreme Court decision hints that an individual has a constitutional right not to be placed in a position where while undressed he or she risks observation or physical contact by persons of the opposite sex. For example, it seems highly unlikely that a female public school student could succeed in a §1983 action against a male gym teacher who improperly touched or spied on her, despite whatever tort remedies she might pursue in state court.

Of course, no one can safely predict that the Supreme Court will never articulate a right of privacy broad enough to include a right to same-sex gym teachers, police officers (at least those who conduct searches), locker room attendants, and prison guards. But despite the myriad privacy claims it has encountered, the Court has resisted the temptation to expand the constitutional right of privacy beyond the area of contraception and child bearing.[13]

Despite the absence of doctrinal support, however, several district court cases since *Rawlinson* have recognized a constitutional right to privacy which encompasses protection against intimate touching or viewing by opposite sex guards. The California district court in *Bowling v. Enomoto* (1981) ruled that male prisoners at San Quentin had a constitutional right not to be surveyed during the night by female officers who, if stationed in the cell houses, could look into the open cells and thereby view prisoners while undressed or performing excretory functions. A similar decision was rendered by a Maryland

---

[12] For a review of the topic and an effort to clarify privacy, see Tribe 1978:886-990.

[13] *See, e.g., Whalen v. Roe* (1977); *Doe v. Commonwealth's Atty. for Richmond* (1976); *Paul v. Davis* (1976); *Village of Belle Terre v. Boraas* (1974).

district court in *Hudson v. Goodlander* (1980).[14] While I believe that both these decisions go well beyond the right of privacy as it has been shaped by the Supreme Court, I do believe that prisoners' privacy concerns are important and should be accommodated where it is possible to do so without riding roughshod over equal employment opportunity.

Everyday Notions of Privacy

Despite the lack of any recognized constitutional right to have one's modesty respected by the state, one cannot ignore a strong societal concensus that supports certain obvious privacy norms. Separate toilet facilities and locker rooms are so standard a part of American society as to be taken for granted. The propriety of hiring same-sex persons to work in public restrooms and teach high school gym classes seems obvious.

In most public institutions respect for personal dignity and modesty is a matter of common decency and politeness, and the question of constitutional rights rarely arises. Only in public hospitals is it routine for orderlies, nurses, and doctors to have close contact with partially clad members of the opposite sex, and even in this setting every effort is made to avoid embarrassment. A prison, of course, is hardly a hospital. While the professionalism of the medical setting negates any sexual connotations to intimate physical contacts, the prison is a highly sexually charged setting, particularly because of the inmates' enforced heterosexual celibacy.

Privacy in the Prison

Assuming that these everyday norms of privacy, short of constitutional right, recognize the propriety of separating men and women in facilities where nudity or intimate contacts are likely to occur, these norms are not necessarily applicable in the unique world of the prison (*see* Singer 1972). The prison is probably society's least private institution. Prisoners are never out of the sight and presence of guards and other inmates (Schwartz 1972). Close and continuous supervision is more than customary; it is an organizational imperative.

---

[14] In *Sterling v. Cupp* (1981), the Supreme Court of Oregon went to great lengths to avoid the uncharted right-of-privacy waters. Instead, the court focused on the state constitution and found that a provision requiring that prisoners not be treated with "unnecessary rigor" prevents female guards from being assigned to housing units or to posts requiring "pat downs," even if prisoners are clothed. *See also Avery v. Perrin* (1979) (use of female guard to deliver mail at regularly scheduled time in New Hampshire men's prison does not violate inmate right to privacy); *Harden v. Dayton Human Rehabilitation Center* (1981) (even if prison officials have standing to assert prisoners' privacy rights, they have failed to show that job assignments could not be arranged in such a way so as to lessen the clash between privacy rights and employment rights; *Smith v. Fairman* (1982)(a light frisk, not extending to the genital area, conducted by a female guard on a male inmate does not violate the inmate's constitutional rights).

Thus, one might rightly ask whether or not privacy is compatible with incarceration.

There is scattered support for an affirmative answer to this question of prisoners' privacy in federal case law.[15] Most interestingly, the Supreme Court's decision in *Houchins v. KQED* (1978) stated that "[i]nmates in jails, prisons, or mental institutions retain certain fundamental rights of privacy; they are not like animals in a zoo to be filmed and photographed at will by the public or by media reporters, however 'educational' the process may be for others." *Bonner v. Coughlin* (1975) a Seventh Circuit opinion authored by Judge (now Justice) John Paul Stevens, also supports the proposition that some elements of privacy do survive imprisonment. In *Bonner*, a prisoner claimed that a retaliatory "shake-down" of his cell and seizure of legal papers violated his Fourth Amendment rights. Judge Stevens, while holding that a prisoner's Fourth Amendment rights are not coincident with those of free citizens, stated:

> Unquestionably, entry into a controlled environment entails a dramatic loss of privacy. Moreover, the justifiable reasons for invading an inmate's privacy are both obvious and well established. We are persuaded, however, that the surrender of privacy is not total and that some residuum meriting the protection of the Fourth Amendment survives.

A few cases involving strip searches and examination of body cavities hold to the same effect. For instance, the district court in *Hodges v. Klein* (1976) held that the state had no interest in requiring anal examinations before or after a segregation inmate is moved within the segregation area or anywhere in the prison while under escort or observation. While the court's constitutional analysis may be questionable, its recognition that some privacy norms should prevail in prison seems sound. Although it is not possible simply to dismiss prisoners' privacy claims as nonexistent, these claims, like claims of privacy in other settings, must be closely scrutinized, especially when they seem to conflict with employment opportunities of other parties.

Privacy and Title VII's BFOQ Exception

Even if the constitutional right of privacy is not broad enough to encompass the individual's embarrassment at being touched or seen in some immodest state by members of the opposite sex, it is still possible that Title VII does not require or justify hiring persons of both sexes for a job that regularly requires intimate physical or visual contacts between the employee and third parties. On its face,

[15] *See also* the recent prison law reform effort of the American Bar Association, Joint Committee on the Legal Status of Prisoners, *"Tentative Draft of Standards Relating to the Legal Status of Prisoners"* (1977). Standard 6.6 recognizes prisoners' privacy rights and places limits on searches of inmates' cells and persons.

Title VII forbids any employment discrimination on the basis of sex and provides no exemption for jobs in which the privacy interests of third parties might be infringed. Legislative history, consisting of only the most cursory comments by three legislators, barely hints that privacy norms might be considered relevant to the bfoq determination.[16] Equal Employment Opportunity Commission Guidelines, which although lacking the force of law, are often given deference by courts, explicitly state:

> (1)The Commission will find that the following situations do not warrant the application of the bona fide occupation qualification exception . . . (iii)The refusal to hire an individual because of the preference of coworkers, the employer, clients, or customers except as covered explicitly in subparagraph (2) of this paragraph.
> (2) Where it is necessary for the purpose of authenticity or genuineness. . .*e.g.* an actor or actress. [29 C.F.R. §1604.2(a)(1976)]

Obviously, these guidelines do not justify an employer's refusal to hire persons of both sexes as locker room and restroom attendants, gym teachers, or prison guards. Thus, to conclude that privacy interests permit certain jobs to be classified as appropriate for one sex only, requires an interpretation of Title VII found in neither the statutory language nor the clarifying regulations.

Given our strong societal consensus on the impropriety of mixed-sex contacts in certain situations, it is tempting to read Title VII in light of what Congress would have done had lawmakers considered the possibility that this federal law would require male gym teachers to be hired for girls' gym classes or women locker room attendants to be hired for men's locker rooms. Surely, it is inconceivable, particularly in light of the symbolic importance of the "potty issue" for the Equal Rights Amendment debate, that Congress would have imposed such a unisex standard of employment on the entire country.

A few lower courts have considered the privacy interests of third parties as they affect the opportunities of opposite sex employees. Perhaps the best known case is *Ludtke v. Kuhn* (1978), in which a female news reporter demanded the same access as male reporters to a baseball team's locker room immediately following each ballgame. In this case the New York Yankees were following the Major League Baseball Commissioner's order to ban women from the locker room, despite a players' vote in favor of admitting women reporters. Although the commissioner relied in part on the privacy rights of the ballplayers, the district court scarcely considered whether any privacy rights or privacy interests were at stake. Judge Constance Motley spoke of the reporter's fundamental right to pursue her profession and pointed out that there were many alternatives available for protecting the modesty of athletes. For example, they

---

[16] *See* 110 Cong. Rec. 2718 (1964) (remarks of Rep. Goodell); *Id.* at 7212 −13 (interpretative memo introduced by Sens. Clark and Case).

could avoid a woman reporter's line of vision by hanging a curtain over the cubicle that they used for dressing.

A similar issue arose in *Fesel v. Masonic Hospital* (1978), with regard to the refusal of a Retirement Home to hire a male nurse's aid because of the preference of the female residents. The district court found that an employer was obliged to protect its customers' personal privacy interests, and therefore permitted a retirement home to use female sex as a bfoq in hiring nurses' aids who provided intimate personal "total care." The court held, however, that privacy interests could not be the basis of a bfoq unless the employer can pass a two-part test:

> The employer must prove not only that it had a factual basis for believing that hiring of any members of one sex would directly undermine the essence of the job involved or the employer's business, but also that it could not assign job responsibilities selectively in such a way that there would be minimal clash between privacy interests of the customers and the nondiscrimination principles of Title VII. [1978:1351]

Both the *Ludtke* and *Fesel* cases suggest that privacy interests of lower stature than rights are entitled to some consideration in determining Title VII's employment requirements, as well as in limiting a third party's right to pursue a calling.

Reconciling Privacy and Equal Employment Opportunity in Prisons

Prior to *Rawlinson*, state courts rejected sex discrimination suits by women seeking employment in correctional facilities — with little attempt to explore possible ways of reconciling privacy with equal employment oportunity. The district court in *Rawlinson* recognized that under some circumstances opposite sex guards might infringe upon inmates' privacy, but stated that a reasonable compromise could be found. The district court referred to selective job assignments and shoulder-high partitions in toilet areas as possible solutions. The *Gunther* court (1979) refused to permit the Iowa Reformatory to exclude women from correctional officer II positions because some of the duties involved would infringe upon the male prisoners' privacy. Instead, the court ordered the department to eliminate duties that would infringe upon privacy from c.o. II positions held by women. Even those courts that hold that prisoners have a constitutional right of privacy have required that efforts be made to accommodate privacy and employment rights.[17]

---

[17] For example, *Bowling v. Enomoto* (1981) found that "plaintiff's privacy interests can be preserved in some way without unnecessarily infringing on the officers' right to equal employment."

Several departments of correction that have pressed forward to hire women guards have made substantial progress in defining workable rules to govern job responsibilities for guards of the opposite sex. California, for example, has promulgated the following guideline:

> Correctional personnel, other than qualified medical staff, will not conduct un-clothed body inspections or searches of inmates of the opposite sex. This does not preclude routine inspections or searches of clothed inmates without regard for the sex of the inmate or of personnel making such inspections or searches.

Likewise, in 1976, the New York Commissioner of Correctional Services issued *Guidelines for Assignments of Male and Female Correctional Officers*:

> 1. Security staff members of the opposite sex to the inmate population are not to be permanently assigned to shower areas where one has to work in open view of showering inmates.
> 2. Escort duty outside a facility should be performed only by officers of the same sex as the inmates to be escorted.
> 3. At least one officer of the same sex as the inmate population at a facility must be assigned to each housing block.
> 4. No assignment is to be made requiring an officer to conduct strip frisks of inmates of the opposite sex.
> 5. Security employees of opposite sex to the inmate population cannot exceed one-third of the total security staff at the facilities designated as maximum or medium security.
> 6. Superintendants, with the approval of the appropriate Deputy Commissioner, can make adjustments in particular assignments based upon specific institutional needs.
> 7. Unless emergency conditions dictate otherwise, correction officers of the opposite sex shall announce their presence in housing areas to avoid unnecessarily invading the privacy of the inmates of the opposite sex.

Both California and New York have used their respective guidelines to go forward with the sexual integration of the guard force. These rules provide precisely the kind of reasonable accommodation between equality of employment opportunity and privacy which is required in the prison setting. The California and New York provisions demonstrate bona fide efforts to find successful solutions.

There is every reason to believe that women can be integrated into corrections, even into front-line positions, without unduly infringing upon the privacy and dignity of male prisoners. My own experience and personal interviews suggest that male guards are more opposed to women correctional officers than are male prisoners.[18] Indeed, I suspect that a vote would show that male prisoners are generally in favor of women guards.[19]

Not all prison guards must be assigned to cell houses, and even those who are so assigned will often work during periods when there is not much nudity (*see Avery v. Perrin* 1979). Guards of either sex can, as a matter of politeness, discretely avoid eye contact with prisoners who are nude or engaged in bodily functions. Structural changes, such as shoulder-high partitions in front of toilets, would promote privacy, whatever the sex of the guards. Whenever possible, body searches should be carried out by same-sex guards, although light "pat downs" would not seem to be overly intrusive, even when conducted by the opposite sex. When male guards are not available or when emergencies require, women may be required to carry out body searches and any other duties that are part of a guard's job, just as male or female police officers, at times, must carry out intrusive searches on members of the opposite sex. As Justice Marshall stated in *Rawlinson*, one may demand and expect that the highest professional standards will be adhered to by prison staffs, especially when called upon to carry out tasks that are sensitive. Disciplinary measures and even civil and criminal penalties remain available to punish guards who abuse their authority.

Male Guards and Women's Prisons

The specter of women guards in men's prisons leads inevitably to speculation and concern about male guards in women's prisons. If Title VII requires women to be hired for front-line positions in men's prisons, it presumably also requires broadening the role of male guards in women's prisons. This possibility is likely to stimulate emotional reactions from the public. A double standard of sexual propriety is deeply rooted in our society. While claims by men that women are humiliating them sexually or are invading their modesty might be treated as quaint and even humorous by various segments of society, a claim that male jailers are humiliating and sexually abusing female prisoners will be seen by the public as a serious matter. Efforts to bring women into corrections however, should not be allowed to founder on this issue.

[18] A female guard at Clinton Correctional Facility in upstate New York reports that some of her fellow officers are less cooperative than the inmates. They also persist in making off-color comments and obscene gestures while female officers are in the duty room waiting for assignments (interview with female guards at Clinton Correctional Facility, Dannemora, N.Y. October 3, 1977). Illinois officials also report that male correctional officers cause women employees far more problems than the prisoners.

[19] In *Harden v. Dayton Human Rehabilitation Center* (1981), the Ohio Department of Corrections relied upon the privacy interests of prisoners in prohibiting employment of women in a men's prison, despite there having been no complaints by the male prisoners.

The propriety of male guards serving in women's prisons arose in New York State in 1976 when the Department of Correctional Services announced that it had acceded to the demands of the guard union for the elimination of sex certification for correction officers. Shortly after this announcement, ten female prisoners brought a class action claiming, *inter alia*, that their constitutional privacy rights were being violated because male guards "look into women's rooms and toilets unannounced and often times when the inmates are nude or partially clad. They have, in this manner, without the women inmates' consent, observed women inmates on various occasions seated on the toilet performing excretory and female hygiene functions."

The female prisoners also alleged privacy violations because male guards stationed themselves in shower areas, conducted searches, and made sexual advances. Without a hearing on the merits or any analysis of the putative constitutional privacy right involved, and despite new state guidelines aimed at respecting prisoner privacy, Judge Richard Owen granted the plaintiffs' motion to enjoin the department from assigning male guards to housing units. He also ordered the department to remove male guards currently assigned (*Forts v. Ward* 1977).

Judge Owen displayed the same kind of stereotyped thinking about relations between the sexes as did Justice Stewart in *Rawlinson*. He rhetorically asked why a woman inmate "must ask a corrections officer (who would often be a man) to come and close her door every time during every day she wished to use the toilet" or "should have to dry off in a damp shower stall instead of an anteroom made for that purpose" or "has to be awakened or observed during sleep by a male guard, her night clothes in possible disarray" or "must discuss personal female problems with hospital staff when male officers are in the room." This case is yet another example of the courts' failure adequately to analyze the constitutional right of privacy in this sensitive area of evolving sex roles in public institutions.

The Second Circuit Court of Appeals reversed the decision and sent the case back for a full factual hearing. After a two-week trial, Judge Owen ruled that male guards could be assigned to the housing units during the daytime inasmuch as inmates were permitted to cover their cell door windows for fifteen-minute intervals while dressing or attending to personal needs. He also found that privacy in the shower area could be protected by the construction of an opaque glass barrier. However, Judge Owen ordered that male guards be completely excluded from the housing units at night, despite the department's willingness to provide inmates with protective sleepwear and to extend the window covering rule. The Circuit Court again reversed:

> The privacy interest entitled to protection concerns the involuntary viewing of private parts of the body by members of the opposite sex. Since appropriate sleepwear can sufficiently protect that interest, its use should be preferred to any loss of

employment opportunities. We do not agree with the inmates that their privacy interest extends to a protection against being viewed while sleeping by male guards so long as suitable sleepwear is provided. Nor do we agree that any legally enforceable rights of inmates sufficient to impair employment rights can arise from an inmate's preference for sleepwear of her choice or for none at all. [*Forts v. Ward* 1980:1217]

The passage is worth quoting because it demonstrates a mature and sensible accommodation of privacy interests and employment rights in the context of a women's prison where, if anything, the privacy interests are more acute, the employment rights less pressing, and the potential for harmful consequences much greater.

The Problem of Sexual Abuse

Throughout history women have been sexually abused by men. Furthermore, some of the worst cases of sexual abuse have been perpetrated by male jailers on women prisoners, as is demonstrated by the recent Joan Little case (Reston 1977). It is one thing to say that women should have the opportunity to work in dangerous occupations, even if there is a threat of sexual assault; it is another to say that women must be placed involuntarily in a situation where they may be sexually abused.

The problem of sexual abuse by male guards in women's prisons should not be lightly dismissed. The desire for consistency and the aspiration for an emerging society in which the sexes can function on an equal footing should not blind us to certain realities based upon long experience. There is little doubt that employing male guards to supervise female prisoners creates a higher risk of sexual abuse of prisoners than does employing women to guard men. Therefore, courts should be less reluctant to permit a bfoq classification for guard positions in women's prisons. Furthermore, much less is at stake for men as a class since men, unlike women, have never been denied equal employment opportunity in corrections and only a small fraction of all guard positions in a state prison system are found in women's facilities since females comprise less than 5 percent of all state and federal prisoners. Nevertheless, the goal should be to adapt all prisons so that men and women can be employed on an equal basis while still protecting prisoners from sexual abuse and unnecessary invasion of privacy.

Conclusion

Pressures to achieve equal employment opportunities have begun to bring about change in American prisons. Some departments of corrections have re-

[199]

sponded to these demands by eliminating sex stereotypical hiring and assignment policies. In some states, such as New York, the union movement has generated pressure to end separate personnel policies for men and women. The most important factor, however, in the change of correctional policy in this area has been the threat of Title VII suits. Correctional officials, like other bureaucrats, are anxious to stay out of court and on the right side of the law.

Dothard v. Rawlinson may prove to be a significant setback for women wishing to serve in corrections. While the decision prohibits the use of arbitrary height and weight requirements to deny correctional jobs to women, similar requirements may yet survive if officials set out to show that height and weight standards are correlated with strength. Quite possibly, strength tests would be upheld. Standards requiring recruits to demonstrate competency in self-defense and effective use of physical force would undoubtedly be found to be job related. In addition, Justice Rehnquist's opinion in *Rawlinson* may encourage corrections departments to attempt to justify excluding women on the basis of the appearance of strength, a proposition that may appeal to judges who are reluctant to interfere with penal management.

Assuming that women can hurdle height, weight, and strength requirements, they may still be barred from most prison jobs because of no contact rules. It is conceivable, of course, that future decisions may limit the reach of *Rawlinson* to the worst prisons in the nation. But all maximum security prisons are dangerous, and none specifically isolate sex offenders. Therefore, the argument that women's vulnerability to sexual assault will increase the instability of the penal environment will be readily available in all such situations. There is no escaping the question of whether women will be permitted to continue serving as cottage parents and as front-line staff in tough juvenile institutions.[20] The future of women parole officers is also in doubt, since deprived sex offenders might be especially disposed to assault them, thereby jeopardizing the safety of fellow officers.

Rank-and-file male guards have often opposed, sometimes strongly, the introduction of women into the men's prisons. Departments may succumb to pressure, stop hiring women and remove those who are employed. This

---

[20] A few state courts, faced with similar problems, reached different results. In *City of Philadelphia v. Pa. Human Relations Comm'n* (1973) the court held that female sex could be a bfoq for supervisor positions in youth centers because the job required supervision of children (ages 7–16) when they are unclothed and because such problem children related better to members of the same sex. The second proposition lacks both a theoretical and an empirical basis. Juvenile institutions were originally staffed by women in order to shield residents from the brutality usually associated with adult facilities. Women have for decades served effectively in institutions for male juveniles. In *Long v. Cal. State Personnel Bd.* (1974) a California court rejected a clergywoman's claim that refusing to consider her application for a chaplain's position in a juvenile institution for males violated Title VII. The court justified its position on the ground that if she were raped, it could have a devastating effect on the youth (ages 18–23) center's rehabilitation program!

would be an unfortunate result. The expansion of Title VII's bfoq exception to limit employment opportunities for women, without any evidence to indicate that women cannot serve as effectively as men, threatens the inroads women have made not only in prison systems but also in other heretofore male-dominated social control organizations.

The privacy problems that inevitably arise as greater numbers of women are integrated in the prison's guard force cannot be ignored, either by courts or by departments of corrections. These problems are neither insignificant nor insurmountable. Courts are beginning to engage in serious analysis of the tension between equality of employment opportunity and personal privacy. Some corrections departments have attempted to anticipate privacy problems and find workable accommodations.

In my view, legal analysis has been inhibited because of the overemphasis upon constitutional rights. Needless to say, not every wrong finds a federal constitutional redress. To constitutionalize all of our privacy norms would go a long way toward merging constitutional law with the private law of torts. This would unduly burden the federal courts, and not necessarily achieve beneficial results. In any case, it is most unlikely that the Supreme Court will expand the constitutional law of privacy to provide a right of action for prisoners who complain of intimate visual and physical contact by guards of the opposite sex. opposite sex.

But simply because prisoners' concerns about privacy do not rise to the level of a constitutional right does not mean that privacy should not count at all. Privacy is a value, and an important one, in American society and it should be accommodated by both law and public policy. Permitting a public or private employer to rely upon the bona fide privacy concerns of third parties as a justification for classifying some positions as bfoq's is a sensible approach. Of course, this is not to say that it should be used to discriminate. Before any job is classified as a bfoq on privacy grounds, every effort must be made to find practical, workable accommodations.

[10]

The Implications of National Service for Corrections

The Idea of National Service

National service is an idea that will not be put to rest. The image of young people realizing their potential by working on behalf of their nation has reappeared throughout the twentieth century since it was first suggested by William James (1968) in his 1910 essay "The Moral Equivalent of War." It achieved partial realization in the Civilian Conservation Corps during the Depression and during the 1960s in a variety of programs such as the Peace Corps, VISTA, and even the Job Corps. Some proponents urged national service as an alternative to the military draft that became increasingly unpopular as the Vietnam War dragged on (Janowitz 1967). They argued that if all young Americans were required to serve their country for a short time, in a military or civilian capacity, not only would the nation meet its military manpower needs, but in doing so it would provide many benefits to young people and to the country. While the draft caused resentment among those chosen to serve, national service, its proponents argued, would universalize and therefore legitimate the duty to serve. Furthermore, national service would be superior to an all-volunteer force because it would strengthen citizenship norms and improve the armed forces.

If the draft had continued a few more years, national service would probably have achieved greater political support. In addition to those who favored national service as the best approach for recruiting military manpower, another constituency saw national service as an answer to a host of problems — unemployment, delinquency, drug abuse, and the alienation of the young — because it offered a transition from school to work with accompanying counseling, training, and job experience (*see, e.g.*, Mead 1967).

[202]

Whether the two proponent groups would have developed a broad-based national coalition in the late 1960s and early 1970s is a matter for conjecture. Former President Nixon preferred an all-volunteer armed forces (AVF); the President's (Gates) Commission on an All-Volunteer Force (1970), which he appointed to study the matter, ratified and provided intellectual support for his position. The commission rejected national service as too expensive and too coercive. With the end of the Vietnam War and the institutionalization of the AVF one might have expected national service to hibernate, but that has not occurred because of persistent and documented problems in the AVF and because of the indefatiguable efforts of those who support the idea.

From the beginning the AVF failed to meet many of the goals projected by the Gates Commission. In the early years, recruiting failures created doubts about the nation's ability to attract personnel through economic incentives. In fact, had the Pentagon not steadily reduced its requirement levels through the 1970s, the all-volunteer force would probably have failed (Janowitz and Moskos 1979). The commission's predictions concerning the quality of personnel who would be recruited also proved incorrect. As studies by Morris Janowitz and Charles Moskos have shown, AVF recruits are less educated, less reliable, and less representative of society than their predecessors. Not surprisingly, the combat-readiness of the AVF has been questioned both at home and abroad.

The prognosis for the future hardly inspires optimism. The capacity to maintain (or increase) force levels, in the face of a shrinking youth group, is doubtful.[1] Thus, the return of a peacetime draft or, alternatively, the introduction of some form of National Service, within the next decade, must be considered.

National service has been kept alive in Congress and in the writings and advocacy of various intellectuals and activists. In 1977 the Senate Subcommittee on Manpower and Personnel of the Armed Services Committee released a comprehensive study, commissioned by Senator Sam Nunn (D.-Ga.) and authored by William King, professor of business administration at the University of Pittsburgh, entitled "Achieving America's Goals: National Service or the All-Volunteer Force?" After reviewing the difficulties with the AVF, the report concluded that some form of national service is desirable and feasible.

Any of the wide variety of national service programs on which the nation might embark would serve to address some of the basic informational and diagnostic

[1] Secretary of Defense Caspar Weinberger reported to Congress in early 1982 that "all four services met or exceeded their recruiting goals for FY '81. But in FY '83 the limits on non-graduates and low-scoring enlistees will become more stringent and the number of recruits needed will increase from 367,000 (FY '81) to 381,000. Together with the continuing shrinkage in the number of males reaching enlistment age each year, this portends 'an extremely challenging task for recruiters in FY '83 and beyond.'" *Congressional Quarterly*, Weekly Report 40, no. 7 (February 13, 1982):252.

needs of American youth as well as to alleviate some of the present and potential problems of the AVF. A broad-scale program of national service could address and alleviate a wide-range of such needs and problems, thus enabling the nation to more effectively pursue its national goals.

Three national service bills have been introduced at recent sessions of Congress. Two of them, those presented by Congressmen McCloskey and Cavanaugh, provide for comprehensive national service programs. The third, introduced by Senator Paul Tsongas (D.-Mass) and ten cosponsors, would establish a national commission "to examine the need and the desirability and feasibility of establishing a comprehensive national service program to meet a broad range of national and local needs." Hearings were held in 1979 and 1980.

Meanwhile, advocates of social programs for youth have also taken up the national service banner. Most notable is the work of the Committee for the Study of National Service, which released its report, *Youth and the Needs of the Nation*, in February 1979. That report enthusiastically endorsed a large-scale voluntary national service system. Also in 1979 the Carnegie Council on Policy Studies in Higher Education endorsed a broad-based voluntary national service as a key feature of its overall youth policy. In 1980 the National Commission on Youth endorsed the idea of a voluntary national service.

This hardly means that passage of national service is imminent. No doubt it is an idea that is philosophically, politically, and fiscally abhorrent to the Reagan administration. (Of course, so, too, was draft registration at one time!) But administrations change, and the challenge of effectively recruiting military manpower will not go away. Neither will the problems of youth.

The discussion, debate, and testimony regarding national service has taken place on a rather abstract and philosophical plane, focusing on the reciprocal rights and obligations of the citizen and the state in a democracy: is national service forced labor or a right and obligation of citizenship? My approach is to ask whether national service is feasible. Could a full-scale national service program be implemented? What would the young recruits do? How would they be utilized in both new and existing programs? More specifically, what impact would national service have on a particular agency, such as corrections?

National Service and Corrections

Donald Eberly (1971) and Morris Janowitz (1967) have included correction facilities in their national service plans, as has Congressman Pete McCloskey (R.-Cal.) in his elaborate program. Corrections is a particularly appropriate agency for placement of national service participants; it is labor intensive and has a long tradition of accepting and even seeking volunteers (Harris 1969;

Schwartz, Jenson, and Mahoney 1977; Parker and LeCour 1978). Whether because of a romanticization of criminals or religious sentiments about raising the fallen, prisons have always attracted idealistic volunteers. Drug and alcohol abuse, community and career counseling, and religious instruction programs are commonly staffed by volunteers in prisons and jails. For example, several dozen volunteers tutor and counsel prisoners several nights per week in the PACE program at Chicago's Cook County Jail. In New York State VISTA workers tutor approximately one thousand prisoners per year (Executive Advisory Committee on Sentencing 1979). There are approximately three thousand regular volunteers serving New York State's correctional system; the majority perform service at pre-release centers, but each of the major maximum security institutions has at least one hundred regular volunteers who provide various types of counseling. Another four to five thousand perform volunteer services on an irregular basis.

A national service program would differ from existing volunteer programs. National service volunteers would be younger and have fewer skills than traditional volunteers. While most volunteer programs consume no more than a few hours per week, national service presumably would be a full-day assignment.

How national service participants would be deployed and what their impact on the prison community would be depends, of course, on the number of national service participants involved. A mere handful of young people could be assimilated with hardly a ripple. But as a point of departure, let us consider the implication of a large-scale program — for example 50,000 national service participants in correctional facilities nationwide. That number would constitute roughly 2.5 percent of all eighteen-year-olds and 20 percent of all personnel now employed in corrections. How would these young men and women be deployed in the prisons?

Their deployment, among other things, would depend upon the skills they bring with them to correctional service. Skill level would depend upon the age at which most young people would serve. Although national service might be delayed until after college, it is far more likely that service would take place immediately after high school, or in the case of those who do not complete high school, at age seventeen or eighteen. Thus young people would enter national service without specialized job training, except perhaps for a limited number trained as office clerks, typists, and educational assistants.

Lack of specialized job skills would not necessarily prove to be a disadvantage. Prisons remain highly labor-intensive organizations. Almost all institutional functions could usefully employ more personnel. Record keeping of all kinds could be vastly improved, thereby contributing to the effective implementation of due process procedures mandated during the past decade. Such mundane tasks as responding to prisoners' requests about parole and mandatory release dates could be expedited with the assistance of more clerks in the re-

[205]

cords office. Visiting procedures could be much improved if there were more personnel to sign the visitors in, conduct routine searches, and handle packages and gifts. Vocational and academic education could be enriched by a corps of tutors.

But the greatest manpower deficiency is in the uniformed ranks. All penal facilities are short-handed, and, at some, industrial, recreational, and social service programs must regularly be canceled because of insufficient supervision. The use of national service personnel as guards could mean more programming, better service delivery, and, ultimately, a reduction of violence.

It could also mean a younger, less "professional," and more idealistic guard force. The mix in age and experience for prison staff would be substantially altered if one-fifth of all positions were filled by young national service participants. A more heterogeneous staff could have distinct advantages, especially for those prisons where turnover is low. (There is considerable variation in turnover rates at different correctional facilities. In New York State, for example, Attica has an annual turnover rate of 5 percent, while Green Haven's annual turnover far exceeds 100 percent.)

It is interesting to compare correctional service to the armed forces, which strives for a mean age of less than twenty-five. To this end, the military limits re-enlistment to approximately 10 to 15 percent of those completing their initial enlistment contract. Rotating national service personnel through prisons on one-year tours of duty would ensure a similar turnover and might reduce the personal fatigue and cynicism of the permanent staff. Of course, using national service participants as uniformed guards raises many more problems than does deploying them as typists, clerks, and tutors.

Is it realistic to believe that seventeen- and eighteen-year-olds could serve successfully as guards? I think it is. It is important to note that in a majority of states eighteen-year-olds are now eligible to become state prison guards. Furthermore, we should not assume that guards are carefully screened and selected for their jobs. In most states, eligibility requirements are few, if they exist at all, and turnover is very high. National service participants, although younger on average than current recruits, would be likely to have better educational and perhaps personal qualifications.

It is inconceivable that a national service program would place young men and women on the front line at correctional facilities without some formal training. But even with good training, we can expect and must plan for a considerable number of dropouts. On the other hand, it is not a job that anyone can handle successfully. Stress is high; danger is continual. The demands of the job push some guards toward collusion with prisoners and others toward brutality (Sykes 1956). National service would serve to focus attention on the critical need for training programs.

In addition to supplying more personnel, a national service program would contribute the enthusiasm and idealism of youth to organizations all too often marked by distrust, hostility, cynicism, and the familiar "burn-out syndrome." This contribution is clearly discernible in the work of those who are currently correctional volunteers.

As many administrators will attest, "people work" is exhausting. Countless individuals enter juvenile and adult correctional facilities with the express intention of "helping" and "working with the inmates," only to lose their idealism to the "bitter realities" and demands of the prison system. National service personnel might counteract this cynicism. Their youth, along with the short term of the assignment, might keep the feeling of "mission" alive in corrections in the face of widespread cynicism about rehabilitation and loss of public support for corrections programs. However, national service's potential to inject corrections with idealism may turn on whether national service is a voluntary or compulsory program. Thus it is worth considering how a national service prototype, such as the McCloskey bill, would actually operate.

National Service Models

McCloskey's proposal (H.R. 1730, 97th Cong.) requires all seventeen-year-old males and females to register, under pain of criminal penalty, with a National Service System. Each registrant must either "volunteer" for two years of active military service, six years of reserve duty, or one year of civilian service or choose not to "volunteer" and thus be vulnerable to a draft lottery for six years. Draftees must serve two years in the military. Although McCloskey labels his proposal "voluntary," it is unmistakably a form of compulsory national service which uses the threat of conscription to induce volunteers for alternative civilian service.

McCloskey's proposal envisions federal administration, with a national director, state headquarters, and local placement centers in each county or comparable political subdivision. A national board, chaired by the national director, would regularly compile, on a nationwide basis, listings of civilian service jobs and distribute these lists to local placement centers, which would provide young people with information on available positions throughout the country. The proposal requires, however, that those who elect civilian service locate their own positions.

Two aspects of McCloskey's proposal — its compulsory nature and its failure to accept responsibility for placing registrants in civilian positions — would undermine national service's potential contribution for corrections. For any agency to reap maximum benefit from national service, it is extremely important that young people view the program as an opportunity to serve the country and not as coercion or punishment. If the latter conception prevails, it is likely

[207]

that many "volunteers" will be recalcitrant, hostile, and indifferent to the goals of corrections.

A voluntary system has a great many advantages in its own right. Over the long term, a voluntary national service system could invigorate citizenship, harness idealism, and create support for serving others and the country (Committee for the Study of National Service 1979). To encourage service norms and the inclination to volunteer, successful completion of national service could be established as a prerequisite for later employment by federal, state, or local governments; or, successful national service could, like veteran's status, constitute a preference in competition for civil service positions. Institutions of higher education could also encourage national service participation through their admission policies (*see* Moskos 1981).

The difficulty, if not the impossibility, of administering a universal or nearly universal national service system that would have to provide meaningful work for several million per year also militates in favor of a voluntary program. Instead of establishing an entire system at once, as McCloskey proposes, a modest step-by-step approach is preferable. During the 1980s the system could target meaningful service opportunities for experimentation. Corrections, with its huge manpower needs, relatively few prerequisites, and attraction for idealistic volunteers, is fertile ground for such experimentation.

The requirement that registrants find their own placement would also reduce the potential benefits of national service for such agencies as corrections. Without a nationwide employment service, most young people would likely limit their search to familiar jobs in their local area. Less benefit would accrue to corrections if national service personnel working in the prisons were sons and daughters or neighbors of prison staff than if they were representative of a wide cross section of the larger society. To encourage diversity there should be a nationally coordinated system of registration, testing, counseling, and job referral. Such a system would not only avoid the problems that attended the localism of the old Selective Service System, but would also create a better fit between individual strengths and weaknesses and service opportunities across the country.

Neither would it be particularly desirable for registrants themselves to serve in their home communities, as this would limit the potential of national service to provide a broadening experience. Like military service, Peace Corps, and VISTA, national service should provide a chance to travel, broaden one's horizons, and mix with other social groups. A truly voluntary and "national" program seems to offer the most benefits for corrections and for the registrants.

Democratizing the Prison

Prisons, like the armed forces and police, have a unique role in democratic society. They implement society's most severe punishments — incarceration and execution. It is not disingenuous to suggest that these punishments be administered democratically, with all social segments participating. Today, capital punishment and the punitive regimen of maximum security incarceration are enforced by a highly unrepresentative social group — poorly educated, white, rural males who live in economically depressed areas. A properly organized and administered national service, operated on a nationwide basis, would take advantage of diverse young men and women from all economic and cultural strata. If a broader cross section of the American population imposed punishment, both the public and prisoners themselves might perceive it as more legitimate, and, more important, prison reform might be easier to accomplish. Diversity within the prison community would stimulate discussion among members of different socioeconomic classes. Prisoners would benefit from contact with a cross section of American youth, including the college-bound. National service participants would gain some understanding of criminality and the problems of the American underclass. They would also benefit from interaction among themselves and with the permanent cadre of prison guards.

National service personnel would alter the guard force's racial and sex mix. Few blacks or Hispanics reside in the rural locales where prisons are located. Efforts to attract minorities to work and live in such towns as Attica continue to be unsuccessful. A national service system would locate, house, and provide a peer group for young minority personnel who would not otherwise seek employment in corrections.

It is possible, of course, that national service could be instituted "for men only," particularly if it were linked to conscription. A compulsory system might totally exclude women or include only a few women, for if women were not vulnerable to the draft, there would be no way to require them to serve in a civilian capacity. If only young men were to serve, however, the norm of service and national service itself would be undermined. And those who oppose equal rights for women would draw strength from a definition of citizenship that assigned disparate obligations on the basis of sex. An additional argument in favor of voluntary national service is that it would be equally available to young men and women.

If women do participate, how will they be deployed in the prisons where the overwhelming majority of inmates are males? Over the last decade, spurred by the women's movement and the 1964 Civil Rights Act (Title VII), women all over the country have demanded equal employment opportunities in prisons and jails (see Chapter 9). Some prison systems have acceded to these demands and voluntarily integrated their guard forces. The majority, however, have resisted this development, and sometimes male prisoners have raised invasion of their privacy as an issue. There have been dozens of lawsuits and even one Supreme Court opinion, which, unfortunately, was not definitive. The current situation is unclear. While women can be found in uniform in many men's prisons, they are not there in equal numbers and their future role is uncertain.

The experience so far has convinced me that women can serve successfully, even as guards, in men's prisons, and that selective work assignment will protect prisoner privacy. But even if I am wrong, there certainly does not seem to be any reason why women could not serve in prisons on an equal footing with men as clerks, tutors, and other nonuniformed personnel. Female national service volunteers should have an opportunity to serve and contribute to corrections along with their male counterparts.

The influx into corrections of national service personnel from a national or regional population base would help break down the excessive homogeneity and parochialism that characterizes most penal facilities' guard forces. It is likely that some national service personnel would be disturbed by what they see; they would not accept things as they are and would ask hard questions and demand cogent explanations. More important, national service volunteers would not easily identify or sympathize with the staff subculture; they would become an institutionalized watchdog that the permanent cadre would not trust to maintain the secrecy and silence that deter public scrutiny. Brutality, excessive force, and racism might decrease.

National service could constitute a vital link between prisons and society. In the last several decades, through ties with the larger society, particularly with federal courts and the federal government, these autonomous, isolated institutions moved closer to society's center (Jacobs 1977). This trend, however, peaked by the mid-1970s. In the 1980s the challenge will be to keep the prisons from reverting to the isolated autonomy of the pre-World War II period. National service, through its participants (and their families) and administrators, would serve as an institutional link tying prisons to the national government and the larger society.

National service also would provide correctional facilities with an unparalleled opportunity to broaden their recruitment base for career staff. Despite the challenges and importance of their mission, penal institutions are not successful in competing for talent, particularly at the entry level. Prison staff are overwhelmingly recruited from the ranks of the unemployed and marginally employed (Jacobs 1978). Few college graduates enter the field through the ranks. No doubt some national service personnel who serve in the prisons would respond to the challenges and remain or return after their schooling is completed.

For the vast majority of national service participants, prison service would constitute but a short career break. The experience should prove profoundly moving, however, enriching their later education and personal development. Corrections would benefit from the consequent emergence of a constituency supportive of prison reform. National service could provide a firsthand prison experience for citizens who, in all probability, would otherwise never come into contact with prisons. These prison "veterans" could then bring about substantial changes in correctional politics and policymaking.

Administrative and Other Potential Problems

What problems might national service cause for the prisons? Would participation in national service be attractive to corrections administrators, employees, and unions? Employees in at least two-thirds of state correctional agencies have formal collective bargaining agreements with their employers. In some states (Rhode Island, for example) these guard unions are very strong indeed. They would be unlikely to accept a program that could, in effect, substitute national service participants for regular employees. Even if both sides agreed that national service participants would only augment the full-time staff, there would surely be controversy over wages and other terms of employment. Unions would object to paying service participants less than the prevailing wage because of the potentially depressing effect on their own wages. To pay these young people regular wages, however, might make the program prohibitively expensive, undermine the "service" rationale, and subject it to sharp criticism from the adult unemployed and low-wage earners. Neither would union leaders tolerate the use of national service workers to operate the prisons during strikes. These objections could pose a serious impediment to the establishment of a national service and must be anticipated and resolved by national service planners.

Another set of problems involves the issues of personnel management. What control would prison officials have over national service participants? Would anyone who wants to work or anyone certified as "qualified" by the national service bureaucracy be accepted? Would prison officials insist on adherence to entrance requirements and examinations?

Once prison officials accept a national service participant for work would they be bound to keep him or her employed? Suppose the young man or woman does not come to work on time? Or shows up on drugs? Or fraternizes with prisoners? Or fails to carry out duties and responsibilities to the satisfaction of the guard corps? Would prison officials have the authority to hire and fire? If history is any guide, a federally funded and administered program would place some restrictions on the correctional administrators' disciplinary options.

A third set of problems deals with the capacity of national service participants to serve successfully in the prisons. Would they be able to handle the danger? Are convicts too "street wise"? I expect that many young people, if properly motivated and trained, could serve successfully; others would neither be up to the challenge nor able to exert the necessary authority over older, hardened convicts. Failures and dropouts must be expected. But this is no dif-

[211]

ferent from the current situation. Prisons typically are unable to exercise much selectivity in recruitment. A high percentage of recruits does not last six months and still fewer make it beyond a year (Jacobs and Grear 1977). There is no reason to assume that national service participants would be any less likely to adapt than those who are now being recruited.

Prisons are dangerous places and inevitably some national service personnel would be injured in conflicts. Of course, peacetime military service also has its dangers; so does the Peace Corps. If the nation can draft eighteen-year-olds into the armed forces, it can surely offer them opportunities for alternative service in law enforcement and corrections. Other problems that cannot yet be envisioned will, of course, present themselves. Some may be readily solvable, others not. Because of such contingencies, experimentation with national service should be on a step-by-step basis. Under any version of national service, correctional officials should be in a position to terminate participation.

Conclusion

For national service to be thoroughly evaluated, it is necessary for proponents to present full plans explaining how programs will be administered and how they will affect each participating agency. The McCloskey proposal is a good beginning. It focuses attention on certain key issues: namely, the relationship of the program with military service, the role of women, exemptions, funding, machinery for job placement, discipline, and appropriate service categories. By examining each of these issues in some depth, we will be able to evolve a prototype and assess the feasibility of the most promising version of national service. Such an exercise has other value as well. For example, for prisons it focuses attention on the legitimacy of punishment in a democratic society and the question of whether punishment is too isolated from society's mainstream. If it is too isolated, then we should consider national service or some other strategy — for example, correctional interns or a correctional cadet corps.

It is possible to reap the advantages of national service even without the passage of a federal or state program. If the analysis here is persuasive, departments of corrections could establish internship or cadet programs on their own. There already exist precedents for such programs. I know of two, but there are undoubtedly more. For many years in the late 1960s and early 1970s the Texas Department of Corrections hired college students for the summer. They served in all institutional capacities without incident.[2] The New York City Department of Corrections is currently planning a similar kind of internship program. If this experiment is successful it will provide concrete support for the suggestions in this chapter.

[2] I am indebted to George Beto, former director of the Texas Department, for calling this program to my attention.

References

Adler, H. G. 1958. "Ideas toward a Sociology of the Concentration Camp." *American Journal of Sociology* 63:513–522.

Alex, Nicholas. 1969. *Black in Blue*. New York: Appleton-Century-Crofts.

———. 1976. *New York Cops Talk Back*. New York: John Wiley & Sons.

Alexander, Elizabeth. 1978. "New Prison Administrators and the Court: New Directions in Prison Law." *Texas Law Review* 56:963–1008.

American Bar Association. 1977. "Tentative Draft of Standards Relating to the Legal Status of Prisoners." *American Criminal Law Review* (Special Issue).

American Bar Association, Commission on Correctional Facilities and Services. 1973. *Minority Recruitment in Corrections*. Washington, D.C.:American Bar Ass'n.

———. 1975. *When Society Pronounces Judgment*. Washington, D.C.: American Bar Ass'n.

American Bar Association, Resource Center on Correctional Law and Legal Services. 1974. "Providing Legal Services to Prisoners." *Georgia Law Review* 8:363–432.

American Correctional Association. 1978. *Accreditation: Blueprint for Corrections*. College Park, Md.: American Correctional Ass'n.

Barker, Frederick. 1944. *The Modern Prison System in India*. London: Macmillan & Co.

Barnes, Harry Elmer, and Negley K. Teeters. 1959. *New Horizons in Criminology*. Englewood Cliffs, N.J.: Prentice-Hall.

Bartollas, Clemens, Stuart Miller, and Simon Dinitz. 1976. *Juvenile Victimization: The Institutional Paradox*. New York: John Wiley & Sons.

Bayer, Ronald. 1981. "Crime, Punishment, and the Decline of Liberal Optimism." *Crime and Delinquency* 27:169–90.

Beans, Maj. Harry C. 1975. "Sex Discrimination in the Military." *Military Law Review* 67:19–83.

Bentham, Jeremy. 1962. *Panopticon: Or the Inspection House*. 1791. The Works of Jeremy Bentham, Vol. 4, ed. John Bowring. New York: Russell & Russell.

Bershad, Lawrence. 1977. "Law and Corrections: A Management-Perspective." *New England Journal of Prison Law* 4:49–82.

References

Bickel, Alexander M. 1962. *The Least Dangerous Branch*. Indianapolis: Bobbs-Merrill Co.

Biderman, Albert. 1968. "Internment and Custody." In vol. 8 of *International Encyclopedia of the Social Sciences*, ed. D. E. Sills, 139–148. New York: Macmillan Co.

Black, Charles. 1960. "The Lawfulness of Segregation Decisions." *Yale Law Journal* 69:421–430.

Bloch, Peter, and Deborah Anderson. 1974. *Police Women on Patrol: Final Report*. Washington, D.C.: Police Foundation.

Blumstein, Alfred, Jacqueline Cohen and Harold Miller. 1980. "Demographically Disaggregated Projection of Prison Populations," *Journal of Criminal Justice* 8:1–26.

Bowker, Lee. 1977. *Prisoner Subcultures*. Lexington, Mass.: Lexington Books.

Breed, Allen F. 1976. "Instituting California's Ward Grievance Procedure: An Inside Perspective." *Loyola of Los Angeles Law Review* 10:113–25.

Breed, Allen F., and Paul H. Voss. 1978. "Procedural Due Process in the Discipline of Incarcerated Juveniles." *Pepperdine Law Review* 10:641–71.

Brest, Paul. 1976. "Forward: In Defense of the Antidiscrimination Principle." *Harvard Law Review* 90:1–54.

Brierley, J. R. 1976. "The Legal Controversy as It Relates to Correctional Institutions — a Prison Administrator's View." *Villanova Law Review* 16:1070–76.

Brodsky, Carroll. 1977. "Long-term Work Stress in Teachers and Prison Guards." *Journal of Occupation Medicine* 19:133–138.

Bronstein, Alvin J. 1977. "Reform without Change: The Future of Prisoners' Rights." *Civil Liberties Review* 4:27–45.

Brown, Claude, 1965. *Manchild in the Promised Land*. New York: Macmillan Co.

Brown, D. W., and D. W. Crowley. 1979. "The Societal Impact of Law: An Assessment of Research." *Law and Policy Quarterly* 1:253–84.

Brownell, Baker. 1958. *The Other Illinois*. New York: Duell, Sloan & Pearce.

Bunker, Edward. 1977. *Animal Factory*. New York: Viking Press.

Burgess, Anthony. 1962. *A Clockwork Orange*. New York: W. W. Norton & Co.

Calhoun, Emily. 1978. "The Supreme Court and the Constitutional Rights of Prisoners: A Reappraisal." *Hastings Constitutional Law Quarterly* 4:219–47.

Cardarelli, Albert P., and M. Marvin Finkelstein. 1974. "Correctional Administrators Assess the Adequacy and Impact of Prison Legal Services Programs in the United States." *Journal of Criminal Law and Criminology* 65:91–102.

Cardwell, Wallace. 1968. "A Survey of Attitudes toward Black Muslims in Prison." *Journal of Human Relations* 16:220–38.

Carnegie Council on Policy Studies in Higher Education. 1979. *Giving Youth a Better Chance: Options for Education, Work, and Service*. San Francisco: Jossey-Bass.

Carroll, Leo. 1974. *Hacks, Blacks, and Cons: Race Relations in a Maximum Security Prison*. Lexington, Mass.: D.C. Heath Co.

Champagne, Anthony, and Kenneth C. Haas. 1976. "The Impact of *Johnson v. Avery* on Prison Administration" *Tennessee Law Review* 43:275–306.

Chayes, Abram. 1976. "The Role of the Judge in Public Law Litigation." *Harvard Law Review* 89:1281–1316.

Chicago-Kent Law Review. 1977. Note, "Inmate Assaults and Section 1983 Damage

Claims." *Chicago-Kent Law Review.* 54:596–613.

Christianson, Scott. 1980. "Racial Discrimination and Prison Confinement: A Follow-Up." *Criminal Law Bulletin* 16:616–21.

Cleaver, Eldridge. 1968. *Soul on Ice.* New York: McGraw-Hill Book Co.

Clemmer, Donald. [1940] 1958. *The Prison Community.* New York: Holt, Rinehart & Winston.

——, and John Wilson. 1960. "The Black Muslims in Prison." *Proceedings of the American Correctional Association,* 147–55.

Cohen, Fred. 1972. "The Discovery of Prison Reform." *Buffalo Law Review* 21: 855–87.

Cohen, Neil and Dean Rivkin. 1971. "Civil Disabilities: The Forgotten Punishment." *Federal Probation* 35–2:19–25.

Committee for the Study of National Service. 1979. *Youth and the Needs of the Nation.* Washington, D.C.: Potomac Institute.

Congressional Budget Office. 1980. *Costs of the National Service Test (H. R. 2206): A Technical Analysis.* Washington, D.C.: U.S. Government Printing Office.

Conrad, John. 1965. *Crime and Its Correction.* Berkeley: Univ. of California Press.

Conrad, John, and Simon Dinitz. 1977. "Position Paper for the Seminar on the Isolated Offender." Academy for Contemporary Problems, Columbus, Ohio.

Corrections Compendium. 1982. "Construction and Overcrowding." *Corrections Compendium* 6(9):1–7. Lincoln, Neb.: Contact.

Cressey, Donald. 1965. "Prison Organization." In *Hornbook of Organizations,* ed. James March. New York: Rand McNally & Co.

——, and W. Krassowski. 1958. "Inmate Organization and Soviet Labor Camps." *Social Problems* 5:217–29.

Dannenmaier, W. D., and F. J. Thumin. 1964. "Authority Status as a Factor in Perceptual Distortion of Size." *Journal of Social Psychology* 63:361–65.

Davidson, Theodore. 1974. *Chicano Prisoners: The Key to San Quentin.* New York: Holt, Rinehart & Winston.

Davis, Alan. 1968. "Sexual Assaults in the Philadelphia Prison System and Sheriff's Vans." *Transaction* 6:8–16.

De Beaumont, Gustave, and Alexis de Tocqueville. 1964. *On the Penitentiary System in the United States and Its Application in France.* Carbondale: Southern Illinois Univ. Press.

Dishotsky, Norman, and Adolph Pfefferbaum. 1977. "Ethnic Polarization in a Correctional System." Paper presented to Boys Town Center for the Study of Youth Development, Stanford University, August 1977.

——. 1979. "Intolerance and Extremism in a Correctional Institution: A Perceived Ethnic Relations Approach." *American Journal of Psychiatry* 136:1438–43.

Eberly, Donald. 1971. "A National Service Pilot Project." *Teachers College Record* 73:65–80.

Eisenberg, Ted, and S. C. Yeazell. 1980. "The Ordinary-Extraordinary in Institutional Litigation." *Harvard Law Review* 93:465–517.

Executive Advisory Committee on Sentencing. 1979. *Crime and Punishment in New York: An Inquiry into Sentencing and the Criminal Justice System.* Albany: Executive Advisory Committee on Sentencing.

[215]

References

European Committee on Crime Problems. 1963. *The Status, Selection, and Training of Prison Staff*. Strasbourg: Council of Europe.

Fiss, Owen. 1978. *The Civil Rights Injunction*. Bloomington: Indiana Univ. Press.

———. 1979. "The Forms of Justice." *Harvard Law Review* 93:1–58.

Flynn, Elizabeth. 1972. *My Life as a Political Prisoner*. New York: International Pubs. Co.

Fogel, David. 1975. *"We are the Living Proof . . . ": The Justice Model for Corrections*. Cincinnati: Anderson Publishing Co.

Fox, Vernon. 1972. "Racial Issues in Corrections." *American Journal of Corrections* 34:12–17.

Frank, Jerome. 1949. *Courts on Trial: Myth and Reality in American Justice*. Princeton: Princeton Univ. Press.

Frankel, Marvin. 1976. "The Adversary Judge." *Texas Law Review* 54:465–87.

Fuller, Lon L. 1978. "The Forms and Limits of Adjudication." *Harvard Law Review* 92:353–409.

Glaser, Daniel. 1964. *The Effectiveness of a Prison and Parole System*. Indianapolis: Bobbs-Merrill Co.

Glazer, Nathan. 1975. "Towards an Imperial Judiciary." *Public Interest* 41:104–23.

Goffman, Erving. 1961. *Asylums*. Garden City, N.Y.: Doubleday & Co.

Gottfredson, Michael, Michael Hindelang, and Nicolette Parisi. 1978. *Sourcebook of Criminal Justice Statistics — 1977*. Washington, D.C.: U.S. Government Printing Office.

Gould, William. 1972. "Labor Relations and Race Relations." In *Public Workers and Public Unions*, ed. Sam Zagoria 147–59. Englewood Cliffs, N.J.: Prentice-Hall.

Haney, C., C. Banks, and P. Zimbardo. 1973. "Interpersonal Dynamics in a Simulated Prison." *International Journal of Criminology and Penology*, 1973, no. 1:69–97.

Harris, Louis. 1969. *Volunteers Look at Corrections*. Joint Commission on Correctional Manpower and Training. Washington, D.C.: U.S. Government Printing Office.

Harris, M. Kay, and D. P. Spiller, Jr. 1977. *After Decision: Implementation of Judicial Decrees in Correctional Settings*. Washington, D.C.: U.S. Department of Justice, Law Enforcement Assistance Administration.

Harvard Center for Criminal Justice. 1972. "Judicial Intervention in Prison Discipline." *Journal of Criminal Law and Criminology* 63:200–228.

Harvard Law Review. Note, 1977. "Implementation Problems in Institutional Reform Litigation." *Harvard Law Review* 91:428–63.

Hawkins, Gordon. 1976. *The Prison: Policy and Practice*. Chicago: Univ. of Chicago Press.

Hayner, Norman, and Ellis Ash. 1940. "The Prison as a Community." *American Sociological Review* 5:577–83.

Hirschkop, Philip, and M. A. Millemann. 1969. "The Unconstitutionality of Prison Life." *Virginia Law Review* 55:795–839.

Hoobler, Raymond L., and J. A. McQueney. 1973. "A Question of Height." *The Police Chief* 40:42–48.

Horowitz, D. L. 1977. *The Courts and Social Policy*. Washington, D.C.: Brookings Institution.

[216]

Hughes, Everett. 1958. *Men and Their Work*. New York: Free Press.

——. 1964. "Good People and Dirty Work." In *The Other Side: Perspectives on Deviance*, ed. Howard Becker. London: Free Press of Glencoe.

Ianni, Francis. 1974. *Black Mafia: Ethnic Succession in Organized Crime*. New York: Simon & Schuster.

Irwin, John. 1970. *The Felon*. Englewood Cliffs, N.J.: Prentice-Hall.

——. 1974. "Memorandum of Convict and Staff Relationships at Stateville." Program Evaluation Design of the Illinois Correctional Training Academy. Washington, D.C.: Metametric.

——. 1977. "The Changing Social Structure of the Men's Prison." In *Corrections and Punishment*, ed. David Greenberg. Beverly Hills, Calif.: Sage Pubs.

——. 1980. *Prisons in Turmoil*. Boston: Little, Brown & Co.

——, and Donald Cressey. 1962. "Thieves, Convicts, and the Inmate Culture." *Social Problems* 10:142−55.

Jackson, George. 1970. *Soledad Brother: The Prison Letters of George Jackson*. New York: Coward, McCann, & Geoghegan.

——. 1972. *Blood in My Eye*. New York: Random House.

Jacobs, James B. 1976. "Stratification and Conflict among Prison Inmates." *Journal of Criminal Law and Criminology* 66:476−82.

——. 1976a. "Prison Violence and Formal Organization." In *Prison Violence*, ed. Albert Cohen. Lexington, Mass: Lexington Books.

——. 1977. *Stateville: The Penitentiary in Mass Society*. Chicago: Univ. of Chicago Press.

——. 1978. "What Prison Guards Think: A Profile of the Illinois Force." *Crime and Delinquency* 24:185−96.

Jacobs, James B. 1979. *Individual Rights and Institutional Authority: Prisons, Mental Hospitals, Schools, and Military*. Indianapolis: Bobbs-Merrill Co.

——. 1982. "The Role of Military Forces in Public Sector Labor Disputes." *Industrial & Labor Relations Review* 35:163−80.

——, and Norma Crotty. 1978. *Guard Unions and the Future of the Prisons*. Ithaca, N.Y.: New York State School of Industrial & Labor Relations.

——, and Mary Grear. 1977. "Drop-outs and Rejects: An Analysis of the Prison Guard's Revolving Door." *Criminal Justice Review* 2(2):57−70.

——, and Harold Retsky. 1975. "Prison Guard." *Urban Life* 4:5−29.

——, and Lynn Zimmer. 1980. "The 1979 Montana Prison Guard Strike: A Case Study." Cornell University, Ithaca, N.Y.

James, William. 1968. "The Moral Equivalent of War." In *Memories and Studies by William James*. New York: Greenwood Press.

Janowitz, Morris. 1967. "The Logic of National Service." In *The Draft*, ed. Sol Tax. Chicago: Univ. of Chicago Press.

——. 1970. "The Logic of Political Conflict." In Janowitz, *Political Conflict: Essays in Political Sociology*. Chicago: Quadrangle Books.

——, and Charles Moskos, "Five Years of the All-Volunteer Force: 1973−1978." *Armed Forces and Society* 5 (1978):171−218.

Joint Commission on Correctional Manpower and Training. 1968. *Corrections 1968: A*

References

Climate For Change. Washington, D.C.: U.S. Government Printing Office.

———. 1969. *A Time to Act: Final Report*. Washington, D.C.: U.S. Government Printing Office.

Kahl, Joseph. 1976. *Modernization, Exploitation, and Dependency in Latin America*. New Brunswick, N.J.: Transaction Books.

Kantrowitz, Nathan. 1969. "The Vocabulary of Race Relations in a Prison." *Publication of the American Dialect Society* 51:23–34.

Karsh, Bernard. *Diary of a Strike*. Urbana: Univ. of Illinois Press, 1958.

Keating, J. M. 1975. "Arbitration of Inmate Grievances." *Arbitration Journal* 30:177–90.

———. 1976. "The Justice Model Applied: A New Way to Handle the Complaints of California Youth Authority Awards." *Loyola of Los Angeles Law Review* 10:126–48.

Kerr, Clark, and Abraham Siegel. 1954. "The Interindustry Propensity to Strike." In *Industrial Conflict*, ed. Arthur Kornhauser, Robert Dubin, and Arthur Ross, 189–212. New York: McGraw-Hill Book Co.

King, William. 1977. *Achieving America's Goals: National Service or the All-Volunteer Armed Force?* Washington, D.C.: U.S. Government Printing Office.

Kogon, Eugene. 1966. *The Theory and Practice of Hell*. New York: Berkley Publishing Corp., Medallion Books.

Koulack, David, and John A. Tuthill. 1972. "Height Perception: Function of Social Distance." *Canadian Journal of Behavioral Science* 4:50–54.

Laber, Jeri. 1976. "Phillipines Torture." *New York Times*, October 30, 1976:23.

LeClaire, Thomas. 1980. "The Strike Aftermath at Elmira Correctional Facility: Problems of Transition." Research paper, School of Industrial & Labor Relations, Cornell University, Ithaca, N.Y.

Leopold, Nathan. 1957. *Life Plus Ninety-nine Years*. Garden City, N.Y.: Doubleday & Co.

Lincoln, C. Eric. 1961. *The Black Muslims in America*. Boston: Beacon Press.

Lipton, Douglas, Robert Martinson, and Judith Wilks. 1975. *The Effectiveness of Correctional Treatments: A Survey of Treatment Evaluations*. New York: Praeger Pubs.

Little, Malcolm. 1965. *The Autobiography of Malcolm X*. New York: Grove Press.

Lockwood, Daniel. 1980. *Prison Sexual Violence*. New York: Elsevier.

Lottman, Michael. 1976. "The Enforcement of Judicial Decrees: Now Comes the Hard Part." *Mental Disability Law Reporter* 1:69–76.

Mannheim, Karl. 1940. *Man and Society in an Age of Reconstruction*. New York: Harcourt Brace Jovanovich.

Marshall, T. H. 1964. "Citizenship and Social Class." In Marshall, *Class, Citizenship and Social Development*. Garden City, N.Y.: Doubleday & Co.

McCleery, Richard. 1960. "Communication Patterns as Bases of Systems of Authority and Power." In *Theoretical Studies in Social Organization of the Prison*, Richard Cloward et al. New York: Social Science Research Council.

McClelland, Peter, and Alan Magdovitz. 1981. *Crisis in the Making: The Political Economy of New York State Since 1945*. Cambridge: Cambridge Univ. Press.

McCormack, Wayne. 1975. "The Expansion of Federal Question Jurisdiction and the Prisoner Complaint Caseload." *Wisconsin Law Review*, 1975:523–51.

McNamara, Donald. 1973. *Analysis of Assaulted and Non-assaulted Officers by Height, Weight, Tenure, and Assignment.*

Mead, Margaret. 1967. "A National Service System as a Solution to a Variety of National Problems." In *The Draft*, ed. Sol Tax. Chicago: Univ. of Chicago Press.

Miller, L. M. P. 1978. "Toward Equality of Educational Opportunity through School Districts in State Bureaus: An Innovation in Correction Education." *Harvard Journal of Legislation* 15:221–96.

Miller, Walter B. 1974. "American Youth Gangs, Past and Present." In *Current Perspectives on Criminal Behavior*, ed. Abraham S. Blumberg, 210–37. New York: Alfred A. Knopf.

Minton, Robert, ed. 1971. *Inside Prison American Style*. New York: Random House.

Morris, Norval. 1975. *The Future of Imprisonment*. Chicago: Univ. of Chicago Press.

—— and Gordon Hawkins. 1969. *The Honest Politician's Guide to Crime Control*. Chicago: Univ. of Chicago Press.

—— and Michael Tonry. 1981. "Blacks, Crime Rates, and Prisons." *Chicago Tribune*, August 18–21, 1980, editorial page.

Moskos, Charles. 1973. "The American Dilemma in Uniform: Race in the Armed Forces." *Annals of the American Academy of Political and Social Science* 406:94–106.

——. 1981. "Making the All-Volunteer Force Work: A National Service Approach." *Foreign Affairs* 60:17–34.

Nathan, Vincent M. 1979. "The Use of Masters in Institutional Reform Litigation." *University of Toledo Law Review* 10:419–64.

National Advisory Commission on Youth. 1980. *From Youth to Adulthood: A Bridge Too Long*. Boulder, Colo.: Westview Press.

National Commission on Criminal Justice Standards and Goals. 1973. *Task Force Report on Corrections*. Washington: U.S. Government Printing Office.

National Council on Crime and Delinquency. 1966. *Standard Act for State Correctional Services.* Paramus, N.J.: National Council on Crime and Delinquency.

——. 1972. *A Model Act for the Protection of Rights of Prisoners*. Paramus, N.J.: National Council on Crime and Delinquency.

Neisser, Eric. 1977. "Is There a Doctor in the Joint? The Search for Constitutional Standards for Prison Health Care." *Virginia Law Review* 63:921–73.

New York State Special Commission on Attica. 1972. *Official Report*. New York: Bantam Books.

New York University Law Review. 1976. Note, "Workers' Compensation for Prisoners." *New York University Law Review* 51:478–92.

Niederhoffer, Arthur. 1967. *Behind the Shield*. Garden City, N.Y.: Doubleday & Co.

Nowak, John, Ronald D. Rotunda, and J. Nelson Young. 1978. *Constitutional Law*. St. Paul, Minn.: West Publishing Co.

Opotowsky, Stan. 1972. *Men behind Bars*. Los Angeles: Pinnacle Books.

Orland, Leonard. 1975. "Can We Establish the Rule of Law in Prisons?" *Civil Liberties Review* 2:57–67.

Park, George. 1976. "The Organization of Prison Violence." In *Prison Violence*, ed. Albert K. Cohen, George F. Cole, and Robert G. Bayley. Lexington, Mass.: Lexington Books.

References

Parker, Jack, and John LeCour. 1978. "Common Sense in Correctional Volunteerism in the Institution." *Federal Probation* 42(2):45−54.

Pell, Eve, ed. 1972. *Maximum Security: Letters from California's Prisons*. New York: E.P. Dutton.

Pfefferbaum, Adolph, and Norman Dishotsky. 1981. "Racial Intolerance in a Correctional Institution: An Ecological View." *American Journal of Psychiatry* 138: 1057−62.

President's Commission on an All-Volunteer Force. 1970. *The Report of . . . .* Washington, D.C.: U.S. Government Printing Office.

President's Commission on Law Enforcement and Administration of Justice. 1967. *Task Force Report on Corrections*. Washington, D.C.: U.S. Government Printing Office.

Reagan, Michael, and Donald Stoughton. 1976. *School behind Bars: A Descriptive Overview of Correctional Education in the American Prison System*. Metuchen, N.J.: Scarecrow Press.

Reimer, Hans. 1937. "Socialization in the Prison Community." *Proceedings of the American Prison Association*, 151−155.

Reston, James. 1977. *The Innocence of Joan Little: A Southern Mystery*. New York: Times Books.

Ross, Beth. 1978. *Changing of the Guard: Citizen Soldiers in Wisconsin Prisons*. Pamphlet. Madison: League of Women Voters.

Rothman, David. 1971. *Discovery of the Asylum: Social Order and Disorder in the Republic*. Boston: Little, Brown & Co.

———. 1973. "Decarcerating Prisoners and Patients." *Civil Liberties Review* 1:9−30.

———. 1980. *Prison Reform in the Progressive Era*. New York: Harper & Row Pubs.

Roucek, Joseph. 1935. "Sociology of the Prison Guard." *Sociology and Social Research* 20:145−51.

Rubin, Sol. 1974. "The Impact of Court Decisions on the Correctional Process." *Crime and Delinquency* 20:129−34.

Rundle, Frank. 1973. "The Roots of Violence at Soledad." In *The Politics of Punishment: A Critical Analysis of Prisons in America*, ed. Erik Olin Wright. New York: Harper & Row Pubs.

Rusche, Georg, and Otto Kirchheimer. 1939. *Punishment and Social Structure*. New York: Russel & Russel.

Scacco, Anthony. 1975. *Rape in Prison*. Springfield, Ill.: Charles C. Thomas Pub.

Scheingold, Stuart A. 1974. *The Politics of Rights*. New Haven: Yale Univ. Press.

Schien, Edgar. 1960. *Coercive Persuasion*. New York: W. W. Norton & Co.

Schrag, Clarence. 1954. "Leadership among Prison Inmates." *American Sociological Review* 19:37−42.

Schwartz, Barry. 1972. "Deprivation of Privacy as a 'Functional Prerequisite': The Case of Prison." *Journal of Criminal Law, Criminology, and Police Science* 63:229−39.

Schwartz, Herman. 1972. "A Comment on *Sostre v. McGinnis*." *Buffalo Law Review* 21:775−93.

———. 1972a. "Prisoners Rights: Some Hopes and Realities." In *A Program of Prison Reform: The Final Report*. Annual Chief Justice Earl Warren Conference on Advocacy in the United States. Cambridge, Mass.: Roscoe Pound American Trial Lawyers Foundation.

Schwartz, Ira, Donald Jenson, Michael Mahoney. 1977. *Volunteers in Juvenile Justice*. National Institute of Law Enforcement and Criminal Justice. Washington, D.C.: U.S. Government Printing Office.

Seashore, Marjorie, and Steven Haberfeld. 1976. *Prisoner Education: Project Newgate and Other College Programs*. New York: Praeger Pubs.

Sherman, Michael, and Gordon Hawkins. 1981. *Imprisonment in America: Choosing a Future*. Chicago: Univ. of Chicago Press.

Shils, Edward. 1962. "The Theory of Mass Society." *Diogenes* 39:45–66; reprint in Shils, *Center and Periphery: Essays in Macrosociology.* (Chicago: Univ. of Chicago Press, 1975).

Sibley, Mulford, and Ada Wardlaw. 1945. *Conscientious Objectors in Prison, 1940-1945*. Philadelphia: Pacifist Research Bureau.

Sichel, Joyce L. 1978. *Women on Patrol: A Pilot Study on Police Performance in New York City.* Washington, D.C.: Law Enforcement Assistance Administration.

Singer, Linda R., and J. M. Keating. 1973. "Prisoner Grievance Mechanisms." *Crime and Delinquency* 19:367–77.

Singer, Richard. 1972. "Privacy, Autonomy, and Dignity in the Prison: A Preliminary Inquiry Concerning Constitutional Aspects of the Degradation Process in Our Prisons." *Buffalo Law Review* 21:669–716.

Skogan, Wesley G. 1981. "On Attitudes and Behavior." In *Reactions to Crime*, ed. Dan A. Lewis. Beverly Hills, Calif.: Sage Pubs.

Skolnick, Jerome. 1966. *Justice without Trial*. New York: John Wiley & Sons.

Solomon, Richard. 1976. "Lessons from the Swedish Criminal Justice System: A Reappraisal." *Federal Probation* 40(3):40–48.

Solzhenitsyn, Alexander. 1973. *The Gulag Archipelago*. New York: Harper & Row Pubs.

——. 1975. *The Gulag Archipelago II*. New York: Harper & Row Pubs.

South Carolina Department of Corrections. 1973. *Collective Violence in Correctional Institutions: A Search for Causes*. Columbia: South Carolina Department of Corrections.

Stanford Law Review. 1973. Note, "Disenfranchisement of Ex-felons: A Re-assessment." *Stanford Law Review* 25:845–64.

Stark, Rodney. 1972. *Police Riots*. New York: Barnes & Noble Books, Focus Books.

State of New Mexico, Office of Attorney General. 1980. *Report of the Attorney General on the February 2 and 3, 1980 Riot at the Penitentiary of New Mexico*. Distributed by Office of Attorney General.

Steele, Eric, and James B. Jacobs. 1977. "Untangling Minimum Security: Concepts, Realities, and Implications for Correctional Systems." *Journal of Research in Crime and Delinquency* 14:68–83.

Sutherland, Edwin, and Donald Cressey. 1974. *Criminology*. 9th ed. Philadelphia: J. B. Lippincott Co.

Swanson, Cheryl G., and Charles D. Hale. 1975. "A Question of Height Revisited: Assaults on Police." *Journal of Police Science and Administration* 3:183–88.

References

Sykes, Gresham. 1956. "The Corruption of Authority and Rehabilitation." *Social Forces* 34:257–62.

———. 1958. *The Society of Captives*. Princeton: Princeton Univ. Press.

———, and Sheldon Messinger. 1960. "The Inmate Social System." In *Theoretical Studies in the Social Organization of the Prison*, ed. Richard Cloward. New York: Social Science Research Council.

Tax, Sol, ed. 1967. *The Draft*. Chicago: Univ. of Chicago Press.

Thomas, Charles W., and David M. Petersen. 1977. *Prison Organization and Inmate Subcultures*. Indianapolis: Bobbs-Merrill Co.

Thomas, J. E. 1972. *The English Prison Officer Since 1850*. London: Routledge & Kegan Paul.

Thorpe, Gregory A. 1977. Note, "Inmate Assaults and Section 1983 Damage Claims." *Chicago-Kent Law Review* 54:596–613.

Tribe, Laurence. 1978. *American Constitutional Law*. Mineola, N.Y.: Foundation Press.

Tulane Law Review. 1977. Note, "Tort-Liability of the State for Injuries Suffered by Prisoners Due to Assult by Other Inmates." *Tulane Law Review* 51:1300–1306.

Turner, William B. 1979. "When Prisoners Sue: A Study of Prisoners Section 1983 Suits in the Federal Courts." *Harvard Law Review* 92:610–63.

U.C.L.A. Law Review. 1973. Note, "Judicial Intervention in Corrections: The California Experience — An Empirical Study." *U.C.L.A. Law Review* 20:452–575.

U.S. Administrative Office of the United States Courts. 1979. *Annual Report of the Director*. Washington, D.C.: U.S. Administrative Office of the United States Courts.

U.S. Commission on Civil Rights. 1971. *Racial Conditions in Indiana Penal Institutions: A Report of the Indiana State Committee*. Washington, D.C.: U.S. Government Printing Office.

U.S. Department of Justice. 1976. *National Prisoner Statistics Special Report, Census of Prisoners in State Correctional Facilities*. Washington, D.C.: U.S. Government Printing Office.

———. 1978. *Federal Standards for Corrections: Draft, 1978*. Washington, D.C.: U.S. Department of Justice.

Ward, David. 1972. "Inmate Rights and Prison Reform in Sweden." *Journal of Criminal Law, Criminology, and Political Science* 63:240–55.

Washington and Lee Law Review. 1968. Note, "The Regulated Practice of the Jailhouse Lawyer." *Washington and Lee Law Review* 25:281–86.

Weber, Max. 1954. *On Law in Economy and Society*. Cambridge, Mass.: Harvard Univ. Press.

Welch, Robert. 1979. "Developing Prisoner Self-Help Techniques: The Early Mississippi Experience." *Prison Law Monitor* 2:105,118–22.

Wexler, David B. 1971. "The Jailhouse Lawyer as a Paraprofessional: Problems and Prospects." *Criminal Law Bulletin* 7:139–56.

White, Thomas N., and Peter Bloch. 1975. *Police Officer Height and Selected Aspects of Performance*. Washington, D.C.: Police Foundation.

Williams, John H. 1975. *Changing Prisons*. London: Peter Owen.

Wilson, Paul R. 1968. "Perceptual Distortion of Height as an Ascribed Status." *Journal of Social Psychology* 74:97—102.

Wright, Erik, ed. 1973. *The Politics of Punishment: A Critical Analysis of Prisons in America*. New York: Harper & Row Pubs.

Wynne, John M., Jr. 1978. "Unions and Bargaining among Employees of State Prisons." *Monthly Labor Review* 101—3:10—16.

Yale Law Journal. 1963. Note, "Beyond the Ken of the Courts: A Critique of Judicial Refusal to Review the Complaints of Convicts." *Yale Law Journal* 72:506—58.

——. 1974. Note, "Mental Illness: A Suspect Classification?" *Yale Law Journal* 83:1237—70.

——. 1975. Note, "The Wyatt Case: Implementation of a Judicial Decree Ordering Institutional Change." *Yale Law Journal* 84:1338—79.

Yee, Minn S. 1973. *The Melancholy History of Soledad Prison*. New York: Harper's Magazine Press.

Table of Cases

Notes on Coauthors

LAURA BERKOWITZ conducted research while an undergraduate at Cornell University. She will receive her B.A. in June 1983 and plans to attend law school.

HELEN A. BROOKS conducted research while an undergraduate at Cornell University. She is now in private law practice in New York City.

NORMA CROTTY conducted research while a law student at Cornell University. She is now in private law practice in Albany, New York.

LAWRENCE J. KRAFT conducted research while a graduate student in sociology at Cornell University. He nows works in Boston as a medical care delivery administrator.

LYNN ZIMMER conducted research while a graduate student in sociology at Cornell University. She is now Assistant Professor of Sociology, State University of New York at Geneseo.

Index

Library of Congress Cataloging in Publication Data

Jacobs, James B.
  New perspectives on prisons and imprisonment.

  Includes index.
  1. Prison—United States—Addresses, essays, lectures. 2. Prisoners—Legal status, laws,
etc.—Addresses, essays, lectures. 3. Prisons and race relations—United States—Addresses,
essays, lectures. 4. Prisons—Officials and employees—United States—Addresses, essays,
lectures. I. Title.
  HV9304.J3 1983   365'.973   82-22222
  ISBN 0-8014-1586-1